Measuring **Sex, Gender Identity,** and **Sexual Orientation**

Committee on Measuring Sex, Gender Identity, and Sexual Orientation

Nancy Bates, Marshall Chin, Tara Becker, *Editors*

Committee on National Statistics

Division of Behavioral and Social Sciences and Education

The National Academies of
SCIENCES · ENGINEERING · MEDICINE

THE NATIONAL ACADEMIES PRESS
Washington, DC
www.nap.edu

THE NATIONAL ACADEMIES PRESS   500 Fifth Street, NW   Washington, DC 20001

This activity was supported by contracts between the National Academy of Sciences and the National Institutes of Health (HHSN263201800029I, 75N98021F00001). Any opinions, findings, conclusions, or recommendations expressed in this publication do not necessarily reflect the views of any organization or agency that provided support for the project.

International Standard Book Number-13: 978-0-309-27510-1
International Standard Book Number-10: 0-309-27510-5
Digital Object Identifier: https://doi.org/10.17226/26424
Library of Congress Control Number: 2022937869

Additional copies of this publication are available from the National Academies Press, 500 Fifth Street, NW, Keck 360, Washington, DC 20001; (800) 624-6242 or (202) 334-3313; http://www.nap.edu.

Suggested citation: National Academies of Sciences, Engineering, and Medicine. 2022. *Measuring Sex, Gender Identity, and Sexual Orientation*. Washington, DC: The National Academies Press. https://doi.org/10.17226/26424.

The National Academies of
SCIENCES · ENGINEERING · MEDICINE

The **National Academy of Sciences** was established in 1863 by an Act of Congress, signed by President Lincoln, as a private, nongovernmental institution to advise the nation on issues related to science and technology. Members are elected by their peers for outstanding contributions to research. Dr. Marcia McNutt is president.

The **National Academy of Engineering** was established in 1964 under the charter of the National Academy of Sciences to bring the practices of engineering to advising the nation. Members are elected by their peers for extraordinary contributions to engineering. Dr. John L. Anderson is president.

The **National Academy of Medicine** (formerly the Institute of Medicine) was established in 1970 under the charter of the National Academy of Sciences to advise the nation on medical and health issues. Members are elected by their peers for distinguished contributions to medicine and health. Dr. Victor J. Dzau is president.

The three Academies work together as the **National Academies of Sciences, Engineering, and Medicine** to provide independent, objective analysis and advice to the nation and conduct other activities to solve complex problems and inform public policy decisions. The National Academies also encourage education and research, recognize outstanding contributions to knowledge, and increase public understanding in matters of science, engineering, and medicine.

Learn more about the National Academies of Sciences, Engineering, and Medicine at **www.nationalacademies.org**.

The National Academies of
SCIENCES · ENGINEERING · MEDICINE

Consensus Study Reports published by the National Academies of Sciences, Engineering, and Medicine document the evidence-based consensus on the study's statement of task by an authoring committee of experts. Reports typically include findings, conclusions, and recommendations based on information gathered by the committee and the committee's deliberations. Each report has been subjected to a rigorous and independent peer-review process and it represents the position of the National Academies on the statement of task.

Proceedings published by the National Academies of Sciences, Engineering, and Medicine chronicle the presentations and discussions at a workshop, symposium, or other event convened by the National Academies. The statements and opinions contained in proceedings are those of the participants and are not endorsed by other participants, the planning committee, or the National Academies.

For information about other products and activities of the National Academies, please visit www.nationalacademies.org/about/whatwedo.

v

Preface

Sex, gender identity, and sexual orientation are core to an individual's understanding of who they are, and these characteristics shape each person's experiences, relationships, and opportunities throughout their lives. Together, these important demographic characteristics are the axes through which personal and societal beliefs about sex (gender) differences play out within people's lives, structuring behaviors and creating gender-based inequality that can manifest itself in many ways, including as segregation, discrimination, violence, sexism, homophobia, and transphobia. Understanding the wide-ranging effects of sex, gender identity, and sexual orientation, their causes and their consequences, is crucial, but doing so requires the development and use of validated measures that can represent the underlying complexity of constructs that are often assumed to be simple and uncomplicated.

Collection of sex and gender data occurs routinely in research, health, and administrative data collection efforts. Most of these efforts have long treated sex and gender as binary, mutually determined (usually at birth), and interchangeable constructs that can each serve as a proxy for the other. Although it is less routinely collected, sexual orientation is also based on a binary that assumes there is unity between sex and gender because it is generally defined on the basis of the sex/gender of one's preferred partner(s) relative to one's own: same-sex/gender, opposite-sex/gender, both sexes/genders.

This simple binary, however, masks a more complicated reality in which a constellation of sex traits may not all correspond to the same sex; and an individual's gender identity may not be the same as their sex and may lie outside the binary of male/female. Thus, these simple, binary measures of either sex or gender do not represent this complexity and may pose difficulties for respondents whose sex traits do not all correspond to the same sex or whose sex is different from their gender identity, namely, intersex and transgender people. These difficulties then extend to other measures that are derived from sex/gender, such as sexual orientation. These measurement issues are not purely academic: they can have severe consequences for sexual and gender minorities in health care and other areas in which measures of sex/gender and sexual orientation are often used for determining appropriate and necessary care.

It was within this context that 19 separate institutes, centers, and offices of the National Institutes of Health (NIH) asked the National Academies of Sciences, Engineering, and Medicine (the National Academies) to undertake a study to examine the measurement of sex, gender identity, and sexual orientation and produce recommendations for specific measures that can be used in surveys and research, administrative, and clinical and other health settings. Underscoring the importance of this issue within many fields of interest, the 19 NIH entities included: the National Cancer Institute; the National Human Genome Research Institute; the National Institute on Aging; the National Institute of Allergy and Infectious Diseases; the Eunice Kennedy Shriver National Institute of Child Health and Human Development; the National Institute of Environmental Health Sciences; the National Institute of Mental Health; the National Institute of Minority Health and Health Disparities; the National Institute of Neurological Disorders and Stroke; the Office of the Director, All of Us; the Office of the Director, Chief Officer for Scientific Workforce Diversity; the Office of the Director, Division of Program Coordination, Planning, and Strategic Initiatives, Office of AIDS Research; the Office of the Director, Division of Program Coordination, Planning, and Strategic Initiatives, Office of Behavioral and Social Sciences Research; the Office of the Director, Division of Program Coordination, Planning, and Strategic Initiatives, Office of Disease Prevention; the Office of the Director, Division of Program Coordination, Planning, and Strategic Initiatives, Office of Research on Women's Health; the Office of the Director, Division of Program Coordination, Planning, and Strategic Initiatives, Office of Strategic Coordination; the Office of the Director, Division of Program Coordination, Planning, and Strategic Initiatives, Sexual & Gender Minority Research Office; Office of the Director, Office of Equity, Diversity, and Inclusion; and the Office of the Director, Office of Intramural Research, Office of Intramural Training and Education. In response to this request, the National Academies appointed the Committee on Measuring Sex, Gender Identity, and Sexual Orientation (under the standing committee of the Committee on National Statistics) to carry out this task. Nine scholars representing a broad array of disciplines—medicine, psychology, public health, sociology, survey methodology, and statistics—were included on the committee, which met virtually seven times over the 9-month period between May 2021 and January 2022.

This report presents an accounting of the process the committee used to evaluate existing measures of sex, gender identity, and sexual orientation and recommend specific measures to be used to standardize federal data collection efforts. This evaluation revealed not only how much progress has been made in the development and refinement of sex, gender identity, and sexual orientation measures that identify sexual and gender minority populations, but also how much progress remains to be made. Although measures of sex and gender that enable the identification of transgender respondents and measures of sexual orientation have improved and become more widely implemented in data collection efforts, few of the measures in use are explicitly inclusive of gender identities that lie outside of the gender binary, and many continue to rely on terminology or language that is considered invalidating or offensive to some sexual and gender minorities. And to date, much less progress has been made in developing measures that identify people with intersex traits. Thus, this report serves as a starting point not only for those looking to expand their sex, gender identity, and sexual orientation data collection efforts, but also for those who wish to focus on further improvement and refinement of these measures. To this end, the report recommends specific areas for future research and question development.

This report would not have been possible without the contributions of many people. Special thanks must be extended to members of the study committee, who devoted extensive time, thought, and energy to this endeavor. The committee received useful information and insights from presentations from outside experts at open sessions of committee meetings. We thank Sari van Anders (Queen's University), Ethan Fechter-Leggett (National Institute for Occupational Safety and Health, Centers for Disease Control and Prevention), Kirk Greenway (Indian Health Service), Elliot Kennedy (Administration for Community Living, U.S. Department of Health and Human Services), Mahri Monson (Environmental Protection Agency), Jennifer Truman (Bureau of Justice Statistics), Courtney Finlayson (Lurie Children's Hospital of Chicago), Elizabeth Reis (City University of New York), Jason Flatt (University of Nevada, Las Vegas), Harper Jean Tobin (HJ Tobin Policy Consulting), Vadim Shteyler (University of California, San Francisco), Jack Byrne (University of Waikato), Jaimie Veale (University of Waikato), Micah Davison (Statistics New Zealand), Sean Cahill (The Fenway Institute), Juno Obedin-Maliver (Stanford University), and Clair Kronk (Yale University). Additionally, Robert Cronin (Vanderbilt University) provided statistical information from the All of Us study.

A number of staff members of the National Academies made significant contributions to the report. Jordyn White and Katrina Stone served as program officers and provided important research support. Eric Grimes made sure that committee meetings ran smoothly, and he and Rebecca Krone assisted in preparing the manuscript and otherwise provided key administrative and logistical support; Kirsten Sampson Snyder managed the report review process; Yvonne Wise managed the report production process; and Brian Harris-Kojetin, director of the Committee on National Statistics, provided valuable guidance and oversight. We also thank Eugenia Grohman for her editing of the report.

This Consensus Study Report was reviewed in draft form by individuals chosen for their diverse perspectives and technical expertise. The purpose of this independent review is to provide candid and critical comments that will assist the National Academies in making each published report as sound as possible and to ensure that it meets the institutional standards for quality, objectivity, evidence, and responsiveness to the study charge. The review comments and draft manuscript remain confidential to protect the integrity of the deliberative process.

We thank the following individuals for their review of this report: Elizabeth L. Cope (AcademyHealth), Kari J. Dockendorff (Colorado State University), Margo Edmunds (AcademyHealth), Jason D. Flatt (University of Nevada, Las Vegas), M. Paz Galupo (Towson University), Kirk Greenway (Indian Health Service), Jody L. Herman (Williams Institute, University of California, Los Angeles), Michelle M. Johns (NORC at University of Chicago), Charles F. Manski (Northwestern University), Kristina Olson (Princeton University), Tonia Poteat (University of North Carolina), Samuel H. Preston (University of Pennsylvania), Kristen Schilt (University of Chicago), and Carl Streed (Boston University School of Medicine).

Although the reviewers listed above provided many constructive comments and suggestions, they were not asked to endorse the conclusions or recommendations of this report nor did they see the final draft before its release. The review of this report was overseen by Yu Xie (Princeton University) and Bradford Gray (Urban Institute). They were responsible for making certain that an independent examination of this report was carried out in accordance with the standards of the National Academies and that all review comments were carefully considered. Responsibility for the final content rests entirely with the authoring committee and the National Academies.

Nancy Bates, *Co-Chair*

Marshall Chin, *Co-Chair*

Tara Becker, *Study Director*

Committee on Measuring Sex, Gender Identity, and Sexual Orientation

Contents

Summary

Sex, gender identity, and sexual orientation are complex constructs that are interrelated but conceptually distinct. These concepts are also key indicators of the demographic diversity in the United States. Sex and gender are often conflated under the assumptions that they are mutually determined and do not differ from each other; however, the growing visibility of transgender and intersex populations, as well as efforts to improve the measurement of sex and gender across many scientific fields, has brought to light the limitations of these assumptions and demonstrated the need to reconsider how sex, gender, and the relationship between them are conceptualized. This in turn affects the concept of sexual orientation, because it is defined on the basis of the relationship between a person's own sex or gender and that of their actual or preferred partners. Sex, gender, and sexual orientation are core aspects of identity that shape opportunities, experiences with discrimination, and outcomes through the life course; therefore, it is crucial that measures of these concepts accurately capture their complexity.

Better measurement of sex, gender identity, and sexual orientation will also improve the ability to identify sexual and gender minority populations and understand the challenges they face. The social, political, and legal status of lesbian, gay, bisexual, transgender, queer, intersex, and other sexual and gender minorities—the LGBTQI+ population—has undergone considerable change in the past decade. Although there has been growing public acceptance, LGBTQI+ people continue to experience disparate and inequitable treatment, including harassment, discrimination, and violence, which in turn affects outcomes in many areas of everyday life, including health and access to health care services, economic and educational attainment, and family and social support. Though knowledge of these disparities has increased significantly over the past decade, glaring gaps remain, often driven by a lack of reliable data.

A 2020 report from the National Academies of Sciences, Engineering, and Medicine (the National Academies) called on the federal government to develop standards to guide the collection of these data throughout the activities of the federal agencies. Without national standards on how to collect, analyze, and report these data, there are increasing differences in the measures that are used in surveys and other data collections. Some of these differences reflect important attention to the data collection context or to variation in terminology across the population, but other differences reflect a lack of consensus on how to define and measure the constructs of interest. A lack of consistency in data collection measures introduces concerns about data comparability, complicates data analysis and reporting, and hinders efforts to advance research and develop effective programs and policies focused on improving the well-being of LGBTQI+ people.

To improve the quality of data collection efforts and advance research and policy around LGBTQI+ population well-being, the National Institutes of Health asked the National Academies to convene a committee of experts (1) to review current measures and the methodological issues related to measuring sex as a nonbinary construct, gender identity, and sexual orientation in surveys and research studies, in administrative settings (such as grant and job applications), and in clinical settings (such as doctors' offices or clinical trials), and (2) to produce a consensus report with conclusions and recommendations on guiding principles for collecting data on sex, gender identity, and sexual orientation and recommended measures for these constructs in different settings.

Due to the broadness of the settings and the short timeline of study, the committee focused on data collection efforts among adults in the general population; therefore, modifications may be necessary when data is being collected for youth or within LGBTQI+ communities.

To carry out its task, the panel first agreed on the definitions and characteristics of the underlying concepts on which our recommended measures would be based; we also identified and defined terminology that we use to describe specific sexual and gender minority populations: see Table S-1. It is important to note that these populations represent only a subset of sexual and gender minority populations in the United States.

In accordance with federal mandates for data collection on American Indian and Alaska Native (AIAN) populations and in response to recommendations of the National Congress of American Indians and the Indian Health Service 2020 Strategic Vision and Action Plan, the panel affirms the importance of ensuring the representation and visibility of the U.S. Indigenous population. "Two-Spirit" is an intertribal umbrella term that serves as an English-language placeholder for tribally specific gender and sexual orientation identities that are centered in tribal worldviews, practices, and knowledges. Tribes have their own specific term for gender statuses (e.g., in Navajo, *Nádleehí* refers to one who is transformed), and many go beyond the binary construct of male or female and are part of a holistic view of personhood that encompasses not only gender or sexual orientation identity, but also a social and cultural position that shapes and defines all aspects of one's life. Tribal identities cannot be directly translated or mapped to the standard Western conceptions of gender and sexuality. Two-Spirit is a way to reference Indigenous identities, practices, and traditions in the context of Western data collection practices and ensure that Indigenous sexual and gender minorities are represented and counted. Because Two-Spirit is a term by and for Indigenous peoples and is culturally anchored with particular meaning and, potentially, social status, it is not appropriate for use by non-Indigenous populations.

TABLE S-1 Definitions and Terminology for "Sex," "Gender," and "Sexual Orientation"

Sex	A multidimensional construct based on a cluster of anatomical and physiological traits (sex traits)	
	Dimensions	
	Sex traits, which include:	external genitalia, secondary sex characteristics, gonads, chromosomes, and hormones
	Characteristics:	• Usually assigned as female or male • Most often defined at birth based on visual inspection of external genitalia • Sex traits usually assumed to be unambiguous, but may not be • Sex traits usually assumed to correspond to the same sex, but may not • Some sex traits can change or be altered over time
	Minority Populations Defined Based on Sex Traits	
	Intersex/DSD[a]	People whose sex traits do not all correspond to a single sex

continued

TABLE S-1 Continued

Gender	A multidimensional construct that links gender identity, gender expression, and social and cultural expectations about status, characteristics, and behavior that are associated with sex traits	
	Dimensions	
	Identity	A core element of a person's individual sense of self
	Expression	How an individual signals their gender to others through behavior and appearance
	Social and cultural expectations	Related to social status, characteristics, and behavior that are associated with sex traits
	Characteristics	• Often conceptualized as binary (male/female or man/woman) in Western cultures, but also includes categories outside this binary • Often used interchangeably with sex, though it is conceptually distinct • Often assumed to be determined based on sex assigned at birth but may differ • Gender identity, expression, and social and cultural expectations may not all correspond to the same gender • May be temporally and contextually fluid
	Gender Identities	
	Transgender	A person whose current gender identity is different from the sex they were assigned at birth
	Transgender experience	All people who can be classified as transgender, regardless of whether they identify as transgender; also called transgender history
	Transgender identity	People who identify as transgender
	Cisgender	A person whose current gender identity corresponds to the sex they were assigned at birth
	Nonbinary	An umbrella term for gender identities that lie outside the gender binary
	Genderqueer	A person who does not follow gender norms
	Genderfluid	A person who does not identify with a fixed gender
	Two-Spirit	Placeholder term for specific gender and sexual orientation identities that are centered in Indigenous tribal worldviews, practices, and knowledges

TABLE S-1 Continued

Sexual Orientation	A multidimensional construct encompassing emotional, romantic, and sexual attraction, identity, and behavior	
	Dimensions	
	Identity	A person's core internal sense of their sexuality
	Attraction	A multidimensional concept that includes the gender(s) to which a person is attracted and the strength of this attraction, including whether a person feels attraction at all
	Behavior	A multidimensional concept that includes the gender(s) of sexual partners, specific sexual activities, and frequency of activity
	Characteristics	• Often defined in Western cultures based on the gender(s) of a person's desired or actual partners relative to their own gender • The three dimensions of sexuality—attraction, identity, and behavior—may not correspond to the same orientation
	Sexual Orientation Identities	
	Heterosexual, straight	Sexually oriented toward people of a different, usually binary, gender
	Homosexual, gay	Sexually oriented toward people of the same, usually binary, gender
	Lesbian	Women who are sexually oriented toward other women
	Bisexual	Sexually oriented toward both men and women
	Queer	An umbrella term for belonging to the LGBTQI+ community; also used to refer to a person who is sexually oriented toward people of more than one gender
	Pansexual	Sexually oriented toward people of any gender
	Questioning	Uncertain about sexual orientation identity
	Same gender loving	Nonheterosexual sexual orientation identity used by some within African American communities as a resistance to Eurocentric language for sexuality
	Two-Spirit	Placeholder term for specific gender and sexual orientation identities that are centered in Indigenous tribal worldviews, practices, and knowledges

NOTE: Populations and identities listed are a subset of all sexual and gender minority populations.

[a]DSD, differences in sex development.

PRINCIPLES FOR DATA COLLECTION

The panel developed five guiding principles for data collection.

1. **People deserve to count and be counted (inclusiveness).** A key purpose of data collection is to gather information that can help researchers, policy makers, service providers, and other stakeholders understand diverse populations and create policies, programs, and budgets that meet these populations' needs. Both quantitative and qualitative data, regardless of how they are collected, reflect the identities and experiences of people and communities that deserve to be heard and respected. Everyone should be able to see themselves, and their identities, represented in surveys and other data collection instruments.

2. **Use precise terminology that reflects the constructs of interest (precision).** Sex, gender, and sexual orientation are complex and multidimensional, and identifying the components of these constructs that are of interest and measuring them using appropriate terminology is critical for collecting reliable data. Questions should clearly specify which component(s) of sex, gender, and sexual orientation are being measured, and one construct should not be used as a proxy for another.

3. **Respect identity and autonomy (autonomy).** Questions about dimensions of identity, by definition, are asking about a person's sense of self. Data collection must allow respondents to self-identify whenever possible, and any proxy reporting should reflect what is known about how a person self-identifies. All data collection activities require well-informed consent from potential respondents, with no penalty for those who opt out of sharing personal information about themselves or other household members. This principle encompasses data collection for legal documents intended for individual identification; external authorization or attestation should not be required when someone reports, or wishes to change, their gender identity.

4. **Collect only necessary data (parsimony).** Data collection is not an end in itself: data should only be gathered in pursuit of a specific and well-defined goal, such as documenting or understanding disparities and inequities between populations or meeting legal reporting requirements, and data that are not essential to achieve that goal should not be collected.

5. **Use data in a manner that benefits respondents and respects their privacy and confidentiality (privacy).** Once data are gathered, they should be analyzed at the most granular level possible, and research

findings should be shared back with respondents and their communities to ensure that they benefit from data they have shared. Throughout all analysis and dissemination steps, sex, gender, and sexual orientation data—which may be sensitive and vulnerable to misuse—must be used, maintained, and shared only under rigorous privacy and confidentiality standards. Similarly, when data are collected in tribal nations, preapproved tribal research and data collection, analytic, and dissemination protocols should be followed to ensure data integrity and community benefit and to ensure rigorous privacy and confidentiality standards are upheld.

GUIDELINES FOR COLLECTING SEX AND GENDER DATA

The growing visibility of transgender and intersex populations, as well as efforts to improve the measurement of sex and gender in many scientific fields, has led to a recognition that sex and gender are more complex than current measures capture. For sex and gender, most data collection instruments do not separately assess both constructs and instead conflate them by using a single measure. This single measure sometimes specifies that respondents should report their sex, sometimes that they should report their gender, and sometimes does not specify the concept of interest. However, for transgender and intersex people, sex and gender and their dimensions may not fall in the same category, and data collection efforts that are not clear regarding which specific dimension of sex or gender is being measured make it difficult to determine how they should answer.

This imprecision can lead to mismeasurement of the relevant concept (e.g., when gender identity is reported as sex) or misuse of the data (e.g., assuming none of an individual's sex traits differ from their reported sex), and this can have negative repercussions for these individuals, as well as for overall data quality. There is growing recognition of the potential harms that can arise from mismeasurement or misuse of measures of sex and gender, particularly in health care, where tests and treatments are sometimes tied to sex-related differences and where gender identity informs social interactions between health care professionals and patients in ways that can affect the quality of care. In general, when a person's identity documents are not consistent with their reported sex or gender, they can face harassment, discrimination, and restrictions on their activities—such as travel or voting—affecting their ability to live freely in society. Measuring sex as a biological variable based on sex traits is insufficient because it cannot address either the multidimensional nature of sex or the independent role of gender in shaping people's health and life experiences.

CONCLUSION 1: Gender encompasses identity, expression, and social position. A person's gender is associated with but cannot be reduced to either sex assigned at birth or specific sex traits. Therefore, data collection efforts should not conflate sex as a biological variable with gender or otherwise treat the respective concepts as interchangeable. In addition, in many contexts, including human subjects research and medical care, collection of data on gender is more relevant than collection of data on sex as a biological variable, particularly for the purposes of assessing inclusion and monitoring discrimination and other forms of disparate treatment.

Although the distinction between gender as a social construction and sex as a biological variable can seem clear on its face, in practice, aspects of gender shape most experiences in everyday life, from internalized psychological processes to structural constraints, such as sexism and other forms of gender discrimination. It is difficult to disentangle the independent effects of sex and gender on other outcomes because of their combined biological and environmental or contextual influences. Gender-based social structures and expectations can influence behaviors and both create or magnify differences that might otherwise appear to be based in biology due to correlations with sex as a biological variable; however, these processes can only be understood if measures of gender are also routinely collected.

RECOMMENDATION 1: The standard for the National Institutes of Health should be to collect data on gender and report it by default. Collection of data on sex as a biological variable should be limited to circumstances where information about sex traits is relevant, as in the provision of clinical preventive screenings or for research investigating specific genetic, anatomical, or physiological processes and their connections to patterns of health and disease. In human populations, collection of data on sex as a biological variable should be accompanied by collection of data on gender.

Asking respondents to separately identify their sex and their gender—in particular, their sex assigned at birth and gender identity—improves overall measurement quality and also allows researchers and other data users to identify individuals with transgender experience by comparing their sex assigned at birth to their current gender identity. This two-step gender measure has become an increasingly common and validated way to identify people with transgender experience because it identifies a wider range of transgender people than single-step methods that ask respondents whether they identify as transgender.

The use of a single binary male/female item to measure sex does not capture either the multidimensional nature of this construct or its underlying complexity for those with intersex traits or transgender people, because their sex traits may not correspond to those of a single sex. Introducing a third response category to binary measures of sex, such as "transgender" or "intersex," is thus a poor measure of these populations. Moreover, because gender is socially mediated, binary measures of any dimension of gender are also inadequate for capturing the complex ways in which individuals can identify with, express, or socially experience gender.

MEASUREMENT CONTEXT

The panel was tasked with making recommendations on measures of sex, sexual orientation, and gender identity with attention to how these recommendations may be applied differently in three settings: in surveys and research studies, in administrative settings, and in clinical settings. We found that the most relevant characteristics distinguishing these settings were uses of the data, the identifiability of respondents, and the risk of data disclosure. LGBTQI+ people are often subject to mistreatment, segregation, harassment, discrimination, and violence, and therefore reporting information that identifies an individual as a sexual or gender minority may pose risks to respondents. Consequently, respondents should always be able to opt out of providing this information, particularly in contexts where their responses can be linked to personally identifiable information and where the risk of disclosure is high. Even when individuals are not at risk of being identified, when data are broadly available—even in aggregated form—there is the potential for these data to be misused or misinterpreted to support harmful treatment or policies. Thus, it is important to weigh the need for and benefits of collecting these data with the risk of harm such data collection might pose to respondents.

For surveys and research, data are often collected confidentially and reported in aggregate to prevent disclosure of identifiable information about respondents. When those protections are in place, the risk of disclosure is low for individual respondents, enabling the routine collection of data that identifies LGBTQI+ populations. In clinical settings, data are linked to a specific individual, but the information on sex traits, gender identity, sexual orientation, transgender experience, and intersex traits is also crucial for providing appropriate and necessary care. While health-related data are legally protected from unauthorized disclosure, clear organizational policies, work flows, and training on its use are necessary for appropriate care and to prevent mistreatment of LGBTQI+ people.

Data collected in administrative settings are often linked to specific individuals, such as for vital statistics and other legal identification documents to establish identity. However, these data have sometimes been used to facilitate segregation, harassment, and discrimination. In many administrative settings, strong legal privacy protections like those in health care do not exist, so there may be specific contexts in which the collection of some of these data, such as intersex status or sex assigned at birth, may be considered invasive. For these reasons, it is especially important to establish a clear need to collect these data, minimize the risk of data disclosure and misuse, and allow individuals to opt out of responding.

Much of the research that has been conducted on measures of sex, gender identity, and sexual orientation has been conducted with survey data and in research settings. Although less information evaluating the use of these measures in clinical and public health settings was available, the panel saw little reason to believe that our recommended measures need to be modified for these settings. Very little information is available on measurement practices in administrative settings, and it may be necessary to modify the recommended measures in specific administrative contexts. We note that sex assigned at birth, gender identity, and sexual orientation are not the only types of potentially sensitive information that need to be collected respectfully and confidentially and used appropriately in administrative settings. For these reasons, while we propose one set of measures that can be used across all three settings, users should identify and adopt best practices for implementation when using these measures in settings that present risks of identifiability and disclosure.

RECOMMENDED MEASURES

Sexual Orientation Identity

The measurement of sexual orientation has varied across settings and data collection purposes, with a focus on any one or a combination of the three dimensions of sexual orientation—behavior, attraction, and identity. The complexities of categorizing sexual behaviors and erotic or romantic attractions present unique challenges to assessing sexual orientation. As a result, the panel does not offer recommended measures of the dimensions of behavior and attraction.

Sexual orientation identity is the cognitive as well as social expression of one's sexual orientation. Thus, it is the dimension that is most consistently tied to experiences with material forms of discrimination and most often invoked explicitly in laws and policies aimed at protecting (or harming) sexual minorities. It is also the dimension with the broadest and longest use in population-based data collection settings to enumerate and distinguish between sexual minority and majority adult populations. For these reasons, we focus our evaluation and recommendations on measures of sexual orientation identity.

RECOMMENDATION 2: The panel recommends that the National Institutes of Health use the following question for assessing sexual orientation identity:

Which of the following best represents how you think of yourself? [Select ONE]:
○　**Lesbian or gay**
○　**Straight, that is, not gay or lesbian**
○　**Bisexual**
○　**[If respondent is AIAN:] Two-Spirit**
○　**I use a different term [free-text]**
(Don't know)
(Prefer not to answer)

Table S-2 details a subset of selection criteria for our recommended measure.

The panel also recommends several areas for research, including validation of measures of sexual behavior and attraction and measures that incorporate "queer," asexual, and other emerging identities; alternate wording for the "straight" response category; the utility of including community-specific terminology in response options; performance within adolescent populations; and how proxy reporting affects data quality (Recommendation 3).

TABLE S-2 Selected Evaluation Criteria for Recommendation on Sexual Orientation Identity

Evaluation Criteria	Evaluation
Conceptual Fit	• Measures sexual orientation identity only (i.e., does not conflate attraction, identity, and/or behavior) • Clearly distinguishes people with different sexual orientation identities and broadly between sexual minority and majority populations; allows enumeration of those who do not use listed labels • Allows for culturally specific identification for Indigenous populations; Two-Spirit response category explicitly included only in automated data collection where respondent endorses American Indian or Alaska Native (AIAN) identity
Populations Included in Testing	• Sexual minority and heterosexual/straight identified • Spanish and English speakers • U.S. general population, racially diverse samples, urban and rural residents • Ages 12–85 years
Adjustments to Previously Tested Items Included in Recommended Measure	• Replaces "none of these" response with "I use a different term" followed by a free-text field • Includes Two-Spirit category in automated data collection where racial identity is collected and AIAN is indicated
Weaknesses and Challenges	• Narrow set of responses does not reflect current culture and terminology • Write-in sexual orientation identity field will have to be cleaned and coded for reporting; newer terms not listed (e.g., "pansexual") may grow in popularity and need to be assessed for inclusion as explicit options • Does not provide a clear option to indicate when a person might lack certainty about an appropriate label (e.g., "questioning") • Though testing showed a need for the "that is, not gay" phrase, it is not clear this is still needed and, as written, is a conceptually inaccurate description of what it means to be straight • Response options are not presented in order of prevalence or other standard ordering

Gender Identity

Although many different strategies have been proposed for measuring gender identity, we focus on measures that allow for the enumeration of both transgender and cisgender people. We recommend using a "two-step" gender measure that includes both sex assigned at birth and a broad measure of gender identity because this approach is designed to include people with transgender experience who may not identify with the term "transgender"; it also replaces current nonspecific measures of sex/gender used in most data collection contexts.

RECOMMENDATION 4: The panel recommends that the National Institutes of Health use the following pair of questions for assessing sex assigned at birth and gender identity:

Q1: What sex were you assigned at birth, on your original birth certificate?
○ Female
○ Male
(Don't know)
(Prefer not to answer)

Q2: What is your current gender? [Mark only one]
○ Female
○ Male
○ Transgender
○ [If respondent is AIAN:] Two-Spirit
○ I use a different term: [free text]
(Don't know)
(Prefer not to answer)

Table S-3 details a subset of the selection criteria for our recommended measure.

The panel also recommends areas for future research and question development, including the need for additional gender identity response options (e.g., nonbinary), alternative two-step measures that do not rely on sex assigned at birth, the effect of changes in the recording of sex on birth certificates, how proxy reporting affects data quality, and expanded testing among youth and non-English speakers (Recommendation 5).

TABLE S-3 Selected Evaluation Criteria for Recommendation on Gender Identity

Evaluation Criteria	Evaluation
Conceptual Fit	• Clearly distinguishes between sex assigned at birth and current gender, which allows for enumerating the broadest definition of the transgender population • Cross-tabulation of the two items provides data for cisgender and transgender people, including counts for cisgender men; cisgender women; transgender men; transgender women; people who identify primarily as transgender; and people identifying with other terms via write-ins, which may include terms such as nonbinary, genderqueer, and gender nonconforming • Allows for culturally specific identification for Indigenous populations; Two-Spirit response category should be displayed only in automated data collection where racial identity is collected and respondent endorses American Indian or Alaska Native (AIAN) identity
Populations Included in Testing	• Transgender and cisgender people • Spanish and English speakers • U.S. general population, racially diverse samples, urban and rural residents • Ages 12–85 years
Adjustments to Previously Tested Items Included in Recommended Measure	• Female-first response list corresponds with both alphabetical and population size ordering • Replaces "none of these" response with "I use a different term" followed by a free-text field • Includes Two-Spirit category in automated data collection where racial identity is collected and AIAN is indicated
Weaknesses and Challenges	• Format for current gender question is forced choice, but response options are not necessarily mutually exclusive • Write-in gender identity field will have to be cleaned and coded for reporting; newer terms not listed (e.g., nonbinary) may grow in popularity and need to be assessed for inclusion as explicit options • Asking for sex assigned at birth is considered sensitive for some transgender people and may not be appropriate in settings where privacy and confidentiality cannot be assured (e.g., employment contexts) • Sex assigned at birth question offers only binary responses, though some states have begun to allow nonbinary options on birth certificates

Intersex/DSD Status

The measurement of intersex status is complicated by the unique experiences of intersex people and a limited research base. Biologically, intersex variations are highly heterogeneous, can involve any sex trait, and may not be apparent from an external examination. Most people with intersex traits are assigned male or female sex at birth. The majority of people with intersex traits are not identified as having an intersex variation until later in life—if at all. Intersex status is an important demographic characteristic and aspect of identity that also involves private medical information. While there are barriers to disclosure, people with intersex traits appear to want to disclose.

> **RECOMMENDATION 6: When the National Institutes of Health seek to identify people with intersex traits (differences of sex development) in clinical, survey, research, and administrative settings, they should do so by using a stand-alone measure that asks respondents to report their intersex status. They should not do so by adding intersex as a third response category to a binary measure of sex.**

Unfortunately, there is very little evidence regarding the language or impact of measurement of intersex status in research, clinical, and administrative settings. Based on the available research, historical context, and community recommendations, there are three measures that appear to have the strongest grounding in evidence. Of these three measures, the panel prefers the following measure, because it is the only measure that has been tested among intersex populations—although it is potentially cumbersome to administer:

> **Have you ever been diagnosed by a medical doctor or other health professional with an intersex condition or a difference of sex development (DSD) or were you born with (or developed naturally in puberty) genitals, reproductive organs, or chromosomal patterns that do not fit standard definitions of male or female?**
>
> ○ Yes
> ○ No
> (Don't know)
> (Prefer not to answer)

In some situations, it might be necessary to identify a respondent's specific intersex variation, and the panel recommends using the list of conditions developed by InterACT Advocates for Intersex Youth.

The panel also recommends that the National Institutes of Health fund or conduct research that comparatively evaluates the quality of the three measures of intersex status with the strongest grounding in the evidence to determine which measure most effectively identifies the intersex population. We further recommend research that tests the utility of including definitions and examples of terms used in intersex status questions, such as "intersex," "DSD," and specific intersex variations; examines the prevalence of "intersex" as a gender identity; and assesses proxy reporting of intersex/DSD status, particularly of parents reporting their children's status (Recommendation 7).

The panel's recommendations provide for consistent measurement of sex, gender, and sexual orientation across each data collection setting, while the research recommendations offer a detailed program that can refine these measures and ensure that they remain in step with cultural and historical developments. The consistent use of validated measures of these complex concepts and continued efforts to refine them will advance science that can be used to improve the well-being of sexual and gender minorities well into the future.

1

Introduction and Background

Sex, gender identity, and sexual orientation are complex, interrelated constructs that are conceptually distinct. In practice, sex and gender are often conflated under the assumption that they are mutually determined and do not differ from each other, despite a widespread understanding that sex refers to biological characteristics and gender refers to social and behavioral characteristics (Hall et al., 2021; Schudson, Beischel, and van Anders, 2019; Westbrook and Saperstein, 2015).[1] Sexual orientation is conceptually linked to sex and gender because individuals are classified on the basis of the relationship between their own sex or gender and that of their actual or preferred partners. This has sometimes led to the conflation of gender (non)conformity and sexual orientation, even though gender and sexual orientation are separate concepts (Rubin, 1984).

The growing visibility of transgender and intersex populations, as well as efforts at the National Institutes of Health (NIH) to improve the measurement of "sex as a biological variable," have underscored the limitations of the prevailing assumptions and demonstrated the need to reconsider how sex, gender, and the relationship between them are conceptualized. This conceptualization also affects how people think about and define sexual

---

[1]In practice, this distinction between the social and biological aspects of gender and sex is not so clear-cut (Springer, Stellman, and Jordan-Young, 2012).

orientation, including how people identify their own sexuality. Sex, gender, and sexual orientation are core aspects of identity that shape people's opportunities, their experiences with material forms of discrimination, and the outcomes through their life courses (NASEM, 2020). A reevaluation of the measurement of these concepts is needed because data collection based on clear measures can provide important insights into the mechanisms through which sex, gender, and sexual orientation operate at the individual, organizational, and societal level to produce inequality among both sexual and gender minorities and majorities.

Better measurement of sex, gender identity, and sexual orientation will also improve identification of sexual and gender minority populations and understanding of the challenges they face. Current estimates suggest that there were over 11 million lesbian, gay, bisexual, and transgender (LGBT) people in the United States in 2020, comprising about 5.6 percent of the U.S. adult population (Jones, 2021). The proportion of the U.S. population that identifies as LGBT is substantially larger among younger generations: 9.1 percent of people born in 1981–1996 and 15.9 percent of people born after 1997 identified as LGBT in 2020 (Jones, 2021). An estimated 1.7 percent of people have an intersex trait (Blackless et al., 2000). Overall, lesbian, gay, bisexual, transgender, queer, intersex, and other sexual and gender minorities—sometimes referred to as LGBTQI+ people—are a significant and growing proportion of the U.S. population.

There have been major changes in the social, political, and legal status of LGBTQI+ people in the past decade. To assess these changes, a recent report, *Understanding the Well-Being of LGBTQI+ Populations* (NASEM, 2020), provided a comprehensive review of what is currently known about sexual and gender minority populations over the life course and across many domains, including family and social relationships, community and civic engagement, education, economics, law and policy, physical and mental health, and health care access. The report detailed the remarkable progress that has been made in research about these populations, but it also highlighted glaring knowledge gaps caused by a lack of reliable data. Most national surveys and other important sources of data in the United States do not yet collect demographic data on sexual orientation, gender identity, or intersex status: although measures of sexual orientation are increasingly included on population surveys, measures that allow researchers to identify transgender populations remain less common, while measures that identify populations with differences in sex development (DSD), sometimes referred to as intersex populations, are almost nonexistent.

STATEMENT OF TASK

To improve the quality of data collection efforts and advance research and policies to improve the well-being of LGBTQI+ populations, NIH asked the National Academies of Sciences, Engineering, and Medicine to convene a committee of experts to address the following statement of task:

> An ad hoc panel of the National Academies of Sciences, Engineering, and Medicine will review current measures and the methodological issues related to measuring sex as a non-binary construct, gender identity, and sexual orientation in surveys and research studies, in administrative settings (such as grant and job applications), and in clinical settings (such as doctors' offices or clinical trials). As part of its information-gathering activities, the panel will hold a public workshop to get input from researchers in sexual and gender minority health and well-being, academic and government researchers doing work on measuring these concepts, members of sexual and gender minority populations, and policy makers and other users of these data on these populations. The panel will produce a consensus report with conclusions and recommendations on 1) guiding principles for collecting data on sex, gender identity, and sexual orientation, and 2) recommended measures for these constructs in different settings, such as surveys, clinical settings, and administrative forms.

In response to this request, the National Academies appointed the Committee on Measuring Sex, Gender Identity, and Sexual Orientation, under the standing committee of the Committee on National Statistics, to carry out this task. The panel is comprised of multidisciplinary experts in the fields of medicine, psychology, public health, sociology, survey methodology, and statistics. The panel met seven times over a 9-month period to identify the most promising measures of sex, gender identity, and sexual orientation that would enable the identification of members of LGBTQI+ populations in each of the contexts outlined in the statement of task.

TERMINOLOGY

Measurement Concepts

The panel began its task to develop measures that captured aspects of the three distinct concepts—sex, gender, and sexual orientation—by defining the underlying concepts on which the measures are based. To develop these consensus definitions, each panel member submitted a definition for each concept, and the panel then discussed these submissions to identify their common elements and arrive at a consensus understanding of each concept. Although definitions from previously published literature were sometimes used as a starting point for these discussions, those definitions were modified as part of the panel's discussions: the definitions used in this report reflect the panel's consensus.

- *Sex* is a multidimensional construct based on a cluster of anatomical and physiological traits that include external genitalia, secondary sex characteristics, gonads, chromosomes, and hormones.

Sex in Western cultures is typically assigned at birth by medical professionals as either male or female, based solely on visual inspection of external genitalia. Sex traits are often assumed to be unambiguous and correspond to a single sex; however, sex traits may not all correspond to the same sex or with these binary categories, and thus with sex assigned at birth. For example, people who are *intersex* or have *differences in sex development (DSD)* have traits that do not correspond to a single sex.[2] Some sex traits may change or be altered over time, making sex both a complex and temporally fluid concept.

- *Gender* is a multidimensional construct that links *gender identity*, which is a core element of a person's individual identity; *gender expression*, which is how a person signals their gender to others through their behavior and appearance (such as hair style and clothing); and cultural expectations about social status, characteristics, and behavior that are associated with sex traits.

As noted above, gender and sex are conceptually distinct, but they are often used interchangeably due to normative assumptions that sex is binary and immutable and that sex assigned at birth defines gender. Neither gender identity nor gender expression is defined by sex traits, however, and both can be temporally and contextually fluid. Gender is often conceptualized in Western cultures as man/male and woman/female, although it also includes categories that lie outside this binary, such as **nonbinary** (an umbrella term for the identities outside of the binary), **gender-fluid** (does not identify with

---

[2]There is considerable variation in preferred terminology for this population and no consensus among people with intersex traits. For example, one study of members of a support group for androgen insensitivity syndrome (a DSD group), which includes both caregivers and affected individuals, found that 55 percent preferred the term "intersex" and 50 percent preferred the term "differences of sex development" (Johnson et al., 2017). Participants were able to select more than one term, and some preferred both terms, while others preferred something else. Throughout this report we refer to this population variably as "people with intersex traits" and "intersex/DSD populations."

a fixed gender), or, for Indigenous[3] populations, **Two-Spirit** (see next section). Throughout this report, we focus on measures of gender identity, but it is important to keep in mind that measuring gender identity is one facet of gender. When we discuss the overall concept that encompasses identity, expression, and social and cultural expectations, we use the broader term: gender.

Transgender refers to a person whose gender identity is different from the sex they were assigned at birth; **cisgender** refers to a person whose gender identity corresponds to the sex they were assigned at birth or is sometimes used to describe someone who is not transgender (Aultman, 2014). This definition of transgender encompasses a wide range of gender minority populations, such as those with nonbinary identities and some people with intersex traits. It is important to note, however, that not all individuals who are classified as transgender under this definition identify themselves as transgender.[4] For this reason, within this report we make a distinction between **transgender experience**[5]—when someone currently identifies with a gender identity that is different from their sex assigned at birth—and **transgender identity**—when someone currently identifies oneself as transgender.

- *Sexual orientation* is a multidimensional construct encompassing emotional, romantic, and sexual attraction, identity, and behavior.

In Western cultures, sexual orientation is often defined on the basis of the gender(s) of a person's desired potential or actual sexual or romantic partners relative to the person's own gender. These dimensions of sexuality—attraction, identity, and behavior—may not correspond to the same sexual orientation. For example, a man may be attracted to other men but exclusively engage

---

[3]The U.S. Office of Management and Budget identifies American Indian or Alaska Native as persons having origins in any of the original peoples of North, Central, or South America and who maintain tribal affiliation or community attachment. Native Hawaiians (Kānaka Maoli) and Indigenous Pacific Islanders of Guam (Chamorro), Marshall Islands (Marshallese), American Samoa (Samoan) are the original peoples of their respective Islands and are also recognized as Indigenous for purposes of this report. When referring to these populations in general we use the term "Indigenous"; when referring the federal government's recognition and measurement of this population, we follow the official terminology and use "American Indian or Alaska Native."

[4]Florence Ashley (2021) has recently proposed a new dimension of gender, "gender modality," as a way to identify an individual who is a person of transgender experience who identifies as cisgender.

[5]Some people view the term "transgender experience" as dismissive or skeptical of transgender identities and people. However, the panel deliberately selected this term because of its common use in transgender and intersex communities to describe individuals with the lived experience of being transgender (also see, e.g., Puckett et al., 2020).

in sexual behaviors with women or a woman may be attracted to men but also identify as lesbian.

The most common sexual orientation identity terms are based on a gender binary and include **heterosexual,** or **straight; homosexual, gay,** or **lesbian;** and **bisexual.** However, there are other less prevalent terms that may eschew the gender binary, such as **queer** (an umbrella term for belonging to the LGBTQI+ community that can also refer to a nonbinary gender identity, which is also referred to as **genderqueer**) or **pansexual** (oriented toward partners of any gender); denote uncertainty (e.g., **questioning**); or be used only among specific populations (e.g., **same gender loving,** used in Black communities,[6] or **Two-Spirit,** used in Indigenous populations). It is important to note that these terms are only a subset of the ever-evolving sexual orientation terminology that is currently in use and that some of the more common terms (gay, bisexual) are also used to reflect gender diversity in attraction (Callis, 2014; Paz Galupo, Ramirez, and Pulice-Farrow, 2017).

To this point, we have used two different umbrella terms to refer to populations defined by their sexual or gender minority status: "LGBTQI+" and "sexual and gender minority." Each term has both benefits and drawbacks. LGBTQI+ is a term that is well recognized and the acronym can be shortened to clearly specify which populations are under discussion; however, it is not easily recognizable if the leading letters in the acronym, LG, are excluded from the list, which makes it of limited utility when the focus is gender rather than sexual minorities. Of particular concern, this term conflates gender and sexual orientation, because it does not clearly distinguish between minority populations defined by their sexuality and those defined by their gender. The term "sexual and gender minority" does make this distinction, but it is less well known and less explicit regarding the specific populations that are being discussed. Because the benefits of using one term or the other depend on the context of their use, we use both of these terms throughout the report.

Gender Identity and Sexual Orientation in an Indigenous Context

There are 574 federally recognized American Indian and Alaska Native (AIAN) tribes that are sovereign governments and, as such, have a nation-to-nation relationship with the United States. Two-Spirit is an intertribal term first coined in 1990 that serves as a placeholder for tribally specific gender and sexual orientation identities that are centered in tribal worldviews, practices, and knowledges (see Wilson, 1996). Tribes have their own specific terms for gender statuses (e.g., in Navajo, *Nádleehí* refers to one

---

[6]"Same gender loving" is a term for a nonheterosexual sexual orientation identity used by some Black communities as a resistance to Eurocentric language for sexuality.

who is transformed), and many of these terms go beyond the binary categories of male or female. For these tribal identities that cannot be directly
translated or mapped to the Western conception of gender, "Two-Spirit"
can be used as the English-language placeholder term. For many tribal nations, gender is not limited to a Western binary construct or expression; in
fact, some tribes have as many as five genders. Thus, Two-Spirit often represents a third or fourth gender status that is nonbinary but is linguistically
or socially contextualized within a particular tribal nation worldview and
cultural understanding, often with certain social, cultural, or ceremonial
roles attached to the status (Jacobs, Thomas, and Lang, 1997). Under this
holistic view of personhood, Two-Spirit is a placeholder term that captures
not only gender identity or sexual orientation identity, but also a social
and cultural position that shapes and defines all aspects of one's life. Because Two-Spirit is a term by and for Indigenous peoples and is culturally
anchored with particular meaning and, potentially, social status, it is not
appropriate for use by non-Indigenous populations.

Although it is widely recognized and used across many Indigenous
communities (Robinson, 2020; Cassels et al., 2010; Walters et al., 2006),
the term Two-Spirit is not universally recognized or accepted. Moreover,
the term encompasses a large number of heterogeneous identities that may
otherwise share little in common. It has been criticized for erasing the
specific cultural histories and practices of individual tribes and for evoking
(and, in some cases, romanticizing) an ahistorical conception of gender and
sexuality that may be more grounded in colonial depictions of Indigenous
peoples as deviant than in Indigenous cultural practices (see, e.g., Pember,
2016). Despite these criticisms, the term Two-Spirit is a way to reference
Indigenous identities, practices, and traditions in the context of Western
data collection practices and ensure that Indigenous sexual and gender
minorities are represented and counted (Davis, 2019).

The U.S. government has a trust responsibility to the tribes, derived
partly from treaties, executive orders, judicial actions, or legislation, to
ensure protection of Indian trust lands and tribal sovereignty, as well as
provision of social, medical, and educational services for tribal members.
The National Congress of American Indians (NCAI) notes that the collection of accurate, adequate, meaningful data is critical to the health and welfare of tribal nations (Sahota, 2007). In recent years, tribes have exercised
sovereign authority over data collection efforts and research in tribal lands
and of tribal members.

Currently, the decennial U.S. census and the American Community
Survey (ACS) are the two major sources of data on AIAN people and form
the main basis of funding for many tribal programs and policies (Connolly
and Jacobs, 2020). Tribes have noted that AIAN and other Indigenous
populations tend to be undercounted in the ACS as well as in other national

surveys due to inadequate data collection and reporting or being collapsed into "other" categories due to small sample sizes. NCAI[7] reports:

> American Indians and Alaska Natives may be described as the "Asterisk Nation" because an asterisk, instead of data point, is often used in data displays when reporting racial and ethnic data due to various data collection and reporting issues, such as small sample size, large margins of error, or other issues related to the validity and statistical significance of data on American Indians and Alaska Natives.

Recognizing that a parallel problem of invisibility often arises in LGBTQI+ data collection methods and research, the panel is highlighting the specific cultural needs of Indigenous populations as part of our evaluation of measures of sex, gender, and sexual orientation.

CONNECTING CONCEPTS TO THE MEASUREMENT OF LGBTQI+ POPULATIONS

The growing visibility of transgender, intersex, and emerging sexual minority populations is an important factor contributing to the increasing recognition that sex, gender, and sexual orientation are more complex than current measures of these concepts may suggest. That recognition, in turn, has prompted a reconsideration of how they can be more accurately defined and measured. With regard to sex and gender, most data collection instruments do not separately assess each construct and instead conflate them by using a single measure. This single measure sometimes specifies that the respondents should report their sex, sometimes their gender, and sometimes does not specify the concept of interest (Westbrook and Saperstein, 2015).

In addition, the use of single measures of both sex and gender does not account for the complexity of the constructs by specifying the dimension of interest. For transgender and intersex people, sex and gender and their constituent dimensions may not correspond to the same response category, and data collection efforts that do not clarify whether they are asking respondents to report based on a specific dimension of their sex or gender make it difficult for respondents to determine how they should answer. The result may be mismeasurement or misrepresentation of the relevant concept, which can have negative repercussions for these individuals, as well as for scientific research and society more broadly. These repercussions for individuals can be serious: for example, if individuals are misclassified or viewed as belonging to a different category than they report in a clinical setting, they may not receive appropriate or adequate health care services

---

[7]See https://www.ncai.org/policy-research-center/research-data/data.

or treatment (Burgess et al., 2019). People whose identity documents are not consistent with the sex or gender they report in some administrative contexts can face harassment and discrimination and restrictions on their activities, including travel or voting (Fielding, 2020; Quinan and Bresser, 2020), thus restricting their ability to live and move freely through society.

In addition to improving the construct validity of measures of sex and gender, asking respondents to separately report their sex and their gender—in particular, their sex assigned at birth and their gender identity—also allows the identification of people with transgender experience. This "two-step" method of collecting sex and gender identity information has become an increasingly common and validated method of identifying people with transgender experience because it identifies a wider range of transgender people than "single-step" methods that ask whether respondents identify as transgender (Saperstein and Westbrook, 2021).

Introducing separate measures of sex and gender to allow these to be reported independently may not adequately address the limitations of these measures if each is measured using a single, binary measure. The use of a single binary male/female measure to capture sex may not adequately capture the underlying complexity of this concept for those with intersex traits or some transgender people who have received gender-affirming care because their sex traits may not all correspond to those of a single sex. Because the differences occur between sex traits that in most cases are male or female, most intersex people identify their sex within this binary, and thus, introducing a third response category to binary measures of sex is unlikely to either identify the intersex population or clarify which sex trait(s) the respondent's report of their sex is based on. For people with transgender experience, there is considerable variation in the gender-affirming care they have received, as well as in whether they are living their day-to-day lives as the gender associated with their sex at birth, their current gender identity, or some combination of the two (Scheim and Bauer, 2014). When asked to report on either their sex or their gender, it is not clear whether these respondents should answer based on their current gender identity or on their sex assigned at birth.

Because gender is socially constructed and expressed, binary measures of specific dimensions gender are also inadequate for capturing the complex ways in which individuals can identify with, express, or socially experience gender (Beischel, Schudson, and van Anders, 2021; Matsuno and Budge, 2017; Richards, Bouman, and Barker, 2017; Beemyn, 2015; West and Zimmerman, 1987). The umbrella term of nonbinary is used as a way to designate understandings of gender identity that lie outside of the gender binary of man/boy and woman/girl: it encompasses a multitude of identities that may reflect identification with both categories of the gender binary, no fixed identification with a specific gender, or identification with no gender at all (Richards, Bouman, and Barker, 2017). A significant proportion of people with transgender experience—by some estimates one-third or more (James et al., 2016)—identify with a nonbinary gender identity, such as "nonbinary," "genderqueer," or "transgender."

The inclusion of a nonbinary gender category—or another method of allowing respondents to report outside of the male/female (man/woman) binary—would allow researchers to assess gender-based disparities within the cisgender and transgender populations. Gender-based disparities across a wide range of outcomes have been well documented, but there are important differences in outcomes for U.S. adults with transgender experience by gender identity. For example, people with transgender experience who identify outside the binary options or who are perceived by others as gender nonconforming report worse health outcomes (Reisner and Hughto, 2019; Streed, McCarthy, and Haas, 2018; James et al., 2016; Miller and Grollman, 2015). Transgender men (men who were assigned female at birth) and transgender women (women who were assigned male at birth) experience differences in a variety of outcomes that are consistent with broader patterns of gender inequality (Shannon, 2021; James et al., 2016; Schilt and Bratter, 2015). These differences within the transgender population further underscore that the need for measures of gender identity extends beyond their utility in identifying those with transgender experience.

Moving beyond a binary understanding of gender also has implications for the measurement of sexual orientation. As noted above, the most commonly reported sexual orientation identities are defined on the basis of a binary understanding of gender and classify individuals on the basis of whether their emotional, romantic, or sexual partner(s) are the same gender or the "opposite" gender as themselves. Nonbinary individuals or those with (actual or potential) nonbinary partners may not see themselves in these sexual orientation identities. In fact, in a survey of LGBTQ+ medical professionals, half of nonbinary and all transgender respondents reported their sexual orientation identity as "something else" rather than classify themselves within any of the gender-binary-based categories provided on the survey (Eliason and Streed, 2017).

IDENTIFYING LGBTQI+ POPULATIONS

Importance

LGBTQI+ populations experience differential and inequitable treatment and outcomes in many areas of everyday life, including in health and access to health care services, educational attainment, economic outcomes, and family and social support (NASEM, 2020). The disparities for these populations include higher prevalence of physical and mental health problems, such as HIV and depression; worse self-reported health and health-related quality of life; lower socioeconomic status; and less support from family members and important social institutions, such as schools.

Recent research has sought to describe the origins of these disparities by exploring the multilevel and intersecting factors that influence the well-being of LGBTQI+ populations. These factors include minority stress exposures, including stigma, violence, and discrimination and barriers in access to education, employment, housing, and health care (NASEM, 2020; National Public Radio, Robert Wood Johnson Foundation, and the Harvard T.H. Chan School of Public Health, 2017). At the same time, they are mitigated by factors that help promote and build resilience, such as community and political engagement and strong social relationships (NASEM, 2020). The intensity and effects of these factors can vary across the life course and among different LGBTQI+ populations on the basis of such factors as race, age, and gender. A lack of data on the characteristics, needs, and experiences of LGBTQI+ populations is a major barrier both to better understandings of these disparities and how they are produced and to the development of effective programmatic and policy interventions to address them.

This report lays out a set of recommendations for how best to measure the concepts of sex, gender identity, and sexual orientation in the United States. Everyone has a sexual orientation, a gender identity, and sex traits, and reliable and valid measurement of these constructs are core to understanding population characteristics and outcomes: like race and ethnicity and other demographic characteristics, they are central components of individual identity and experience that shape social relationships and structural opportunities throughout one's life. Conceptually, sex, gender identity, and sexual orientation are multidimensional, incorporating both social and individual identity components. Social components reflect the interpersonal and societal interaction and recognition aspects of these concepts, while identity refers to an individual's internal sense of self—whom one understands oneself to be as a person. With respect to gender and sexual orientation, identity is the dimension that is most consistently tied to experiences with material forms of discrimination and health disparities (NASEM, 2020) and is noted explicitly in the application of sex discrimination laws and policies to sexual and gender minority populations.[8]

Measures of identity are the most relevant when the goal of measurement is to enable the identification of sexual and gender minority populations that are most consistently at risk for differential treatment and outcomes (NASEM, 2020). Thus, although the report discusses multiple

---

[8]For example, see https://www.eeoc.gov/sexual-orientation-and-gender-identity-sogi-discrimination.

dimensions of sexual orientation, gender, and sex, its recommendations are primarily focused on identity, including measures that make it possible to ascertain the populations who identify as lesbian, gay, bisexual, or another sexual minority term. This report also discusses recommended measures to identify people with intersex traits—a concept we address in this context because this population motivates the need to rethink current measures of sex and because the discrimination and marginalization that people with intersex traits experience often mirror experiences of discrimination on the basis of sexual orientation or gender identity (NASEM, 2020). This is a complicated task because sexual and gender minority populations (and cultures) are dynamic and extremely diverse, and the recognition and study of them is relatively new.

Developing Consistent Data Collection Practices

The 2020 National Academies report recommended that measures of sexual orientation, gender identity, and intersex status be routinely collected within at least three types of data collection activities:

1. survey research;
2. nonsurvey research, including clinical trials, electronic health records, biomedical research, public health surveillance, program evaluations, and assessments of discrimination; and
3. administrative and program data systems, including intake forms, applications, and civil rights and criminal justice enforcement data.

The report called on the federal government to develop standards to guide the collection of these data throughout the activities of the federal agencies that work and collect data within these domains. It also called on private entities, such as hospitals, to collect these data in a consistent and structured manner that would allow for comparisons across data sources.

This growing recognition of the need to identify LGBTQI+ populations is driving changes to the ways in which demographic data are collected in population surveys and research, health and clinical contexts, and administrative records, both within the United States (Baker, Streed, and Durso, 2021; Keuroghlian, 2021; Streed et al., 2020) and internationally (see, e.g., Statistics Canada, 2021, 2020; Stats NZ, 2021, 2019; United Nations Economic Commission for Europe, 2019). Though the United States has not yet established federal standards for data collection specifically on LGBTQI+ populations, a growing number of federal surveys have introduced measures of sexual orientation and gender identity into their routine data collection efforts (NASEM, 2020; Patterson, Jabson, and Bowen, 2017). At the national level, the Federal Committee on Statistical

Methodology (FCSM), an interagency committee dedicated to improving the quality of federal statistics, has released several reports assessing existing sexual orientation and gender identity data collection practices and discussing key implementation issues for the general population (FCSM, 2020; Federal Interagency Working Group on Improving Measurement of Sexual Orientation and Gender Identity in Federal Surveys, 2016a, 2016b, 2016c).

The NIH Sexual and Gender Minority Research Office maintains a comprehensive website[9] devoted to methods and measurement in sexual and gender minority health research and has helped ensure that the NIH PhenX Toolkit[10] for biomedical research includes standardized measures of sexual orientation and gender identity. Federal regulations already require most electronic health record systems to have the capacity to collect, store, and retrieve structured data on sexual orientation and gender identity,[11] and in July 2021 the U.S. Department of Health and Human Services included sexual orientation and gender identity in the U.S. Core Data for Interoperability standards. A number of states have also moved to require the collection of sexual orientation and gender identity data across the activities of their departments of health, aging, and other administrative agencies (State Health Access Data Assistance Center, 2021; San Francisco Human Services Agency, 2020).

Several other countries have similarly introduced or begun to develop recommendations and guidelines for standardized approaches to identifying LGBTQI+ populations. For example, Australia, Canada, and the countries of the United Kingdom have introduced new sex and gender measures on their national census in order to count transgender people. Australia and New Zealand also recently revised their national standards for data collection on sex, gender, and sexual orientation (Australian Bureau of Statistics, 2021; Stats NZ, 2021, 2019), while Canada[12] and the United Kingdom[13] are currently developing new or revised standards.

While gender identity and sexual orientation are increasingly becoming more common to collect, intersex status is still not routinely assessed in population surveys, research, health care, or administrative settings. In addition, intersex status is often erroneously conflated with or subsumed into discussions of sexual minority and transgender populations. Much of the available research on intersex populations focuses on clinical aspects of specific intersex variations, which hinders the ability of researchers, clinicians, and policy makers to understand the well-being of the intersex population

---

[9]See https://dpcpsi.nih.gov/sgmro/measurement.
[10]See https://www.phenxtoolkit.org/.
[11]See https://www.healthit.gov/isa/sex-birth-sexual-orientation-and-gender-identity.
[12]See https://www.statcan.gc.ca/en/concepts/consult-variables/gender.
[13]See https://www.ons.gov.uk/census/censustransformationprogramme/consultations/the2021 censusinitialviewoncontentforenglandandwales.

more broadly, in general health care settings and in nonmedical contexts, such as education, housing, or employment (NASEM, 2020). The invisibility of intersex populations reflects, in part, a historical trend that is "largely one of erasure" of sex diversity by medicine and societies (Reis, 2021). This erasure has led to a large deficit in knowledge about intersex people and populations relative to other sexual and gender minoritized groups.

Another major issue in the collection of data on sexual orientation, gender identity, and intersex status is inconsistency in measurement. Without national standards on how to collect, analyze, and report these data, there is increasing heterogeneity in measures deployed across U.S. surveys and in other data collection activities. Some of this heterogeneity may appropriately reflect important cultural attention to specific populations of interest, such as surveys among AIAN communities that specifically include references to Indigenous identities such as Two-Spirit or specific tribal identities (see, e.g., HONOR Project: see Cassels et al., 2010; Walters et al., 2006). However, other forms of heterogeneity reflect a lack of consensus on how to define and measure the constructs of interest. A lack of consistency in data collection measures introduces concerns about data quality; complicates data analysis and reporting; and hinders efforts to advance research and develop effective programs and policies to address the disparate treatment and outcomes in LGBTQI+ populations. It also affects non-LGBTQI+ populations by obscuring essential variation in important characteristics, such as sex and gender, that are routinely used in research, policy, and law.

There are concerns that collection of sexual orientation, gender identity, and intersex status data will expose LGBTQI+ people to harm, given a long history that includes interpersonal and structural violence targeting of LGBTQI+ people (NASEM, 2020; National Public Radio, Robert Wood Johnson Foundation, and Harvard T.H. Chan School of Public Health, 2017), mistreatment by clinicians and other service providers (Peek et al., 2016), and exposure to harmful practices, such as conversion and aversion therapies and other medically unnecessary procedures, including lobotomies and chemical castration of LGBTQI+ adolescents and adults, and genital surgeries on the bodies of intersex children too young to consent. Not collecting these data, however, makes discrimination and mistreatment harder to address: without tracking experiences by sexual orientation, gender identity, and intersex status, it is impossible to identify and rectify patterns of poorer access, treatment, and outcomes for LGBTQI+ people. Routine and standardized measurement over time is also essential for building datasets large enough to permit robust analyses of the needs of groups that face mistreatment and disparities in outcomes at the intersections of multiple axes of identity, such as LGBTQI+ people with disabilities and LGBTQI+ Black, Indigenous, and other people of color (Bi, Cook, and Chin, 2021; Crenshaw, 2017, 1989; Tomlinson and Baruch, 2013).

Based on the utility of sex, gender identity, and sexual orientation data in enumeration of populations and identifying differences between population groups, we conclude that these constructs are important demographic variables that are essential for more fully understanding the broad diversity of people and populations in the United States.

SCOPE OF THIS REPORT

Interpretations and Limitations

The panel was tasked with developing recommended measures of sex, gender identity, and sexual orientation within three broad contexts: surveys and research settings, clinical and medical settings, and administrative settings. Each of these are settings in which respondents are drawn from the general population and none specifically focus on sexual and gender minority populations. Consequently, the recommended measures had to be broad and easily understood by the general population, including those who are not members of sexual and gender minority communities. Moreover, the short time frame allotted to this study, along with the specific needs of the study sponsor, forced the panel to constrain our evaluation in several important ways.

First, the panel limited our evaluation to measures that would capture the relevant dimensions of sex, gender identity, and sexual orientation within the general adult population of the United States. Although the panel believes that understanding the process and experience of sexual and gender identity formation and development in childhood is crucial for understanding how the unequal treatment of sexual and gender minorities cumulates throughout the life course, identifying age-appropriate terminology and concepts for each stage of the developmental process was not possible in the time available to the panel. When possible, we indicate the age ranges in which the recommended measures have been tested and when these measures can be used with young populations.

Similarly, the panel would have liked to have been able to offer recommendations that focused on data collection efforts in specific sexual and gender minority populations that are often ignored and do not see themselves reflected in most data collection efforts. We also would have liked to offer recommendations for populations with low English proficiency who might benefit from translations of these questions into their native language. Each of these populations is important in their own right and deserves to be represented in data and policy discussions; however, the timeline of this study precluded this work. We hope that there will be future efforts to address these gaps and ensure that these populations can be included and accurately captured in data collection efforts. Doing so will enrich understanding not only of these specific populations, but also of the diverse array of experiences of sexual and gender minorities in the United States.

The second limitation to the scope of the panel's efforts was the decision to focus on the identity dimension of sexual orientation. As noted above, the concepts of sex, gender, and sexual orientation are multidimensional, with dimensions that separately capture their social, behavioral, and identity aspects. With respect to gender, the study title, statement of task, and project description for this study specifically focused on measures of gender identity rather than other dimensions of gender; however, this is not the case for sexual orientation.

In comparison with the measurement of sexual orientation identity, which is (relatively) straightforward, the measurement of sexual orientation attraction and behavior is more complex, because both attraction and behavior are multidimensional concepts. Sexual orientation attraction can be conceptualized as encompassing not only the direction or orientation of attraction (the gender[s] to which an individual feels attraction), but also the strength of that attraction, including whether an individual feels attraction at all. Moreover, even for one person, the orientation and strength of sexual orientation attraction may differ depending on whether it is reported based on emotional, romantic, or sexual attraction.

Sexual behaviors are similarly complex, and their relevance for data collection is often context-specific. Depending on the purpose for including such measures, it may be relevant to identify specific sexual activity or activities, the gender(s) or sex traits of a sexual partner or partners, or the frequency with which an individual engages in specific activities. The panel was concerned both that the measurements of sexual orientation attraction and behavior were too complex to be addressed within the study's time frame and that there would be insufficient guidance in the extant research literature to allow us to make specific recommendations for these dimensions.[14]

The identity dimension is most relevant for measuring disparities in treatment and outcomes, and greater effort has been spent on developing and deploying measures of identity than of other dimensions (Patterson, Jabson, and Bowen, 2017). Identity measures are also better suited for identifying members of sexual minority populations. For these reasons, the panel understood its task to include developing recommendations of specific measures that capture the identity dimensions of sexual orientation. Although the panel focused on measures of identity, we acknowledge the importance of other social and behavior dimensions of these concepts and

---

[14]In consultation with the study sponsor, the panel decided to prioritize measures of identity.

hope that development of measures that capture the complexity of these dimensions continues.

Measures and Information that Informed the Panel's Work

The panel began its task by evaluating the set of measures of sexual orientation, gender identity, and intersex status that have been included in federally sponsored surveys (see Appendix A). To compose this list, we first listed the measures that were included in the 2020 report on LGBTQI+ well-being (NASEM, 2020), and then supplemented it with information from newer and other non-federally funded surveys that were conducted of the general adult population in the United States. The panel further supplemented this list by considering guidelines on collecting sexual orientation, sex, and gender identity data that were recently issued by several English-speaking countries. Although the social and political contexts within these countries differ, these guidelines and the procedures through which they were developed were informative for the panel's deliberations.

The panel also held two public information-gathering sessions that provided additional data and contextual information that informed our discussions. The first session convened a panel of federal employees who had used sexual orientation and gender identity data or had implemented such data collection efforts in different data collection contexts, including survey research, electronic health records, human resources management and measurement of discrimination, and assessing workplace effects. The second session was a 1-day workshop that included panels of experts who discussed the measurement of sex and gender for intersex/DSD populations; legal and administrative issues surrounding the collection of sex, gender identity, and sexual orientation; and the measurement of sex, gender identity, and sexual orientation with clinical and medical contexts. Together, these information-gathering sessions provided a rich knowledge base that informed the panel's discussions and decision making. The agendas for these sessions can be found in Appendix B.

STRUCTURE OF THIS REPORT

The remainder of this report is presented in two parts, the first covering Chapters 2–4 and the second covering Chapters 5–7. Chapter 2 outlines the data collection principles and guidelines that provided the framework for the panel's deliberations when evaluating existing measures of sex, gender identity, and sexual orientation. It also critically examines the most common measures of sex and gender currently in use in order to demonstrate the ways in which sex and gender are often conflated in research and argue for greater conceptual clarity in data collection going forward. Chapter 3 considers each of the three broad settings for data collection (surveys and research, administrative, and clinical) to assess the purpose of data collection within each setting and the characteristics of that setting that could affect how data on sex, gender, and sexual orientation are collected. Chapter 4 provides an overview of standard methods that are used to establish the construct validity and the overall quality of survey questions and outlines the key criteria the panel used to evaluate each survey measure to develop our recommendations.

The second part of the report lays out the panel's final recommendations for measures of sex, gender identity, and sexual orientation identity and identifies important outstanding areas of research that could refine and improve these measures in future. Chapter 5 focuses on the panel's measure and research recommendations for sexual orientation identity. Chapter 6 focuses on the measurement of sex, gender identity, and transgender experience. Chapter 7 considers the more limited body of research on measures of intersex status and recommends future directions for research that would make it possible to develop recommendations for a specific measure in the future.

Part I

Measurement Principles, Contexts, and Methods

2

Principles and Concept Clarity

DATA COLLECTION PRINCIPLES

Part of the panel's charge was to develop principles and guidelines for evaluating measures of sex, gender identity, and sexual orientation and making modifications to these measures to tailor them for specific data collection circumstances and populations. The panel developed the five guiding principles for data collection.

1. **People deserve to count and be counted (inclusiveness).** A key purpose of data collection is to gather information that can help researchers, policy makers, service providers, and other stakeholders understand diverse populations and create policies, programs, and budgets that meet these populations' needs. Both quantitative and qualitative data, regardless of how they are collected, reflect the identities and experiences of people and communities that deserve to be heard and respected. Everyone should be able to see themselves, and their identities, represented in surveys and other data collection instruments.

2. **Use precise terminology that reflects the constructs of interest (precision).** Sex, gender, and sexual orientation are complex and multidimensional, and identifying the components of these constructs that are of interest and measuring them using appropriate terminology is critical for collecting high-quality data. Questions should clearly reflect which component(s) of sex, gender, and sexual orientation are being measured in order to maximize the reliability of

the description of the U.S. population, and one construct should not be used as a proxy for another.

3. **Respect identity and autonomy (autonomy).** Questions about dimensions of identity, by definition, are asking about a person's sense of self. Data collection has to allow respondents to self-identify whenever possible, and any proxy reporting should reflect what is known about how a person self-identifies. All data collection activities also have to require well-informed consent from potential respondents, with no penalty for those who opt out of sharing personal information about themselves or other household members. This principle encompasses data collection for legal documents intended for individual identification, and external authorization or attestation should not be required when someone reports, or wishes to change, their gender identity.

4. **Collect only necessary data (parsimony).** Data collection is not an end unto itself: data should only be gathered in pursuit of a specific and well-defined goal, such as documenting or understanding disparities and inequities between populations or meeting legal reporting requirements, and data that are not essential to achieve that goal should not be collected.

5. **Use data in a manner that benefits respondents and respects their privacy and confidentiality (privacy).** After collection, aggregate data should be analyzed at the most granular level possible, and research findings should be shared with respondents and their communities to ensure that they benefit from the data they have shared. Throughout all the steps of analysis and dissemination, data on sex, gender, and sexual orientation, which may be sensitive and vulnerable to misuse, has to be analyzed, maintained, and shared only under rigorous privacy and confidentiality standards. Similarly, when data are collected within tribal nations, preapproved tribal research and data collection, analytic, and dissemination protocols need to be followed to ensure data integrity and community benefit and to ensure that rigorous privacy and confidentiality standards are upheld.

These principles establish criteria that can be used to assess the measures of sex, gender identity, and sexual orientation presented in this report. The panel focused on identifying measures of these concepts that would be appropriate for use in the general population. We recognize that they may not be adequate for use with specific subpopulations, such as within LGBTQI+ communities, and that these measures may need to be adapted or modified for use in those communities. These criteria can also be used when considering modifications to the recommended measures. They are in keeping with standard practices for ethical data collection in human subjects, such as those developed as evaluation criteria by the Office of Management and Budget (1997) for reviewers to use when considering revisions to federal measures of race and ethnicity.

The panel developed these principles and criteria at the outset of our task and then modified and refined them throughout our deliberative process to ensure that our recommendations adhere to them.

SEX AND GENDER CONSTRUCT CLARITY

As noted in Chapter 1, data on sex and gender have often been conflated, though they are conceptually distinct and may differ from each other (Westbrook and Saperstein, 2015). For example, some surveys ask a single question, "Are you male or female?" that is sometimes referred to as a measure of sex (e.g., National Health Interview Survey), other times as a measure of gender (e.g., Pew Research Center, California Health Interview Survey), and sometimes variably referred to as both in the same survey (e.g., Health and Retirement Survey, General Social Survey). Although the terms "male" and "female" are conceptually sex-specific terminology, and the terms "woman," "man," "girl," and "boy" are conceptually gender-specific terminology, in practice, clear differentiation between sex and gender response categories is not common in large population surveys and other data collections. Moreover, most people do not recognize a conceptional distinction between sex terminology and gender terminology (Hall et al., 2021; Schudson, Beischel, and van Anders, 2019; Pryzgoda and Chrisler, 2000), which is likely both a cause and a consequence of continued conceptual conflation and inconsistent use of terminology in data collection and everyday life (Stuhlsatz, Bracey, and Donovan, 2020). This conflation suggests that use of the appropriate terminology may not be sufficient to signal to respondents what they are being asked to report.

When the question stem wording does not specify the information being collected (i.e., sex or gender), respondents must decide which to report, and the resulting data will conflate these concepts. Data users will be unable to determine whether the data reflects sex or gender for any given respondent, which may lead to mismeasurement among those for whom sex and gender differ: in fact, this occurred with data from the U.S. Department of Veterans Affairs after a 2011 directive required medical providers to provide care based on gender identity (Burgess et al., 2019). Thus, it is important that efforts to collect sex and gender data are precise and make it clear to respondents which information is being collected and why.

Beyond the conflation of the concepts of sex and gender, surveys that use a single measure of sex or gender do not capture the underlying complexity and fluidity of these concepts. As noted in the panel's conceptual

definitions in Chapter 1, individuals may have sex traits or gender characteristics (identity, expression, social and cultural expectations) that inter-
nally correspond to different sex or gender categories, respectively. For such
people, a single overall measure of sex (or gender) will serve as imperfect
proxies for them, creating opportunities for misinterpretation and misuse.
And because both sex traits and gender characteristics may also change over
time, there are opportunities for misinterpretation and misuse. For example,
when these concepts are treated as immutable—such as when longitudinal
surveys assume that sex and gender are stable over time and collect this
information only during the first interview and then carry this information
forward over time (e.g., the Panel Study of Income Dynamics, the Medical
Expenditure Panel Survey, and the Health and Retirement Survey)—this
can lead to misinterpretation or misapplication of these data to subsequent
waves of data collection. Consideration of the experiences of two populations that fall under the LGBTQI+ umbrella, people with intersex traits and
transgender people, highlights the problems with this approach.

Individuals with variations in sex traits, including sex chromosomes,
sex hormones, reproductive anatomy, and secondary sex traits, with which
a person is born or naturally develops are referred to as people with intersex traits. Biologically, intersex variations are highly heterogeneous, can involve any sex trait, and may not be apparent from an external examination.
Those that result in obvious external anatomic diversity, sometimes called
"ambiguous genitalia," are relatively uncommon, accounting for about 1 in
2,000 (0.05%) births (Blackless et al., 2000). Some children may be identified as having intersex traits through prenatal testing. While experts report
that this is occurring more commonly than previously, the frequency of this
is unknown (Smet, Scott, and McLennan, 2020). Most people with intersex
traits are born with genitals that appear to be male or female; consequently,
the majority of people with intersex traits are not identified as having an
intersex variation until later in life, often in adolescence or adulthood. Some
people with intersex traits may go undiagnosed entirely, and most children
born with any intersex trait are assigned a binary sex at birth.

When a child is born with genital differences, the process of assigning
sex at birth is highly complex. Best practices recommend that a team of
medical, surgical, and mental health experts work together with the child's
family to recommend a binary sex assignment (Finlayson, 2021). Clinicians
consider available research on gender identity outcomes along with the
child's anatomy, sex chromosomes, hormone exposure, and likely puberty,
as well as the family's individual culture and values. For some children,
this process may involve genetic testing and exploratory surgery over the
course of months, during which many parents experience high levels of
stress and uncertainty. The end goal is to recommend a sex assignment that

reflects the gender with which the child is most likely to identify, with the understanding that this may shift over time. In fact, evidence suggests that people with intersex traits are far less likely to have cisgender experiences than people without intersex traits.[1] For example, one systematic review and meta-analysis found that the overall rate of gender dysphoria[2] among persons with intersex variations was 15 percent, with variability among specific conditions (Babu and Shah, 2021). This is markedly higher than is found in the general population, in which even the highest estimates of prevalence using the broadest definitions of gender dysphoria range from 0.5 to 1.3 percent (Zucker, 2017).

Thus, experiences within the intersex/DSD (differences in sex development) population highlight the complexity of defining sex, as well as how differences between sex traits can emerge over time. Similar complexities arise for transgender people, whose gender is different from the sex they were assigned at birth. Some transgender people pursue medical gender affirmation, which may change some sex traits, making a single measure of sex a poor proxy for other sex traits or for gender.

Like sex, gender is a multidimensional concept, and therefore single measures are unlikely to capture its complexity. Conceptually, gender comprises identity, expression, and social status and norms, and without explicit direction regarding the dimension on which they should base their response, respondents may report their gender on the basis of any of these dimensions, although these dimensions may differ and may be fluid across social contexts. In many ways, the measurement of gender remains in its nascent stages, with research proceeding primarily along the lines of developing a two-step measure that seeks to identify transgender populations by separately assessing sex assigned at birth and gender identity. A more limited line of research has focused on the development of measures of gender expression that broadly fall into two types: continuum measures of femininity and masculinity (e.g., Gender Identity in the U.S. Surveillance, 2014) and classification into categories such as androgynous, butch, femme, or gender nonconforming (Malatino and Stoltzfus-Brown, 2020).

---

[1] There is considerable diversity in the intersex/DSD (difference of sex development) population on the point of whether intersex is an identity. One of the only population-based studies of intersex people (Rosenwohl-Mack et al., 2020) asked respondents to report their current gender identity. Respondents were allowed to select "all that apply"; more than 60 percent of respondents selected "Intersex" as their gender identity. Thus, it appears that many intersex people see intersex as a gender identity.

[2] Gender dysphoria refers to "clinically significant distress or impairment related to a strong desire to be of another gender, which may include desire to change primary and/or secondary sex characteristics. Not all transgender or gender diverse people experience dysphoria" (American Psychiatric Association, 2013).

Although scholars have long stressed the need to distinguish between sex and gender in social and medical research (Annandale and Hunt, 1990; Bird and Rieker, 1999), there is growing recognition of the potential harms that can arise from mismeasurement (e.g., when gender identity is reported as sex or vice versa) or misuse (e.g., using binary sex as a universal proxy for sex traits). These concerns are particularly acute in health care, where clinical decisions are sometimes tied to sex-related differences and where gender identity affects social interactions between health care professionals and patients in ways that can affect the quality of care (Morrison, Dinno, and Salmon, 2021; Clayton and Tannenbaum, 2016; Heidari et al., 2016).

The European Association of Science Editors convened in 2016 to discuss how to ensure better representation of sex and gender in medical and social research. They issued the Sex and Gender Equity in Research (SAGER) guidelines for more systematic collecting and reporting of sex and gender in research (Heidari et al., 2016). These guidelines recommend that researchers report and justify the use of both sex and gender data, as well as detail the implications of each in research discussions whenever possible. Acknowledging the problems with the measurement of sex in medical re- cords, the guidelines further recommend that medical records that include a measure of sex also include information documenting how that information was collected (e.g., through patient self-report or genetic testing) in order to better assess its suitability and reliability for specific uses in medical contexts. The SAGER guidelines have been endorsed by groups such as the U.K. Commission on Publication Ethics and have been influential in chang- ing publication standards for research journals internationally and (more unevenly) in the United States (Hankivsky, Springer, and Hunting, 2018).

In recent years there has also been a movement among international statistical agencies to develop measures for collecting data on gender. In 2019, the Economic Commission for Europe Conference of European Stat- isticians issued an in-depth review of the measurement of gender identity that noted that though sex and gender are often "used interchangeably in everyday life unless the distinction is made clear in the context" (United Nations Economic Commission for Europe, 2019, p. 3), in English, they are conceptually separate dimensions. The English-speaking countries of Australia, Canada, and New Zealand and the countries of the United Kingdom, have all begun to revise their national data collection standards, and in some cases, their national census, to include measures of gender (Australian Bureau of Statistics, 2021, 2020; Office of National Statistics, 2021; Statistics Canada, 2021; Stats NZ, 2021). Each of these countries has moved towards standards that require their data collection agencies to collect data on gender by default.

In the United States, the National Institutes of Health (NIH) draws a similar conceptual distinction between sex and gender. Consistent with an Institute of Medicine (2001) report focused on exploring the biological contributions to human health, NIH policy requires that differences in health-related risks and outcomes related to sex as a biological variable be considered to strengthen the rigor of science (Clayton, 2018) and improve understanding of sex differences. In the guidance, NIH describes sex and gender (National Institutes of Health, 2015, pp. 1–2):

> [Sex is] a biological variable defined by characteristics encoded in DNA, such as reproductive organs and other physiological and functional characteristics. Gender refers to social, cultural, and psychological traits linked to human males and females through social context. In most cases, the term "sex" should be used when referring to animals. Both sex and gender and their interactions can influence molecular and cellular processes, clinical characteristics, as well as health and disease outcomes.

CONCLUSION AND RECOMMENDATION

CONCLUSION 1: Gender encompasses identity, expression, and social position. A person's gender is associated with but cannot be reduced to either sex assigned at birth or specific sex traits. Therefore, data collection efforts should not conflate sex as a biological variable with gender or otherwise treat the respective concepts as interchangeable. In addition, in many contexts, including human subjects research and medical care, collection of data on gender is more relevant than collection of data on sex as a biological variable, particularly for the purposes of assessing inclusion and monitoring discrimination and other forms of disparate treatment.

Although the distinction between gender as a social construction and sex as a biological factor can seem clear on its face, in practice, aspects of gender shape most experiences in everyday life, from internalized psychological processes to structural constraints (e.g., through sexism and other forms of gender discrimination). It is difficult to disentangle the independent effects of sex and gender on other outcomes because of their combined biological and environmental or contextual influences. Gender-based social structures and expectations can influence behaviors and both create or magnify differences that might otherwise appear to be based in biology due to correlations with sex as a biological variable; however, these processes can only be understood if measures of gender are also routinely collected by default.

RECOMMENDATION 1: The standard for the National Institutes of Health should be to collect data on gender and report it by default. Collection of data on sex as a biological variable should be limited to

circumstances where information about sex traits is relevant, as in the provision of clinical preventive screening or for research investigating specific genetic, anatomical, or physiological processes and their connections to patterns of health and disease. In human populations, collection of data on sex as a biological variable should be accompanied by collection of data on gender.

The panel acknowledges that sex as a biological variable is often meaningful to measure in surveys, research studies, and clinical settings as it can affect the health and well-being of people or populations in terms of reproductive anatomy, biologic mechanisms linked to hormones, cell physiology, metabolism, and chromosomal configurations in biological systems. However, because these aspects of sex may differ from each other and do not exclusively determine gender, standard binary measures of sex are an inadequate proxy for the primary measurement of gender and sex traits, especially among sexual and gender diverse populations.

To address our statement of task, we attend to the constructs of sex and gender by focusing on the measurement of sex assigned at birth, gender identity, and intersex status in self-reported data collection efforts. Together, these measures allow for the identification of individuals for whom binary measures of sex serve as a poor proxy for sex traits, as well as those for whom sex and gender may be different. These measures do not represent the full complexity of either sex or gender, but they do improve on the measurement of gender by distinguishing gender identity from other dimensions of gender, as well as from sex assigned at birth. Providing measures of sex and gender that allow both intersex and transgender people to accurately represent themselves are important steps in aligning measurement practices with the diversity of human experience.

3

The Role of Measurement Context

SETTING-SPECIFIC MEASUREMENT

The panel was tasked with making recommendations on measures of sex, gender identity, and sexual orientation, with attention to how these recommendations may be applied differently in three specific settings: surveys and research studies, administrative settings, and clinical settings. To address the setting-specific question, we considered two primary aspects of data collection for each setting:

1. the purpose of collecting sex, gender identity, and sexual orientation data; and
2. why data collection would change in each setting.

In this chapter we discuss the purpose of data collection in each setting to determine which measures are relevant, and we touch on how the purpose and characteristics of each setting might influence how these data are collected.

The committee first categorized data collection contexts into the three settings included in the statement of task (surveys and research, administrative settings, and clinical settings) based on the purpose of data collection and the subject of the data being collected. Though these three settings at first seem very different, in practice the committee found that some data collection contexts served multiple purposes and thus defied easy classification. For example, clinical trials could be considered under both research and clinical settings, while vital statistics could be considered under both research and administrative settings. Classifying health data was also complicated because the purpose and mode of data collection for public health purposes and for clinical trials can be similar to surveys and research. However, data collected in medical settings, clinical trials, and public health surveillance often include detailed medical and biometric information whose measurement and interpretation may vary by sex traits and sex assigned at birth in ways that are not relevant for general population surveys or nonhealth-related research.

The panel ultimately defined surveys and research settings to include population enumeration, social research, and demography. Health surveys were classified with public health surveillance, medical records, and clinical trials under the broad heading of clinical settings to account for the role sex traits and sex assigned at birth, alongside gender, may play in all these contexts. We defined administrative settings as reflecting two distinct data collection realms: (1) vital statistics and other data collection for the purpose of legal identification and (2) program and personnel administration. These administrative settings are distinguished from each other because, although vital statistics data are often used for research purposes, their use for legal identification and other administrative purposes mean that they often need to meet regulatory or legal requirements that do not apply to other data collection contexts.

ENUMERATION, SOCIAL RESEARCH, AND DEMOGRAPHY

The most common data collection method for enumeration, social research, and demographic data collection is general population surveys. General population surveys are characterized by their ability to enumerate and collect data from representative samples of the population. They describe demographics at a high level and provide generalizable data about large groups in the population. As such, surveys aim to obtain consistent, comparable, and reliable information about a population as a whole. Federal statistical agencies, social scientists, demographers, and policy makers alike depend on data from general population demographic surveys and censuses for a variety of purposes. For example, data from these sources are used to assess social and political attitudes; develop research, policy, program, and funding priorities; and assess population-level disparities in order to identify groups most at risk of negative outcomes and to plan responses accordingly.

Collecting data on sex, gender, and sexual orientation can inform national population estimates, allow for prevalence estimation within and among geographic or sociodemographic categories, and allow for statistical comparisons on socioeconomic, demographic, and survey-specific topics, (e.g., health measures, crime victimization, unemployment, and program participation; see Federal Committee on Statistical Methodology, 2021). Such variables are also used to compute statistical weights and as demographic controls and covariates in statistical models. The lack of data collection on sexual orientation, gender identity, transgender experience, and intersex status as demographic measures in the decennial census or other large-scale federal population surveys, such the American Community Survey, means there is no "gold standard" against which data collections can perform weighting adjustments or assess data quality and nonresponse bias for LGBTQI+ populations.

Although general population surveys in the United States have not consistently included measures to identify LGBTQI+ populations, over the past two decades a number of surveys have introduced measures of sexual orientation and—to a lesser extent—gender identity. Most population surveys that are not focused on collecting health-related information include topics that represent the social and behavioral aspects of an individual's life, which suggests that gender, rather than sex traits, is more relevant for understanding these outcomes in the population. Even in surveys that collect health-related information, this information is generally collected to assess health and health disparities in the population, as well as the role played by interpersonal and structural determinants of health. Therefore, the more important measures to gather in these surveys are those associated with proximal and distal minority stressors: gender identity, transgender experience and identity, intersex status, and sexual orientation. In these survey contexts, data about specific sex traits are needed only in circumstances in which knowledge of these traits is necessary to accurately direct skip patterns for survey questions, interpret responses, or calculate values for composite measures.

The wording of questions on general population surveys has to be understood by the population as a whole and short enough to be administered in a reasonable amount of time to maintain respondents' interest and participation. Therefore, to produce high-quality estimates of LGBTQI+ populations, general population survey measures that are used to collect sexual orientation, gender identity, transgender experience and identity, and intersex status must reduce respondent burden by being simple to administer and understandable to both members of LGBTQI+ communities and the general population who are not LGBTQI+. When survey data collection efforts are focused on LGBTQI+ populations, however, it is less important that measures be comprehensible to those who are not LGBTQI+. In these circumstances, using community-specific terminology allows for better measures of the diverse array of identities in these populations.

ADMINISTRATIVE SETTINGS

Vital Statistics and Legal Identification

In the context of vital statistics and legal identification, there are multiple purposes for data collection because vital statistics—such as birth, death, and marriage certificates—are used in two primary ways: (1) by researchers to generate population estimates and conduct research related to the demographic characteristics and health of the population and (2) by individuals to establish identity and make legal or financial claims.[1] Other personally identifiable legal and administrative documents, such as passports, Social Security records, and Internal Revenue Service files, are also used by researchers and demographers to study characteristics of the population and are sometimes linked to survey data and other administrative records.[2] When used for research purposes, these data are typically deidentified and aggregated to protect personal privacy; however, when used for other purposes, this information is often directly linked to a specific individual. This combination of data needs and uses that cross between public and private domains highlights both the importance of consistent measurement to facilitate data quality and linkage across domains, and the need to establish a clear rationale and process for collecting these data to ensure that individuals are not required to disclose personal information in ways that may put them at risk for discrimination or violence (Ashley, 2021).

For vital statistics and legal identification, the only measure of sex, gender identity, or sexual orientation that is routinely collected is a single binary measure of sex or gender. As in other domains, there is considerable variation in whether data collection fields, internal coding, and public reporting explicitly reference "sex," "gender," some combination of the two, or neither. The clearest designations are the single measure of sex of an infant or decedent on original birth certificates and death certificates, respectively, both of which are completed by a proxy respondent and based on physical examination of one or more of the individual's sex traits (that

---

[1]The Supreme Court recently noted that birth certificates are "more than a mere marker of biological relationships," they are "a form of legal recognition" (*Marisa N. Pavan, et al. v. Nathaniel Smith*. 582 U.S. Supreme Court of The United States. No. 16-992; cited in Epps, 2018). The case involved a dispute in Arkansas over whether female spouses of women who give birth should be listed as parents on a child's birth certificate. The Court ruled for the plaintiffs because male spouses who are not the child's biological father have routinely been listed as parents on birth certificates.

[2]Examples are the National Longitudinal Mortality Study (2014), Mortality Disparities in American Communities (2017), and the U.S. Census Bureau's Small Area Health Insurance Estimates Program; see https://www.census.gov/data/datasets/time-series/demo/sahie/estimates-acs.html.

may not all correspond to the same sex). In other instances, sex or gender information is not queried explicitly but rather inferred from gendered relationship status terms that are built into the form's design, such as when parents are identified as "mother" and "father" on their child's birth certificate or spouses are designated as "bride" and "groom" on marriage licenses.[3] Thus, many of the problems that plague the measurement of sex or gender that are discussed in Chapter 2, including a lack of precision in terminology and failure to include gender identities beyond the female/male binary, also arise in administrative data collection.

Overall, in the vital statistics, data collection on transgender experience or sexual orientation is rare, while data collection on intersex status is nonexistent. This is partly because many of these documents serve foremost as forms of identification, and sexual orientation, transgender experience, transgender identity, and intersex status are not necessary for identification purposes. Similarly, most protected characteristics that were once thought to be necessary for identification, such as race and ethnicity, are no longer included on U.S. identity documents (including the public versions of birth certificates) because doing so facilitated segregation and discrimination (Adair, 2019; Erhardt, 1962). In contrast, data on sex or gender are routinely collected and reported on identity and other administrative documents in ways that may facilitate sex segregation in such settings as the military, restrooms, education, and athletics (Cohen, 2011). In general, data on protected characteristics, including sex and gender, are collected and widely reported across a range of administrative data without a clear and documented purpose (Ashley, 2021).

In vital statistics data, a clear distinction can be made between the data needed for statistical purposes, such as monitoring population health, and the data used for individual identity documents. For example, the U.S. standard birth certificate was revised in 1949 to include a line that specifically demarcates the fields above the line as ones that appear on certified birth certificate copies and the fields below the line as for statistical purposes only. At that time, both race and parents' marital status were moved below the line (Shteyler, Clarke, and Adashi, 2020, citing Wipfler, 2016). This approach separates the information necessary to fully document the circumstances surrounding a "live birth" from information provided for the purposes of individual identification. Similar "lines of demarcation" also appear on marriage and death certificates.

The data below this line of demarcation are collected purely for research and population estimates and are generally reported in aggregate, which makes disclosure of the individual data unlikely. This separation

---

[3]In California, however, it is possible for parents to choose whether to be listed as "mother," "father," or "parent" on their child's birth certificate (Maier, 2019).

opens the possibility that information about sexual orientation, gender identity, transgender experience and identity, and intersex/DSD [differences in sex development] status could be added to vital statistics data to document social and economic disparities in treatment and outcomes experienced by LGBTQI+ people without increasing their risk of discrimination or mistreatment.

The possible implementation of routine data collection of measures of sexual orientation, gender identity, and transgender experience in vital statistics data poses several challenges that may affect data quality, particularly for measures of identity. One challenge is the role of proxy reporting, in which the respondent is providing information on someone else, a practice that is necessary when collecting data on infants and decedents. The primary concern with proxy reporting is that the resulting data will not reflect how a person would have identified if they could have responded for themselves, which can depend on the degree to which the respondent may have personal knowledge about the person whose data are being reported. For example, while spouses may report their own or their partner's characteristics in marriage records, death records are generally completed by a more distal proxy respondent (e.g., a physician or a coroner) who may never have met the decedent. Proxy reporting is likely to result in undercounts for marginalized populations: evaluations of such proxy reporting of racial and ethnic identity on death records has found misclassification rates of more than 40 percent for American Indians and Alaska Natives (National Center for Health Statistics, 2016), which has limited the use of these data for research and public health surveillance for this population.

Similar concerns about proxy reporting for sexual orientation and gender identity data have prompted some to suggest that a system that links death certificates with electronic health records would be preferable to better reflect an adult decedent's self-identification (Mays and Cochran, 2019). Other researchers are exploring the feasibility of using proxy reports to collect sexual orientation and gender identity data for death certificates (Haas et al., 2019); California recently passed legislation to initiate a 3-year pilot study of collecting both sexual orientation and gender identity data on death certificates (Bajko, 2021; California Legislative Assembly, 2021). Such data collection would enable much-needed research on mortality disparities faced by sexual and gender minorities, but additional pilots in more jurisdictions would be needed to demonstrate widespread feasibility.

Data collection in the context of vital statistics is further complicated by wide variations in jurisdictional control over both the collection and associated statistical standards. The National Center for Health Statistics (NCHS) publishes federal guidelines for data collection on birth, marriage, and death certificates.[4] However, the actual design of certificates is determined at the state level and implemented variously in hospitals, funeral homes, and local government offices (see, e.g., National Research Council, 2009; Hahn et al., 2002). These data are reported electronically by state administrative agencies to NCHS, which then produces standardized vital statistics data for the United States.

The number and variety of jurisdictions for the same type of vital statistics record creates a patchwork of practices across the United States. At least 14 U.S. states have also begun to allow nonbinary designations on birth certificates,[5] which is currently implemented through petitions to change the original birth certificate designation, either by an adult or by the parents of a newborn child. Only "female" and "male" are currently available for designation at birth on the standard U.S. birth certificate, and NCHS data record standards do not currently recognize a third category, such as nonbinary, on birth certificate data when they are transferred electronically to the federal government. Moreover, because the United States does not have a population registry system, when an original birth certificate is modified to reflect an individual's current gender, this information is not transferred to the federal government or reflected in national vital statistics data.

Policies and practices for collection of sex and gender data related to legal identification are also changing rapidly but unevenly across the United States. For example, the federal government recently announced that it is now accepting self-identified "female" and "male" designations for all U.S. passport applications (U.S. Department of State, 2021).[6] The U.S. Department of State subsequently announced that the first passport with a nonbinary designation had been issued (Reuters, 2021) with plans to expand availability once the relevant changes can be implemented in its data systems.[7] At least 18 states allow nonbinary designations on driver's licenses or state IDs (as of October 2021), though they vary in whether a change can be obtained through self-identification alone or whether medical

---

[4]Although each state determines how its vital statistics data will be collected, state-level data are reported to and aggregated at the national level by the National Center for Health Statistics (NCHS). To improve comparability across states, NCHS publishes standardized birth certificate (https://www.cdc.gov/nchs/data/dvs/birth11-03final-acc.pdf) and death certificate (https://www.cdc.gov/nchs/data/dvs/DEATH11-03final-ACC.pdf) forms, and a standard marriage license (https://www.cdc.gov/nchs/data/misc/hb_marr.pdf) that individual states can choose to adopt.

[5]The Movement Advancement Project maintains information on state identity document laws and policies: see https://www.lgbtmap.org/equality-maps/identity_document_laws.

[6]Prior to this change, "female" and "male" designations required external attestation from a recognized source, such as a birth certificate or documentation from a medical professional, and could not be based solely on a self-report.

[7]As of January 2022, no timeline for the implementation had been announced.

documentation or other legal requirements must also be met.[8] These policy changes have implications beyond the context of vital statistics and legal identification: broader recognition of nonbinary designations in administrative settings could also raise awareness of gender identity terminology and prompt broader acceptance of this language.

Similar policy changes are occurring around the world, with at least a dozen countries implementing nonbinary designations on passports and other legal identification documents or beginning the process of removing gender from their identity documents entirely (BusinessTech Staff, 2021; González Cabrera, 2021; Holzer, 2018). As these changes are made, it is important for policy makers and data systems administrators to recognize that barriers to changing these legal sex and gender markers—and inconsistency across documents—can restrict the ability of transgender people to travel and vote and may subject them to harassment and discrimination if the accuracy of their identity documents is called into question (Fielding, 2020; Quinan and Bresser, 2020). For immigrants to the United States who are recognized as nonbinary in their country of origin, navigating the complex patchwork of identification practices across jurisdictions that may inconsistently recognize their gender can affect their ability to conduct the business of their everyday lives.

In summary, unlike data collected in surveys and research settings, the collection and coding of data in vital statistics and legal identification settings are constrained by regulatory and legal policies and requirements. Furthermore, most of these data collected are linked to specific individuals for the purposes of establishing identity, and thus, reported demographic characteristics could be used to facilitate segregation, discrimination, and violence against individuals. In these settings, information on sexual orientation, gender identity, transgender experience and identity, and intersex/DSD status are generally not collected, because they are not needed for purposes of identification. At the same time, data on sex or gender are often collected without a clearly designated purpose and without clarity regarding which of the two constructs is of interest. The collection of sex and gender data on legal identification documents can have negative repercussions for people whose recorded sex or gender on their documents does not match their current gender, which underscores the need to ensure that both the collection and reporting of this information is done with a clear purpose that outweighs the potential harms.

The introduction of sexual orientation, gender identity, transgender experience, and intersex/DSD status to vital statistics data could potentially

---

[8]Several states have also attempted to explicitly bar such changes. The Movement Advancement Project provides up-to-date information on state policies: see https://www.lgbtmap.org/equality-maps/identity_document_laws.

be done at low risk to individuals when information that is collected for research purposes can be clearly separated from data that are used for legal identification purposes. Although the need for proxy reporting of identity on death records could affect the quality of these reports, as noted above, there are preliminary efforts to assess whether measures of sexual orientation and gender identity can be feasibly collected for research purposes. If such efforts demonstrate this can be done, it will provide important data for population enumeration and monitoring discrimination of LGBTQI+ people. Meeting those needs is likely to require national standards for data collection on sex, gender identity, and sexual orientation.

Program and Personnel Administration

Program and personnel administration includes data systems that facilitate the functioning of many systems: employment; schools and other educational institutions; child welfare departments; the criminal justice system; and federal- and state-funded programs providing social and human services related to health, insurance coverage, housing, employment, credit and other economic resources, and nutrition. Administrators in these systems and programs collect data on the people they encounter for multiple reasons: to maintain records and ensure individuals are receiving appropriate services; to describe the populations of people needing and using services, including demographic characteristics that may relate to disparities in access, quality, or outcomes; to determine access or assignment to "sex-segregated" facilities or programs, such as bathrooms, prisons, detention centers, locker rooms, sports teams, sex-segregated schools; and to determine eligibility for funding and programs.

Measuring sex or gender, sexual orientation, and transgender experience is important in these contexts because of documented disparities, discrimination, and barriers in access to services in all of them (NASEM, 2018, 2020). In addition to well-documented discrimination and disparities among women—both cisgender and transgender—across many of these areas (Wilson et al., 2021), there are demonstrated disparities for people identified as lesbian, gay, bisexual, transgender, and questioning in incarceration (Wilson et al., 2017; Meyer et al., 2016; Marksamer and Tobin, 2014), housing (Wilson, O'Neill, and Vasquez, 2021; O'Neill, Wilson, and Herman, 2020; Romero, Goldberg, and Vasquez, 2020; Wilson et al., 2020), child welfare (Irvine and Canfield, 2016; Wilson and Kastanis, 2015), and education (Aragon et al., 2014). Some studies show disparities for sexual minority populations as defined by same-sex sexual behavior in prisons and jails (Zaller, et al. 2020; Brinkley-Rubinstein et al., 2019; Harawa et al., 2018) and for gender nonconforming populations in relation to food insecurity and in such settings as foster care, prisons and jails, homeless shelters, and health care (Russomanno and Jabson Tree, 2020; Ecker, Aubry, and Sylvestre, 2019; Eisenberg et al., 2019; Glick et al., 2019; Lagos, 2018; Streed, McCarthy, and Haas, 2018; Gonzales and Henning-Smith, 2017; Irvine and Canfield, 2016; Wilson et al., 2014).

Due to the wide range of contexts that are covered under program and personnel administration, it was not possible for the committee to evaluate the full range of data collection practices that are currently in use in all of them. Even in the same context, data collection practices can vary widely. For example, although the Equal Employment Opportunity Commission requires all private-sector employers with 100 or more employees to report specific demographic data describing their workforce by sex, employers have flexibility in designing their data collection tools, and there is considerable variation in whether their data collection fields and internal coding explicitly reference sex, gender, some combination of the two, or neither. For applicants, some employers collect data on gender, transgender, or sexual orientation identities.[9] These practices are consistent with Supreme Court rulings, which have found that the legal prohibition of discrimination based on sex extends more broadly to protections against discrimination based on sexual orientation and gender identity.[10] To our knowledge, information on intersex status has not been collected in any administrative setting.

As is the case for vital statistics and legal identification data, an important feature of these administrative data is the ability to link this information to a specific individual. Although these data are often collected to monitor and measure disparities in treatment, this linkage to identifiable individuals can also contribute to segregation, discrimination, and harassment of individuals. Thus, collection of information on sex, gender identity, transgender experience and identity, sexual orientation, and intersex/DSD status in this setting could put individuals at risk if their data is disclosed or misused. When combined with the well-documented disparities faced by cisgender women and LGBTQI+ people, it underscores the importance of only collecting the minimum data that are necessary to meet specific administrative goals and to ensure protections are in place that restrict the use of these data to the furthering of those goals. For example, in some settings, such as in employment records or applications for social or business services, asking about an aspect of sex, such as sex assigned at birth, can be considered invasive or inappropriate by transgender people who do not wish to disclose this information to an employer, business contact, or social services coordinator. In other settings, however, asking about a specific

---

[9]For example, the Biden administration employment application form asks applicants to report their gender, transgender identity, and sexual orientation: see: https://www.whitehouse.gov/get-involved/join-us/.

[10]See https://www.eeoc.gov/sexual-orientation-and-gender-identity-sogi-discrimination.

definition of sex, such as sex assigned at birth, may be important: these settings include programs and residential facilities that allow for assignment based on gender identity and yet are required to provide or connect people to health care, such as detention centers and child welfare case management. In these contexts, sex assigned at birth can serve as an imperfect but necessary proxy for specific health care needs.

In addition to ensuring only necessary data are collected, the possibility of disclosure can be minimized in administrative settings by enacting data protections that restrict data access and making disclosure voluntary for respondents. For example, in employment-related contexts, there are legal restrictions on when and how data on protected characteristics, such as age, gender, race, and ethnicity, may be collected. It is illegal for employers ask about this information on employment applications because it can be used to facilitate discrimination in hiring. However, the collection of this information about employees allows employers to monitor their hiring practices and identify potential discriminatory behaviors. It also facilitates mandatory reporting on employee characteristics to the federal government for large employers. For this reason, many employers ask applicants to voluntarily complete a form that asks for information about protected characteristics, which the employer then keeps separated from job application materials.

There is another significant form of data collection in many administrative systems that is consistently needed and likely never used by people outside the system itself: case management notes. On the one hand, a case management file is an opportunity to ask more detailed questions, provide space for personalized labels, and add flexibility to document shifts in identity over time, and thus it may provide a rich source of information both about individual identities and service needs and about population trends more broadly. On the other hand, this level of detail also makes case management files difficult to use outside of the specific purpose for which these data are collected because they require either significant staff time to manually review and extract data or the application of technological approaches, such as natural language processing, that are not currently widely used.

Data collected in case management files may be directly collected by staff from individuals, and they are often used by staff to inform interpersonal interactions and guide the provision of services. As in other administrative settings, this access can leave individuals vulnerable to mistreatment, and some respondents may prefer not to disclose this information due to fear of mistreatment or loss of services. For this reason, data collection and use of case management files requires high levels of competence among staff when they ask about or discuss sexuality and gender, particularly when sexual orientation and gender identity questions are open ended. It remains unclear whether any groups have tested the efficacy of proposed best practices for data collection and management in this context (see, e.g., Wilber and Canfield, 2019; Wilber, 2013).[11]

Summary

In administrative settings, data collection often serves purposes that require data users to be able to link data to a specific individual. This ability to link data heightens the risk of disclosure of individual information and of mistreatment of vulnerable populations through segregation, harassment, discrimination, and violence. LGBTQI+ populations are at increased risk of disparate treatment across a wide range of administrative contexts. Although the collection of data on sex, gender identity, and sexual orientation can facilitate mistreatment, these data are also necessary to document its occurrence, as well as design and implement policies and procedures to counter it. For this reason, it is important that data collection in administrative settings serve a clearly defined purpose, be limited to data that are needed to support that purpose, and minimize the likelihood of data disclosure or misuse.

CLINICAL SETTINGS

Clinical settings include a wide variety of contexts in which sex, gender, and sexual orientation are critical for health and well-being, at both individual and population levels: they include health surveys, public health surveillance, clinical trials, and medical records. In health surveys and public health surveillance, these data are critical for identifying and addressing disparities between groups on health-related outcomes and understanding the social determinants of health. In clinical trials and other biomedical research, these data can help ensure that research questions and findings apply across the diversity of natural population variation in sex, gender, and sexual orientation. In medical care settings, collecting these data is important for building trusting relationships between providers and patients, promoting culturally appropriate care (Bi, Cook, and Chin, 2021), identifying and tracking health conditions and risk factors at both individual and population levels (Sell and Krims, 2021), improving the quality and safety of health care systems (Bonvicini, 2017), and facilitating the processing of administrative functions, such as billing.

Stratifying clinical performance data by social risk category—including not only sexual orientation, gender identity, and intersex status, but also

---

[11]The San Francisco Human Services Agency (2020) does generate an annual report on implementation of data collection for sexual orientation and gender identity across its divisions.

such factors as race, ethnicity, and socioeconomic status—is a foundational step for improving the quality of care and advancing health equity for marginalized populations (Chin, 2021, 2020). Increasingly, public and private payers are reporting stratified clinical performance data and linking the results to financial rewards or penalties, and The Centers for Medicare & Medicaid Services' Innovation Center (2021) lists stratified performance data as a pillar in its strategy to advance health equity. Thus, collecting data on sex, gender identity, and sexual orientation in medical settings is important for quality improvement and the advancement of health equity.

In health contexts, each of these characteristics may be independently relevant: gender identity; sex assigned at birth; transgender experience and identity; intersex status; sex traits, including chromosomes, gonads, internal and external genitalia, secondary sex characteristics, and hormones; the components of sexual orientation, identity, behavior, and attraction; and gender pronouns. It is important not to use any one as a proxy for any other one (see Chapters 1 and 2). Although sex assigned at birth may provide additional information beyond gender identity that is useful for improving care (Burgess et al., 2019), it is insufficient as a proxy measure for sex traits, because specific sex traits can have direct effects on the risk for or manifestation of a range of health conditions (Traglia et al., 2017), ranging from acute abdominal pain (Kim and Kim, 2018) to genetic disorders (Traglia et al., 2017), cancers (Dorak and Karpuzoglu, 2012), infertility, and osteoporosis (Dy et al., 2011). Ranges of some laboratory values, such as hemoglobin concentration or clinical decision tools (e.g., atherosclerotic cardiovascular disease), are interpreted within sexually bivariate ranges that reflect the effect of sex traits on physiologic processes. Anatomic inventories have been proposed as more specific strategies for collecting data regarding sex traits, though these questions may not be relevant or practical in all health care contexts (Grasso et al., 2021). Measures of gender identity and transgender experience can also be independently relevant for assessing patient risk. For example, transgender people demonstrate a higher prevalence of cardiovascular disease than cisgender people (Streed et al., 2021; Caceres et al., 2020).

At the heart of effective patient care is a strong, trusting relationship between clinicians and patients that facilitates clear communication and shared decision making. Collection of data related to sexual orientation, gender identity, transgender experience and identity, and intersex/DSD status by health care providers is critical to fostering that trust and providing care that is respectful and culturally appropriate (Bi, Cook, and Chin, 2021; Cook, Gunter, and Lopez, 2017). This can only be achieved if health care professionals engage in reflection, empathy, and partnership with patients; understand the effects of exposure to marginalization and discrimination; recognize and reduce their personal biases (Vela et al., 2022);

and be sensitive with terminology and language, such as using appropriate pronouns and avoiding invasive questions about identity when they are not relevant for providing care (Suen et al., 2022; Knutson et al., 2016).

As in administrative settings, however, information collected in clinical settings is linked to a specific identifiable individual and informs interpersonal interactions, so the collection of this data can also leave individuals vulnerable to mistreatment. Too often, implicit and explicit bias from health care professionals and discrimination by health care delivery organizations harm LGBTQI+ people (National Public Radio, Robert Wood Johnson Foundation, and Harvard T.H. Chan School of Public Health, 2017; Peek et al., 2016). Robust nondiscrimination policies, training of health care providers, and other structural changes to health care delivery organizations to promote better care for marginalized populations have become increasingly recognized as essential to the provision of high-quality care (Bi, Cook, and Chin, 2021; Cook, Gunter, and Lopez, 2017; DeMeester et al., 2016; U.S. Department of Health and Human Services, 2013).

The collection and use of data on sex traits, sexual orientation, gender identity, and intersex status are challenging areas for health care delivery organizations, health plans, and payers. These data have to fill a complex set of needs that include measurement of disparities to improve population health, information for health care and health services research, enabling respectful patient-provider interactions, and identifying sex-trait-related differences to provide appropriate health care to individuals. These needs create many points of access to the data in these systems. Although health data are protected from unauthorized disclosure by the Health Insurance Portability and Accountability Act (HIPAA), it remains crucial for organizations to have policies in place that clearly establish procedures and conditions under which authorized access to the data is granted to those within health care systems in order to minimize the possibility that providing the data can result in an individual's mistreatment.

When data are collected in clinical settings, it is important to consider which data elements are needed for patient screening and population health purposes (i.e., demographic analysis) and which are needed for specific clinical purposes (e.g., Pap tests are indicated only for people with a cervix). It is then necessary to develop privacy protections around the disclosure and sharing of these data both in and outside of the clinical context. Unlike population surveys, clinical settings provide many points of contact in which information can be collected, which necessitates the development of work flows and organizational policies that identify when, how, and by whom data are collected to ensure that patient privacy is adequately protected (Antonio et al., 2022).

Data in clinical settings are most commonly collected and accessed through electronic health record systems, which have utility not only for clinical care, but also for research and public health purposes. These systems have different interfaces for collecting data on sex, gender identity, transgender experience and identity, intersex status, and sexual orientation. The underlying terminology involves international code sets, such as Systematized Nomenclature of Medicine[12] and Health Level 7 International (HL7),[13] that affect how these data are collected and transmitted among systems. The U.S. Office of the National Coordinator for Health Information Technology has identified various terms that can be used to capture sex assigned at birth, gender identity, and sexual orientation in electronic health records,[14] but little work has been done on how to measure intersex status as a demographic measure.

Although electronic patient health records are an important source, it is important to note that administrative decisions do not entirely depend on the data that have been collected by the health care provider. Despite what information is entered into the patient's medical record, health insurers may make their decision to cover some procedures on the basis of the sex that is noted on the patient's insurance policy. This sex designation may or may not be the same as the patient's sex assigned at birth. In the electronic health records systems used by many institutions in health care, a common additional data element is "administrative sex/gender," which refers to the designation of people as male, female, or another gender for such activities as hospital room assignments and insurance billing. This data element cannot be readily mapped onto self-identified sex or gender and cannot be considered a demographic measure, but it nevertheless affects the treatment individuals receive in a clinical setting.

CONCLUSIONS

The panel was tasked with making recommendations on measures of sex, sexual orientation, and gender identity with attention to how these recommendations can be applied differently in three settings: surveys and research studies, administrative settings, and clinical settings. We found that the most relevant factors that distinguished these settings were the use of the data, the identifiability of respondents, and the risk of data disclosure. In considering the collection of data on sex, gender identity, and sexual orientation, it is important to recognize that LGBTQI+ people are often subject to mistreatment, segregation, harassment, discrimination, and violence; consequently, reporting this information may pose risks to respondents in some situations. Because of this potential risk, we strongly advise

---

[12]See https://www.snomed.org/.

[13]See http://www.hl7.org/.

[14]See https://www.healthit.gov/isa/united-states-core-data-interoperability-uscdi.

that respondents always be able to opt out of providing this information, particularly in contexts where their responses can be linked to personally identifiable information and where the risk of disclosure is high. Even when individuals are not at risk of being identified, such as when data are made publicly available in aggregated form, there is the potential for this data to be misused or misinterpreted to justify harmful treatment or policies. Thus, it is important to weigh the need for and benefits of collecting these data with the risk of harm that doing so may pose to respondents.

The three broad settings differ from each other in important ways that can affect the collection of sex, gender identity, and sexual orientation data. The first—and most important—factor is the potential for data disclosure. In considering this factor, surveys and research settings can be distinguished from the other settings because the information is usually reported in aggregated form or with personally identifiable information removed, which means the possibility of disclosure is low. In contrast, information that is collected in administrative and clinical settings can generally be linked to a specific individual. When LGBTQI+ individuals can be identified as such, it increases the risk that they can be targeted as members of these communities and suffer harm.

In clinical settings, data privacy is protected through HIPAA, which imposes penalties for the disclosure of medical record data. However, these protections cannot prevent mistreatment by those within the health care system, so it is imperative that in this setting there are clear organizational policies and workflows in place to control the collection of, access to, and use of these data. Although such clear legal protections against disclosure do not exist in all administrative contexts, clearly defined plans to restrict unauthorized access to the data need to be in place before they are collected, particularly when such data are used to inform interpersonal interactions. When this information is collected and reported in the identification portion of vital statistics records or in other identification documents, it may be inappropriate and potentially harmful to collect data that enable the identification of sexual and gender minority populations.

Another way in which the three settings differ is the purpose that the data collection serves. Although sex, gender identity, and sexual orientation data can be used to document group-based disparities in treatment and outcomes in all three data collection settings, data collection also serves a unique purpose in each setting that informs the specific measures of sex, gender identity, and sexual orientation that are collected:

- When data collection is conducted solely for the purposes of establishing identity, measures of gender identity, sexual orientation, transgender experience or identity, or intersex/DSD status are not needed, and their collection could facilitate segregation, harassment, and discrimination.

- When data are collected to improve interpersonal interaction and communication between case managers or health care personnel and service recipients or to provide appropriate services and care, measures of gender identity, sexual orientation identity or behavior, and transgender experience or identity may be relevant. In some circumstances, information on sex as a biological variable may also be needed as an imperfect proxy for sex traits in order to establish need or qualification for specific programs and services.
- Data that are collected to ensure that an individual receives appropriate health care services require the inclusion of detailed measures of sex, gender identity, and sexual orientation, including information about specific sex traits, intersex/DSD status, sex assigned at birth, gender identity and pronouns, transgender experience and identity, and sexual orientation identity, attraction, and behavior.
- When data are collected to enumerate populations and conduct research that elucidates the structural mechanisms through which population-based disparities are created and could be addressed, measures that can identify the relevant sexual and gender minority populations, such as sexual orientation identity, gender identity, transgender experience, and intersex status are the most relevant.

Even when collecting data on sex, gender identity, and sexual orientation is relevant in a specific context, data collection efforts need to balance the benefits of the data with the risks associated with unauthorized data disclosure and the potential misuse of data by those with authorized access. Protections need to be in place to minimize the risk to individuals of providing this information, particularly when it can be linked to specific individuals. When possible, data should be deidentified and aggregated. These protections serve not only to protect sexual and gender minorities, but also to ensure the collection of reliable data that accurately reflect the experiences of these populations.

4

Scientific Criteria for Recommended Measures

This chapter lays out the evidentiary basis that the committee used to assess the recommended measures that are presented in the subsequent chapters of this report. It presents a synthesis of methods and criteria that are commonly used to test and evaluate survey questions, emphasizing evidence suggesting that a measure works well within both sexual/gender minority *and* majority populations. The panel is not aware of unique criteria that specifically address testing and evaluation of demographic measures collected in clinical settings, but we found little reason to use different evaluation criteria to assess these measures across these settings. Nor is the committee aware of unique criteria for evaluating measures collected for administrative records. Official federal forms (e.g., passport applications) are reviewed and approved by the Office of Management and Budget's Office of Information Regulatory Affairs using criteria that include many of the factors used to evaluate survey measures, such as respondent burden. After discussing commonly used evaluation criteria, the chapter concludes with a set of criteria the committee used to assess and ultimately select the recommended measures in the rest of the report.

CRITERIA FOR DEVELOPING AND EVALUATING MEASURES

When developing standardized questions, the primary goal is to establish their construct validity—alignment between what the item(s) is (are) measuring and the underlying concept being measured. The purpose of establishing validity is to reduce measurement error and craft questions that meet the desired content, cognitive, and usability standards (Groves et al., 2009; Beimer et al., 1991; Converse and Presser, 1989).

- The content standard evaluates whether the question is asking about the right construct.
- The cognitive standard evaluates whether respondents understand the questions and are willing and able to answer them.
- The usability standard evaluates whether respondents (and potentially, interviewers) can complete the question easily and as it was intended.

There are a number of metrics that are commonly used to evaluate measure quality, including respondent comprehension; cognitive load (the amount of working memory required to respond) and retrieval (the ability to recall the requested information from memory); interviewer administration issues; response time; response bias; item response distributions; and item nonresponse, refusal, and do not know rates. Some measures may speak to more than one of the three standards. For example, measures of respondent comprehension can help establish content validity (content standard) and whether respondents understand what is being asked of them (cognitive standard). Similarly, item nonresponse rates can provide information regarding whether questions meet cognitive and usability standards.

Methods of Assessing Measure Validity

Pretesting is perhaps the most common method for evaluating question quality, and there are a variety of methods that are used to do so, including:

- *expert review*, in which content experts provide evaluations of question quality (see, e.g., Olson, 2010);
- *focus groups*, in which a group of participants are recruited as a panel to develop, evaluate, or provide feedback on a specific topic, most commonly to develop new measures (see, e.g., Krueger, 1994);
- *cognitive interviews*, in which a small set of respondents is interviewed to discuss in detail their thought processes as they interpreted and responded to potential items (see, e.g., Willis, 2005; Desimone and La Floch, 2004);
- *respondent debriefings*, in which respondents are provided with additional information about the data collection process and asked to provide feedback on specific questions after they have completed the instrument (see, e.g., Campanelli, Martin, and Rothgeb, 1991);
- *field pretests and behavior coding*, which monitor small numbers

of interviews with respondents to evaluate question performance (see, e.g., Ongena and Dijkstra, 2006; Presser et al., 2004); and
- *randomized split-panel experiments,* in which the effects of question wording or administration conditions (e.g., mode) are tested by randomly assigning respondents into panels that are administered different questions or conditions (Presser et al., 2004).

These evaluation methods are generally introduced at different stages of the question design process, with focus groups most commonly occurring early in question development and field tests, behavior coding, and split-panel experiments occurring during administration. Key indicators that are used to assess the quality of questions differ across the various evaluation methods. For example, focus groups and cognitive interviews produce indicators of comprehension, readability, cognitive load and retrieval, and sensitivity. Behavior coding and field pretests yield interviewer administration problems, as well as respondent comprehension. Split-ballot experiments produce indicators such as differential item nonresponse rates, refusal and don't know rates, response bias, and response distributions, that are used to evaluate different question wordings.

When discussing response options, ordering is also considered. Because sex, gender identity, and sexual orientation are nominal variables, there is no inherent ordering to their response categories. However, the order of response categories is important as it does affect how respondents answer. Studies have documented two types of order effects: primacy and recency effects. Primacy effects occur when respondents tend to "satisfice" and select options early in a list (Krosnick, 1999). Alternatively, when respondents hear categories in interviewer-administered surveys, the opposite can happen with respondents selecting options toward the end of the list (Krosnick and Alwin, 1987). In automated data collection, randomizing the order of categories can reduce this effect. In this case, programming is used to randomize the order such that they are varied across interviews. In data collection that cannot be automated, ordering is sometimes presented alphabetically or according to the predicted size of each category (from largest to smallest). Free-text categories—for example, "Other-specify: _____"—are typically presented at the end of a list.

To the extent possible, the panel considered these types of key indicators in developing our recommended measures. When discussing alternative question designs to recommend, the panel also considered evaluation approaches that reflect our guiding principles (specifically, precision, inclusiveness, autonomy, parsimony, and privacy [see Chapter 2]). For example, a measure needs to be representative, allowing respondents to see themselves and their identities, while balancing the need to collect accurate information without undue burden; needs to clearly specify which component(s) of sex, gender, and sexual orientation are being measured; and must allow respondents to self-identify without requiring external authorization or attestation of identity. Finally, given the statement of task's focus on data collection among the English-speaking adult population, the panel was keenly interested in quality indicators coming from current measures used in large-scale nationally representative data collections.

Community-Specific Considerations

The panel recognizes the complex and nuanced identities that characterize some small minority groups, and additionally how misreporting of these identities can increase overall measurement error if these identities are not well known or are misunderstood by the broader population. It is also important for researchers to use community-appropriate terminology and ensure that data collection is culturally grounded. As such, there are several dimensions of community responsiveness that need to be balanced in the development of questions that allow the identification of these populations, including how the questions are understood by respondents, the use of appropriate language that understands how dynamic terminology and niche jargon are understood by both minority and majority people, and abiding by principles of not doing harm (McDonnell, Goldman, and Koumjian, 2020; Kelley et al., 2019; Moore, 2018; Harper and Schneider, 2003).

Adjustments to existing well-tested measures that appear on prominent national surveys, such as the National Health Interview Survey sexual orientation identity item, are often proposed by minority communities as a way of giving the community voice, better representation, or legitimation within the data collection process. One type of adjustment that is commonly requested (and sometimes implemented) is to increase the number of response options by adding additional unique identity terms to the question response options. While it is important for respondents to be able to find a suitable category for themselves in the response options, as the number of categories increases, so does statistical noise due to misidentification. When categories representing small minority populations are introduced, these categories may not be well understood outside of these minority communities, and respondents from the majority population may misinterpret the response option and select it, leading to (potential) overreporting within the new category and (potential) underreporting within the original category.

Misreporting as a small minority by the majority population—sometimes referred to as "false positive" reports—does not only affect the data from those who misreported their identity. The effects of this misreporting can actually be more consequential for members of the smaller group. Even if only a small fraction of the majority population are "false positives," it can lead to a biased understanding of the size, characteristics, and outcomes of people in the smaller group. This occurred in the 2010 census, when a tiny fraction of straight couples mismarked the sex question which resulted in upwards of one-quarter of same-sex couples being misclassified (DeMaio, Bates, and O'Connell, 2013). These effects can be compounded if the item also leads to a significant number of "false negative" reports, which occur when members of the small minority group do not select that response category. This can occur when a person fits the definition of a category or experience but does not recognize the terminology provided, finds the response options offensive, or is otherwise uncomfortable reporting an identity that is marginalized or stigmatized. Although it is almost impossible to entirely eliminate false positives and false negatives, careful pretesting of items through cognitive interviews and experimental studies that compare results from different wordings help to minimize these misclassifications and improve data validity.

A further complication can arise when data are tabulated and reported because categories with few people in them are often later collapsed into broader categories and are sometimes even dropped from analysis. When this occurs, although respondents may have initially had the opportunity to express their unique identity in data collection, the end result is that their voice is erased.

A similar outcome can occur when a question uses an open-response or free-text question format. In this format, respondents are allowed to write in their personal identity. This type of approach requires recoding each written response into a broad category that can be used in statistical analysis. This coding process requires the coder or analyst to make decisions on how to categorize the information that the respondent provided. This means that the coder will choose the best way to recategorize an individual's identity into usable data groups, and this recategorization comes with implicit biases that may not be consistent with the individual's understanding of their own identity (Guyan, 2022). Additionally, this process can be very time consuming and resource intensive, particularly when a large number of responses have to be coded. Nonetheless, write-ins allow respondents to record terms outside of a fixed list and allow analysts to monitor the use of terms over time to determine if the inclusion of a new category is warranted going forward, which is particularly useful when terminology is in flux.

Determining when a write-in response is "sufficient" to warrant its own category requires several considerations. First, has previous research indicated respondents identifying with the potential new category have different outcomes than those identifying with existing categories? For example, do people writing in "nonbinary" or "gender-fluid" have different outcomes than those currently being classified as transgender? Second, has the potential new category seen an increase in frequency *over time* and over different data collections? In other words, will the terminology have "staying power" or is it a temporarily popular term? Third, is the frequency of the potential new category as large as or larger than an existing category? Furthermore, is the number of responses large enough to pass disclosure avoidance thresholds such that it can be published in public data tables? If these conditions are met, then pretesting the new category is essential to understand whether it might confuse some respondents—a narrow niche might know what it means, but what impact will it have on the general population? Finally, if resources permit, a randomized split ballot experiment can be conducted testing the old set of categories against the expanded group to examine who selects the new category and with what frequency (as well as a comparison of the new group's demographics to original write-in group demographics).

Summary

Although we recognize that all kinds of data can inform public policy and community action, the statement of task stipulated that the panel's recommendations be focused on the types of information collected in population-based surveys, large-scale administrative contexts, and other data collection activities that track entire populations or large general samples, not just those that target sexual and gender minorities. These contexts almost always use multiple-choice questions that capture the vast majority of respondent identities and minimize the need for further data coding and processing. Moreover, because many sexual and gender minority groups are small populations, mismeasurement can have an outsized impact on data quality, which means that pretesting of measures is particularly important. For this reason, the panel decided to base our evaluation on existing measures that had undergone testing, and, when possible, have been used in general populations.

Measures that primarily have been used and tested in LGBTQI+ communities may better capture the diverse range of identities and experiences in those populations, but they may be less comprehensible to the general population. Similarly, the use of specific terminology may vary with age or other respondent characteristics, such as race, ethnicity, and geography. Data collection efforts that target these populations may wish to consider modifying the recommended questions and response options. We strongly urge any adjustments to the recommended questions be properly tested to understand the potential impact on the resulting data.

CRITERIA FOR MEASURES USED FOR SEXUAL ORIENTATION, GENDER IDENTITY, AND INTERSEX STATUS

Given the generally accepted criteria for assessing measures and the concerns about balancing community responsiveness with usability in a general population that are discussed above, we used the following criteria for selecting which measures for sexual orientation identity, gender identity, and intersex status to recommend:

1. consistency with the data collection principles discussed above (e.g., precision, inclusiveness, autonomy);
2. comprehensibility to the general population as well as the LGBTQI+ populations of interest;
3. tested in *both* general population and LGBTQI+ populations;
4. requires that respondents select only a single response option in order to simplify enumeration, tabulation, and analysis of the resulting data;
5. provides consistent estimates when measured across data collection contexts; and
6. tested or previously administered with adequate performance using multiple administration modes (i.e., web-based, interviewer-administered, computer-assisted, and telephone administration).

For the *response options*, we used the following criteria:

1. comprehensibility to the general population;
2. consistency with terminology that is currently used in both the general population and LGBTQI+ populations;
3. ability to measure current trends;
4. ability to measure, assess, and incorporate changes with less well-known terminology;
5. balance in providing comprehensive options with minimizing complexity and respondent burden that arises from considering a longer list of response options;
6. produces a sufficient number of respondents per category to minimize the need to collapse categories and reclassify respondents; and
7. considers the effects of response item ordering, including relevant factors, such as:
   a. population prevalence,
   b. alphabetical listing,
   c. previous testing, and
   d. randomization.

In Part II of this report, the panel's recommended measures were weighed against these criteria using the evaluation methods described earlier. Both qualitative and quantitative evidence are cited to demonstrate degrees of understandability and comprehension, usability, item-nonresponse rates, frequency of category responses, and other psychometric measures of construct validity. In some cases, such as for intersex status, we highlight promising measures and recommend testing for inclusion in future data collection efforts.

The panel was charged with recommending measures for use in each of three context settings: surveys and research, administrative, and clinical. Much of the research that has been done to evaluate these measures has been done in surveys and other research settings. For this reason, we have greater confidence in the performance of our recommended measures in this setting than in the other two.

For clinical settings, the panel reviewed the available information on measures, including data collection guidance from a variety of sources, including government agencies, such as the Centers for Disease Control and Prevention and the National Institutes of Health, as well as research and practice from public and private health care organizations. We did not find any reasons to modify our recommended measures for data collection in this setting.

For administrative settings, which cover a wide range of contexts and practices, and, with the exception of vital statistics and legal identification documents, tend to be privately maintained, very little information is available on the practices that are in use, and even less information is publicly available on how those measures perform. As noted in Chapter 3, there may be specific contexts in administrative settings in which the collection of some of these data, such as sex assigned at birth, may be considered invasive; therefore, it may be necessary to modify the recommended measures for these contexts. Unfortunately, the panel did not have a sufficient evidentiary base for data collected in this setting to allow us to recommend possible alternative measures. Thus, we propose one set of measures that can be used across all three settings; however, users need to exercise caution when using these measures, particularly in administrative settings.

Part II

Recommended Measures

5

Measuring Sexual Orientation and Identifying Sexual Minority Populations

This chapter reviews approaches to assessing sexual orientation in large-scale population-based settings. We begin with an overview of the construct of sexual orientation and an explanation of how the measures we highlight in this report relate to the broader construct. Following this brief overview, we review existing approaches for assessing sexual orientation identity as an indicator of sexual orientation, allowing for the enumeration of sexual majority and sexual minority populations. We then offer our recommendations for measurement practices to document sexual orientation identities, and we conclude with recommendations for future research.

As noted in Part I, sexual orientation is a multidimensional construct reflecting in some way the gender(s) of a person's desired potential or actual sexual or romantic partners relative to the person's own gender.[1] The measurement of sexual orientation has varied across settings and data collection purposes, with a focus on one or a combination of the three dimensions of sexual orientation: behavior, attraction, and identity (van Anders, 2015; Tolman at al., 2014; Diamond, 2003; Coleman, 1987). Given the complexities of categorizing sexual behaviors and erotic or romantic attractions across a range of diverse gender identities as indicators of sexual orientation (van Anders, 2015), there are unique challenges to assessing sexual orientation through the dimensions of behavior and attraction.

---

[1]Throughout this chapter we use "gender" rather than "gender identity" because, while sexual orientation may be based on gender identity, it may also consider other dimensions of gender, such as gender expression.

SEXUAL ORIENTATION DIMENSIONS:
CONCEPTS AND MEASUREMENT

The construct of sexual behavior is often characterized as the sexually expressed component through physical and nonphysical expression. Sexual behavior can also include sexual abstinence, celibacy, or not yet physically expressed behaviors independent of sexual orientation identity. For example, one can self-identify as gay but decide to be celibate, or one can self-identify lesbian but not yet have experienced sexual physical contact with a woman. Primarily, collecting data on sexual behavior has served to inform public health epidemiological surveillance and intervention, health care practice, and ethnographic assessment of sexuality (Brooks et al., 2018; Wolff et al., 2017; Sell, 1997).

Identifying all of the possible sexual behavior measures and types is beyond the scope of this report. Often, measures of sexual behavior (e.g., number of partners, occasions of engaging in a given sexual act) are selected to meet a specific purpose, such as estimating the risks of pregnancy, HIV, or sexually transmitted infections or understanding or distinguishing among diverse sexual partnerships. Questionnaire design typically involves elaborate skip and filtering instructions (see Fenton et al., 2001) particularly related to partner information—including multiple sexual partners—as well as anatomical information of both respondents and partners (see Webb et al., 2015; Ivankovich, Leichliter, and Douglas, 2013; Fenton et al., 2001).

Similarly, approaches to the measurement of sexual attraction as an indicator of sexual orientation center on categorizing people by the gender(s) to which they are attracted, sexually or romantically. The measurement of sexual attraction may be appropriate when the purpose of the data collection is to assess the complex and fluid ways that individuals may experience attraction across a range of genders and relationships, irrespective of whether they enact these attractions into behavior or how they self-identify (Wolff et al., 2017; Diamond, 2003). Although the study of erotic and romantic attractions can serve many important data collection goals, in administrative setting and general population surveys, measures of sexual attraction have often been included as an indicator of sexual orientation when there are concerns that stigma and prejudice may inhibit individuals' self-disclosure of their sexual orientation identity.

The measurement of sexual attraction has also been used to characterize individuals who are not or not yet sexually active, as done in the National Longitudinal Study of Adolescent to Adult Health (Add Health) (Harris et al., 2009). Approaches include providing response options across a range of genders (men, women, men and women, etc.) or a range of sexual orientation terms that imply the gender to which someone is attracted (e.g., mostly homosexual). Over the years, the measurement of sexual attraction has varied, alongside the terms used to define interrelated phenomena, such as sexual arousal, sexual feelings, sexual desire, sexual attraction, and erotic attraction (for reviews, see Patterson et al., 2017; Sexual Minority Assessment Research Team, 2009; Diamond, 2003; Sell, 1997).

The final dimension of sexual orientation, sexual orientation identity, is often characterized as reflecting a person's sense of self with regard to enduring romantic and sexual attraction to particular gender(s) (Sell, 1997; Laumann et al., 1994). Sexual orientation identity is the cognitive as well as social expression of one's sexual orientation. Thus, sexual orientation identity is the dimension that is most consistently tied to experiences with material forms of discrimination (Drydakis, 2022; Pachankis et al., 2020; Dillbary and Edwards, 2019; Pachankis and Bränström, 2018) and noted explicitly in laws and policies aimed at protecting or harming sexual minorities (e.g., U.S. Equal Employment Opportunity Commission, 2021; U.S. Department of Justice, 2015). It is also the dimension with the broadest and longest use in population-based data collection settings (surveys and administrative data) to enumerate and distinguish among sexual minority and majority populations (Patterson et al., 2017; Federal Interagency Working Group, 2016b). Given the implications for measuring identity when tracking services and outcomes for sexual minority populations and the long-standing inclusion of measures of sexual orientation identity as a tool for assessing sexual orientation, the remainder of the chapter focuses on a review and recommendation of measurement approaches of sexual orientation identity.

EVALUATION OF EXISTING MEASUREMENT APPROACHES

The panel considered existing sexual orientation identity measures included in federal and national surveys and reviewed the prior recommendations published in peer-reviewed journals (e.g., Patterson et al., 2017), in books (e.g., Stall et al., 2020), and in policy briefs and reports (e.g., Federal Interagency Working Group, 2016a; The Gender Identity in U.S. Surveillance Group [GenIUSS], 2014; SMART, 2009) and well-respected think tanks and academic research centers (e.g., the UCLA Williams Institute, the National Opinion Research Center). Tables 5A-1 and 5A-2, in the annex to this chapter, list measures that the panel evaluated based on the measurement criteria outlined in Chapter 4 and our principles for data collection: inclusiveness, precision, autonomy, parsimony, and privacy (see Chapter 2).

Measures of sexual orientation identity have not varied dramatically over the last three decades. There are three general types of approaches: (1) asking whether someone identifies as a sexual minority or LGBT with dichotomous "yes/no" response options; (2) asking a respondent to select from a set of options reflecting combinations of sexual orientation identity and attraction terminologies (e.g., mostly homosexual [gay], but somewhat attracted to opposite sex); and (3) asking a respondent to select from a set of sexual orientation identity labels or terms (e.g., lesbian, straight, bisexual). The dichotomous response approach used by the Gallup Poll provided one of the first and strongest population-based estimates of the total LGBT population in the United States. However, it did not allow for the distinct measurement of sexual orientation separately from gender identity. The response option set, which includes a mix of terminology reflecting attraction and identity, appear to be more common among population-based data collection targeting younger respondents, such as Add Health and the National Survey of Youth in Custody. Most of the measures assessing sexual orientation identity use the third approach in which the focus is documenting which sexual orientation identity labels people use to describe themselves, with slight variations in stems and response options.

Across the surveys assessing identification with sexual orientation labels, slightly different wording is used in the question stems, such as "do you consider yourself," "describe your sexual orientation," or "think of yourself." The panel weighed concerns related to our principle of precision over whether naming the construct "sexual orientation" or "sexual identity" in the question stem was required for adequate performance of the measure. Avoiding the use of technical and theoretical language is a best practice in measurement design, and many scholars have considered the use of the term "sexual orientation" in general population data collection to be too technical (Badgett et al., 2009). Recent qualitative research has suggested that some respondents would prefer the specification of the concept they are being asked about, and yet the study also found that participants ranged in their understanding of "sexual orientation" (Suen et al., 2020). Moreover, in this study, the participants were mostly highly educated, and those who reported a desire to have the term "sexual orientation" specified in the stem were White and identified as a sexual minority, a demographic that represents a narrow subset of the general U.S. population. As such, it appears that while it may seem more precise to add the construct terminology to the stem of the question about sexual orientation identity, it is not yet clear whether it would produce more precise and accurate estimates of sexual orientation.

Additionally, the response options differ slightly in terms of whether a "none of the above" type of option is listed, whether a free text option is provided, and the range of identities offered for selection. Terms used to affirmatively describe people who identify with a sexual orientation indicating a sexual minority status have shifted throughout U.S. history, although some terms have remained popular for decades. "Gay," "lesbian," and "bisexual" have been present in literature and community organizing among sexual minorities since the early to mid-1900s (Morris, 2009). Other terms have been asserted in response or resistance to what is considered the mainstream Eurocentric sexual minority community, including Two-Spirit, same gender loving, and queer. There are also varying terms for sexual orientation identity that reflect plurisexual attractions and behaviors (e.g., pansexual, queer, omnisexual) and terms used to reflect the lack of erotic attraction (e.g., grey, asexual) (Jourian, 2015; Lassiter, 2014; Galupo et al., 2014).

The placement of sexual orientation identity terms varies across data collection contexts and has changed over time. In several early versions of surveys including measures of sexual orientation identity, the question was placed near questions about sexual risk and health care (e.g., in the National Health and Nutrition Examination Survey [NHANES], and the National Survey of Family Growth [NSFG]) or in sections about general life issues (the National Health Interview Survey [NHIS]) (Dahlhamer et al., 2014). The current 2021 NHIS also includes a sexual orientation identity item in the context of questions about social support and relationship status. However, other surveys have had success including it with the demographic items without increasing nonresponse. For example, the Census Pulse Survey, which introduced a question on sexual orientation identity in 2021, includes the item as the eighth question overall following the two-step question on transgender identity (see Chapter 6) and before asking about household size and marital status. However, the placement of sexual orientation identity questions in a survey merits further assessment of its effect on response rates and the response options selected.

In reviewing the available data for each measure's performance, the panel also considered several other factors: the empirical evidence (e.g., cognitive interviews, psychometric evaluation, nonresponse rates) supporting its use in large-scale population studies; its use in both probabilistic and nonprobabilistic sampling frames; the extent to which it has been used in diverse populations (e.g., across races, ages, sexual and gender minority populations, regions); and the extent to which it has been used with different modes of data collection (e.g., interviewer administered, paper-and-pencil administration, computer-assisted interviews with or without audio, web based). The panel also considered whether the measure was indicative of sexual orientation identity and did not conflate its use with other dimensions of sexual orientation (i.e., indicators of attraction or sexual behavior).

Evidence of Measure Performance in the United States

The panel explored whether the existing sexual orientation identity measures use a stem and response options with strong face construct validity (see above and Chapters 1 and 4). We prioritized the recommendation of measures of sexual orientation identity that reflect both the cognitive dimension of identity (i.e., how a respondent sees or thinks of themselves) and the social or political dimension of identity (i.e., provides label options that reflect a social status or community). We also assessed whether the measure met the content standard by including a stem and response options that reflected a focus on sexual orientation identity labels separate from gender identity, sexual behavior, or attraction. Only the measures asking respondents to select an identity label, which we refer to as the "identity label approach," fit this criterion and therefore became the focus of the rest of our evaluation and discussion of a recommended measure of sexual orientation identity.

The sexual orientation identity label approach has undergone a significant amount of cognitive interview and survey design testing to assess whether respondents understood the question and could be categorized into the available response options and whether misclassifications could be minimized. This initial questionnaire development research was conducted between 2001 and 2013 using data collected through the NHIS and NSFG, as well as cognitive interviews (Dahlhamer et al., 2014; Ridolfo et al., 2012; Miller and Ryan, 2011; Miller, 2001). The cognitive interview respondents ranged in age (18–60+ years), ethnicity and race (more than 75% people of color), and sexual orientation and gender identity (more than 40% identified as something other than straight/heterosexual, and 6% indicated their gender was "more complicated" than male or female). This research demonstrated comprehension of the sexual orientation identity measure among sexual majority and minority populations with racially diverse samples; the item based on the testing was ultimately included in the 2013 NHIS.

Another component of the cognitive standard discussed in Chapter 4 is the extent to which items result in respondents being willing and able to answer them (Suen et al., 2022; Bates, García Trejo, and Vines, 2019; Ellis et al., 2018; Fredriksen-Goldsen and Hudson, 2018; Rullo et al., 2018). The feasibility of asking questions about sexual orientation in population-based data collection has been demonstrated across many studies. For example, Meyer and colleagues (2002) conducted a study that found that women would respond to an anonymous random-digit-dial telephone health survey asking a series of questions that included sexual orientation identity and sexual attraction. More recent studies of feasibility provide further evidence that respondents in population-based surveys and health care settings are willing and able to respond to questions about sexual orientation identity (Bates et al., 2019; Rullo et al., 2018; Ellis et al., 2018; Lee et al., 2018). Several of these studies noted that while there are subsets of respondents who find the questions about sexual orientation sensitive, such concerns are not limited to the construct of sexual orientation: for example, questions about disability status were also reported as potentially sensitive and yet feasible to collect.

In current surveys, the nonresponse rate for questions on sexual orientation identity appears more than acceptable. There is no one standard for acceptable item nonresponse rates; however, the U.S. Census Bureau, in a review of changes in responses to specific items between population counts, characterized nonresponse under 5.95 percent as "low."[2] The percentage of respondents in 2020 who refused or did not provide data for sexual orientation on the English versions of the NHIS, Behavioral Risk Factor Surveillance System (BRFSS), Census Pulse Survey, and other probability national samples asking this question were all under 3 percent: see Table 5-1 (also see Bates, García Trejo, and Vines, 2019; Meyer et al., 2019). That is, nonresponse rates are lower than or comparable to other demographic or outcome variables, such as race and family income. The point estimates for the proportion of the U.S. population that is identified as a sexual minority does vary across the surveys that use this measure, but without confidence intervals for the point estimates it is not clear whether these differences are significant or meaningful.

The panel also considered mode of administration. The recommended measure has been used in self-reported surveys and interviewer-administered surveys. A study by Dahlhamer and colleagues (2014) found that the accuracy of the measure in national surveys was not statistically different if respondents completed the measure using an audio computer-assisted self-interviewing mode or a computer-assisted personal interview mode. Household surveys often require proxy reporting on household members. A recent effort to test whether a similar measure of sexual orientation identity could be reliably collected by proxy has concluded that it is feasible (Holzberg et al., 2019). However, given the challenges associated with proxy reporting, the panel concluded that that we did not yet have sufficient evidence to endorse the use of proxy reporting.

Comparison with Other English-Speaking Countries

The panel also reviewed standards for collecting data on sexual orientation identity from other English-speaking countries. Outside the United States, Australia, Canada, New Zealand, and the countries of the United Kingdom have begun or recently completed the process of revising their

---

[2]See https://www.census.gov/newsroom/blogs/random-samplings/2021/08/2020-census-operational-quality-metrics-item-nonresponse-rates.html.

TABLE 5-1 Item Nonresponse Rates and Sexual Minority Population Prevalence for Recommended Sexual Orientation Identity Measure

Survey	Question	Nonresponse/ Unknown Rate	Percentage Lesbian, Gay, Bisexual
2016 NCVS	Which of the following best represents how you think of yourself? ○ Gay/lesbian ○ Straight, that is, not gay ○ Bisexual ○ Something else ○ I don't know the answer	2.8%	1.9% (weighted)
2018 GSS	Which of the following best describes you? ○ Gay, lesbian, or homosexual ○ Bisexual ○ Heterosexual or straight ○ Don't know	1.9%	5.8% (weighted)
2020 BRFSS	Which of the following best represents how you think of yourself? ○ Gay ○ Straight, that is, not gay ○ Bisexual ○ Something else ○ I don't know the answer	1.9%	4.2% (weighted)
2020 NHIS	Do you think of yourself as: ○ Gay/lesbian ○ Straight, that is, not gay/ lesbian ○ Bisexual ○ Something else ○ You don't know the answer	2.6%	3.1% (un-weighted)
2021 Census Pulse	Which of the following best represents how you think of yourself? ○ Gay/lesbian ○ Straight, that is, not gay ○ Bisexual ○ Something else ○ I don't know	2.2%	6.5% (un-weighted)

TABLE 5-1 Continued

NOTE: All data from national samples of U.S. adults. Nonresponse rates calculated by committee members from publicly accessible codebooks for Behavioral Risk Factor Surveillance System (BRFSS) and National Health Interview Survey (NHIS); online data tools for the General Social Survey (GSS); and detailed data tables for the U.S. Census Pulse Survey.
SOURCES: Data from BRFSS (CDC, 2021), NHIS (National Center for Health Statistics, 2021), National Crime Victimization Survey (NCVS; Truman et al., 2019), GSS (Davern et al., 2021), and U.S. Census Pulse Survey (U.S. Census Bureau, 2021).

data collection standards for measuring sexual orientation (see Table 5A-2 in the annex to this chapter). All of the countries defined the concept of sexual orientation as an umbrella term that encompasses the dimensions of identity, attraction, and behavior, and they all stress that these characteristics can change over time and do not necessarily correspond to one another at any given time. These countries also use very similar measures for sexual orientation identity: each country offers the same three major response categories, and all include the option of a write-in response.

A question on sexual orientation identity was included for the first time in the 2021 census for England and Wales and will be included in the 2022 census of Scotland. The Office of National Statistics (ONS) conducted extensive pretesting for the measure and ultimately made it a voluntary response for people ages 16 and up (Office of National Statistics, 2021). The format of the question, "Which of the following best describes your sexual orientation?" is consistent across all three territories (see Table 5A-2);[3] the major difference between this format and most versions in the United States is that the question stem specifies the term *sexual orientation*, and a write-in line is provided to account for responses in addition to "Straight or heterosexual," "Gay or lesbian," and "Bisexual." In addition to the censuses, ONS has also been collecting sexual orientation identity on its Annual Population Survey and Crime Survey for England and Wales. Its original 2009 guidance for measuring sexual identity was among the earliest national publications of its kind; the national harmonized standard was last updated in 2016 (Office of National Statistics, 2016).

Canada did not include a question about sexual orientation in its 2021 census but has asked about sexual orientation identity on the Canadian Community Health Survey since 2003 and on its General Social Survey on

[3]See revised Scotland census form here: https://www.scotlandscensus.gov.uk/documents/scotland-s-census-2022-question-set/.

victimization since 2004. Questions on sexual behavior and sexual attraction were added to Canada's national health survey of adults and youth, in 2015 and 2016, respectively (Statistics Canada, 2020). A proposed national statistical standard for sexual diversity was published in January 2021,[4] but has not yet been implemented. Its currently recommended measure for sexual orientation identity is a close version of the United Kingdom's question stem and response options (see Table 5A-2).

Overall, the panel found it notable that the language used to describe major sexual orientation identities are relatively consistent across countries. There is some divergence in how to label the write-in option (ranging from New Zealand's "Other, please state" to Australia's "I use a different term"), and New Zealand's testing suggested that respondents in that country had "variable understanding" of the terms sexual orientation and sexual identity; as a result, New Zealand opted not to include that wording in its recommended question stem (Stats NZ, 2019: 11; Australian Bureau of Statistics, 2021). However, the general consistency of approaches to measuring sexual orientation identity provide additional evidence that supports our conclusions and recommendations for the United States.

In our review of measures in other English-speaking countries, the panel also noted that the consensus minimum age recommendation for asking about sexual orientation identity across most of the countries is 15 (see, e.g., Australian Bureau of Statistics, 2021); the United Kingdom opted for 16 and over because that is their age of consent and minimum age at marriage (Office of National Statistics, 2021). However, the panel found insufficient evidence to support a minimum age recommendation for the United States. We return to this point at the end of the chapter in our recommendations for future research.

CONCLUSIONS AND RECOMMENDATIONS

Sexual orientation identity has been assessed as a demographic variable in population-based national and state surveys and numerous community studies for decades (Sexual Minority Assessment Research Team, 2009). The panel prioritized a measure that would be easiest to implement across population-based, clinical, and administrative data collection efforts. The panel approached the evaluation and recommendation of sexual orientation measures following the principles delineated in Chapter 2 and the criteria outlined in Chapter 4. With regard to evaluation criteria, the panel relied heavily on the measure's demonstrated use and performance in both the general population and LGBTQI+ populations; evidence of conceptual grounding, comprehension, and usability; and record of use as a single

---

[4]See https://www.statcan.gc.ca/en/concepts/consult-variables/gender.

response to enable enumeration across multiple modes of data collection (e.g., interviewer or computer-assisted interviews, administrative forms, etc.).

Our findings are summarized in Table 5-2, following our recommended measure, and then we provide a discussion of how the criteria apply to the recommended measure.

> RECOMMENDATION 2: The panel recommends that National Institutes of Health use the following question for assessing sexual orientation identity:
>
> Which of the following best represents how you think of yourself? [Select ONE]:
> O Lesbian or gay;
> O Straight, that is, not gay or lesbian;
> O Bisexual;
> O [If respondent is AIAN:] Two-Spirit
> O I use a different term [free-text]
> (Don't know)
> (Prefer not to answer)

Question Stem

The stem of the recommended measure does not require knowledge of the term "sexual orientation" and yet frames the question as an issue of identity or how people see themselves, reflecting the cognitive dimension of sexual orientation. The response options all reflect labels used to describe sexual orientation identity, rather than attraction or behavior. The recommended measure allows for respondents to answer their sexual orientation identity using one of these popular terms or to write-in a response for other terms.

Response Categories

In considering the ordering of response categories, the panel decided to list the response options as they appear in existing surveys. The panel considered whether response options could be reordered based on population prevalence, with the most commonly selected category ("straight, that is, not gay or lesbian") presented to respondents first; however, the panel decided against this approach given insufficient evidence to support it.

Testing the effects of reordering is particularly important because the "straight" category is phrased as a negation of the "gay or lesbian"

TABLE 5-2 Summary of Findings on Sexual Orientation Identity Measure and Evaluation Criteria

Question Stem	Question Responses	Evaluation Criteria	Evaluation
Which of the following best represents how you think of yourself?	• Gay; • Straight, that is, not gay; • Bisexual; • I use a different term (Don't know) (Prefer not to answer)	Previous use in population-based data collection	• Close versions of this have been used in: the Behavioral Risk Factor Surveillance System (BRFSS) (since 2014), the National Crime Victimization Survey (NCVS) (since 2016), the National Health Interview Survey (NHIS) (since 2013), and the National Health and Nutrition Examination Survey (since 2013) • Close versions used in electronic medical records (EMR) in health systems following a 2015 final rule by the Office of the National Coordinator for Health Information Technology (ONC) • Recommended by the Federal Interagency Working Group on Improving Measurement of Sexual Orientation and Gender Identity in Federal Surveys (2016)
		Conceptual fit	• Measures sexual orientation identity only (i.e., does not conflate identity with attraction and/or behavior) • Clearly distinguished people with varying sexual orientation identities and broadly between sexual minority and sexual majority populations, while allowing for enumeration of those who do not use any of the listed labels • Allows for culturally specific identification for Indigenous populations; response category needs to be explicitly included only in automated data collection where racial identity is collected and respondent endorses AIAN [American Indian and Alaska Native] identity
		Testing; comprehension and validity	• Debriefing interviews, targeted interviews, cognitive interviewing, and focus groups (Holzberg et al., 2019; Truman et al., 2019; Martinez et al., 2017; Michaels et al., 2017; Wilson et al., 2016; Miller, 2001; Ridolfo, Miller, and Maitland, 2012; Miller and Ryan, 2011; Austin et al., 2007 • Acceptability studies in clinical settings (Rullo et al., 2018; Ruben et al., 2017; Cahill et al., 2014) • Behavior coding and split-sample question format experiments in telephone interviews (West and McCabe, 2021; Dahlhamer et al., 2019; Michaels et al., 2017)

Populations included in testing	• Sexual minority and heterosexual/straight identified • Spanish and English speakers • U.S. general population, including racially diverse samples, urban and rural residents, and ages 12–85
Testing; errors and nonresponse	• Testing options with expanded response list to existing list (Meyer et al., 2019) • Testing response rate and willingness to be asked sexual orientation questions in the census (Bates, García Trejo, and Vines, 2019; Truman et al., 2019; Ruben et al., 2017; Saewyc et al., 2004) • Nonresponse rates on the BRFSS (2020), NCVS (2017), NHIS (2019), General Social Survey (2018) ≤3%
Adjustments to previously tested item included in recommended measure	• Removed "something else" and replaced with open-text and wording of "I use a different term" • Include Two-Spirit category in automated data collection where racial identity is collected and AIAN is indicated
Weaknesses and challenges	• Narrow set of responses that do not reflect current culture and terms used by many sexual minorities (e.g., queer, Two-Spirit) • Write-in sexual orientation identity field will have to be cleaned and coded for reporting; newer terms not listed (e.g., pansexual) also may grow in popularity and need to be assessed for inclusion as explicit options • Does not provide a clear option to indicate lack of sureness about a label that describes them (i.e., questioning) • Though testing showed a need for the "that is, not gay" phrase among some heterosexual respondents, it is not clear this is still needed; also, as written, it is a conceptually inaccurate description of what it means to be "straight" and has implications for the definition of bisexual • Response options are not presented in order of prevalence or other common ordering (e.g., alphabetical)

category, and so, changing their order could affect respondent comprehension. The panel also considered the necessity of still including the clarification term under the heterosexual category (i.e., "straight, that is, not gay or lesbian"). This phrasing places "straight" in contrast with "gay or lesbian," which (1) reinforces "straight" as the normative, unmarked category and (2) in combination with "gay or lesbian" logically appears to include all possible responses ("gay or lesbian" vs. "not gay or lesbian"), but it does not because, for example, bisexual is excluded. Inclusion of the "not gay or lesbian" qualifier was prompted from research a decade ago for the NHIS (Ridolfo, Miller, and Maitland, 2012). Cognitive interviews found that many straight respondents had little need to express a salient sexual orientation identity because they represent the heteronormative majority. Instead, these respondents often disidentified from a gay identity, sometimes referred to as a "not-me" identity (McCall, 2003). For these respondents, identifying as heterosexual (as some described it "not gay" or "normal") served to distance themselves from what they perceived as a stigmatized sexual orientation.

The panel recognizes that the wording of the response category for the heterosexual population is informed by psychometric work that was carried out over the past three decades when social awareness of sexual and gender minority identities was less well understood (Fredriksen-Goldsen and Kim, 2015; Sell, 1997). Evidence from testing this question in recent years, however, suggests that heterosexual respondents may not answer the question correctly without the clarification term. For example, researchers (e.g., Michaels et al., 2017) have noted that among people whose primary language is Spanish, changing the phrasing of the straight option to read the negation portion first (e.g., "not gay [or lesbian], that is, heterosexual") may improve response accuracy compared with the recommended response phrasing (e.g., "straight, that is, not gay or lesbian"); however, the panel did not have sufficient evidence of testing this change in phrasing in other populations to recommend this change. Similarly, there was insufficient empirical evidence that would allow us to determine whether the performance of the measure would be affected if the clarification portion of this response option was removed. Finally, the qualifier is currently used in several of the largest national surveys, including the BRFSS, All of Us, the National Crime Victimization Survey (NCVS), NHANES, and NHIS (starting in 2022; see Table 5A-1). The panel recommends that the clarification included in the heterosexual answer category (i.e., "that is, not gay or lesbian") and its wording order be further studied to ensure sufficient understanding among the general population, including those for whom English is not their primary language.

The list of sexual orientation identity labels in the United States is continuously expanding (e.g., see, Goldberg et al., 2020; Rothblum et al., 2020) as part of the assessment of available measures, and the panel weighed the opportunity costs associated with including a more expansive list of sexual orientation identity categories. For example, the panel discussed whether additional response categories need to be added to the recommended measure to capture the use of sexual orientation identities such as "queer," "pansexual," or "same gender loving." However, the panel did not have sufficient evidence to warrant making such a recommendation at this time. Almost none of the general population survey questions the committee considered included these response categories (see Table 5A-1) and none demonstrated testing for comprehension in the general population. Moreover, there is reason to believe that these terms might be understood or accepted differently among sexual and gender minority people, as well as the general population. For example, the panel noted that the term "queer" has different connotations by age: queer is experienced as a slur by older people while younger people have sought to reclaim the term; moreover, it can be used to refer to both sexuality and gender (see, e.g., Flatt et al., 2022; Barsigian et al., 2020).

All of Us included "queer" and "pansexual" as response options in a follow-up question administered to those who selected "None of these and I would like to see more options." However, even when provided this more extensive list of response options (shown in Table 5A-1), only about half of these respondents selected an identity from the list. Similarly, Meyer and colleagues (2019) conducted an experiment with approximately 9,700 adults age 18 or older, randomly assigning respondents to one of two sexual orientation question wordings. For those who responded "something else," half of the sample got a follow-up question that included "queer," "pansexual," "asexual," "demisexual," "same gender loving," and "none of the above." However, only 0.6 percent of respondents identified as one of these sexual orientations. The study concluded that most respondents (53 percent) who initially identified as "something else" subsequently identified as "none of the above."

The panel decided on the use of a write-in category as a strategy that allowed respondents who did not find the existing response categories captured their identity to respond. The panel considered the likelihood that additional categories would need to be collapsed into broader categories or dropped from analyses entirely if an insufficient number of respondents selected a given term. The panel strongly encourages the reporting of the use of these write-in categories in published tabulations of responses. An increase in the use of write-in responses could indicate that the existing response categories are no longer representative of those used in the general population and could indicate a need to revisit the recommended response categories.[5] The write-in identity categories could assist in assessing which sexual orientation identities have become sufficiently prevalent in the general population to target for testing as new response categories.

Considerations for Indigenous Populations

Recognizing the importance of representation and visibility of the U.S. Indigenous population and in accordance with federal mandates for data collection on American Indian and Alaska Native (AIAN) populations and recommendation of the National Congress of American Indians and the Indian Health Service 2020 Strategic Vision and Action Plan (Indian Health Service, 2020), the panel considered including an additional response category for surveys that include a population-based, representative, or Indigenous-community-based sample of AIAN respondents. In weighing the inclusion of this category, the panel was concerned whether misreporting by non-AIAN people as Two-Spirit would preclude accurate representation of Indigenous Two-Spirit populations. To assess the potential impact of "false positive" reports as Two-Spirit among non-Indigenous populations, the panel reviewed data from the All of Us study,[6] which included Two-Spirit as a sexual orientation response option. These data showed that more than two-thirds of those who identified as Two-Spirit were not AIAN. Given the high probability of producing data on Two-Spirit people that inaccurately reflects AIAN populations, the panel does not recommend making this a response option for all respondents.

However, inclusion of a Two-Spirit response option for AIAN respondents would provide a way for surveys to explicitly include a category that represents sexual and gender minority populations that are culturally specific to the AIAN population. The need for such a response option is demonstrated by the AIAN LGBTQI+ Two-Spirit Study, funded by the National Institutes of Health (HONOR Project; Cassels et al., 2010)—the only nationally representative study of AIAN LGBTQ health. When AIAN respondents were asked, "Which one category best describes your sexual orientation now?" the responses were are follows: 16 percent Two-Spirit, 30 percent gay, 29 percent bisexual, 15 percent lesbian, 7 percent heterosexual, 2 percent reported their specific tribal word for their sexual orientation, and 1 percent reported "other." Thus, one of six AIAN respondents

---

[5]Analysts cannot not assume that all write-in responses for "I use a different term" represent sexual minority identities. Write-ins will need to be examined to determine whether responses represent sexual minority identities and are consistent with existing response categories (and can be recoded accordingly) or need to be treated as (uncodable) missing data. The latter may include "protest" write-ins or other off-topic responses (see Bates, García Trejo, and Vines, 2019).

[6]See https://allofus.nih.gov/.

preferred the Two-Spirit term for sexual orientation. This is underscored by the Indian Health Service's (2020) recommendation that all clinical and research Indian Health Service forms include "Two-Spirit" as a response option for sexual orientation.

Inclusion of the Two-Spirit response category ensures that data will capture the significant portion of AIAN respondents who would otherwise not identify with existing Eurocentric sexual orientation identity response categories. The Indian Health Service recommendation that the Two-Spirit category be included in data collection efforts reflects the fact that this term is used in both rural and reservation environments. The high prevalence of its use within Indigenous populations in combination with the culturally specific role in sexual orientation identity that the term Two-Spirit holds for this population motivated the panel's decision to include a Two-Spirit option for AIAN respondents.

The panel recommends that Two-Spirit be included as a response category for participants who self-identify as AIAN in computer-assisted surveys where the response options may be tailored through an algorithm. In such cases, data collection would also need to include a measure of racial or ethnic identity that offers AIAN as a response option and is asked prior to questions on sexual orientation identity. In an interviewer-assisted or paper-and-pencil survey in which response options cannot be tailored, the Two-Spirit responses can be tallied through the open text response option. Although offering different response options based on previous survey responses is not standard survey practice, it is not unprecedented in this context, where response options have often differed by gender of the respondent. The panel recommends this measurement strategy as a way to reduce misappropriation of an identity that has a very particular meaning in AIAN communities, a population with language describing sexual and gender minority status or identities that predate the terms that predominate in the general population. This option allows AIAN respondents to see their culturally specific sexual identities represented, even in general population surveys, while preserving the autonomy of all respondents to write-in "Two-Spirit" or a tribal-specific term in the open-text field. When automated programming of response options is not feasible, researchers need to be cognizant of possibility of the appropriation of an Indigenous identity category by non-Indigenous people in their analyses and interpretation of results.

RECOMMENDED RESEARCH AREAS

The panel's recommended sexual orientation identity measure is the result of a review of currently available evidence. We concluded there is sufficient evidence to support this approach to asking about sexual orientation identity in large-scale data collection settings, particularly for general population enumeration and research among English-speaking adults. Additionally, there is evidence of acceptable performance in health contexts, including medical settings, clinical trials, and public health surveillance. We also identified potential challenges and limitations to this empirically validated option. Although the sexual orientation identity question used in several federal surveys and electronic health records is the strongest option available, additional research is needed to assess its ongoing use in administrative contexts (see, e.g., Cooper, Wilson, and Choi, 2017), and to respond to concerns expressed by members of sexual minority communities, scholars, and other stakeholders about some aspects of its operationalization to date (see, e.g., Suen et al., 2020). In addition to the issues noted above, these include the following concerns:

- whether concerns about straight people's comprehension of the sexual orientation identity terms are still warranted, in English and other languages;
- whether changes are needed to the ordering of the response options;
- how best to integrate standardized questions for sexual attraction as a measure of sexual orientation and determine under which conditions it is equally or more useful than identity measures;
- the need for further assessment of item performance across all survey modes, including proxy reporting, in languages other than English, in all major U.S. racial and ethnic populations, and among youth; and
- the need to reevaluate and expand answer options over time, particularly with regard to plurisexual response categories (e.g., queer and pansexual).

In the rest of this section we briefly review these considerations and offer recommendations for future research.

Clarification for the Heterosexual Response Category

The panel had serious concerns about the use of negating and imprecise language in the "heterosexual" response option ("straight, that is, not gay or lesbian"). However, we had insufficient empirical evidence to determine whether the performance of the recommended measure would be affected if the clarification portion of the heterosexual response option was removed. Given increased social awareness of different sexual identities in the general population, the panel recommends that the clarification included in the heterosexual answer category ("that is, not gay or lesbian") and its wording order be further evaluated to ensure optimal comprehension by the general public, including those for whom English is not their primary language. Given the evidence suggesting differences in measure performance across different communities, testing the comprehension and performance of the recommended measure across multiple languages and racial, ethnic, and cultural groups is an important area for research.

Ordering of Response Categories

The panel considered the ordering of response categories and whether response options could be reordered based on population prevalence. However, we ultimately decided against this change. To our knowledge, there is no evaluation data that allows us to determine whether reordering the response categories based on their population prevalence would affect the measure's performance. This testing is particularly important because the "straight" category is phrased as a negation of the "gay or lesbian" category, and so changing the order could affect respondent comprehension. Given the limited evidence on whether response order would affect response rates, the panel encourages research to examine whether response ordering affects the measure's performance.

Item Performance of "Attraction"
in General Population Data Collection

Sexual attraction does not require individuals to identify or conform with a sexual orientation identity, nor does it require individuals to engage in sexual behavior. While the etiologic and historical review of the different conceptualizations and measures used to describe sexual attraction are beyond the scope of this report, the panel acknowledges the need to assess the performance of sexual attraction measures in future research. Specifically, the panel emphasizes that any entity requiring data regarding respondents' attractions needs to ensure that the measure is independent of LGBQ status or sexual behavior. Moreover, a future measure of attraction needs to acknowledge multiple forms of attraction (e.g., romantic, erotic), include a response for the absence of attraction in response categories (e.g., asexuality, aromantic), and integrate an expansive conceptualization of the gender identities, bodies, and identities to which a person may be sexually attracted. At this time, there are no measures that have been qualitatively or quantitively tested for use in general population data collection. Future research in this area is warranted.

Evaluating Best Practices for Sexual Orientation Measures among Youth

The statement of task instructed the panel to review and recommend measures to assess sexual orientation and gender identity for the U.S. adult population. However, higher proportions of youth and young adults today identify with a sexual and gender minority identity than previously, and this proportion appears to be growing (Jones, 2021). Also, youth and young adults make up a disproportionate percentage of the sexual minority population (Wilson et al., 2021; Meyer et al., 2019). Moreover, youth surveys served as the site of the earliest administration of population-based measures of sexual orientation (Remafedi et al., 1992). Currently, the national Youth Risk Behavior Surveillance System (YRBSS) and many similar state surveys ask questions about sexual orientation, including identity, and several states and localities collect similar data in their administrative systems, such as child welfare, incarceration, and social services (see, e.g., California Legislative Assembly, 2015). Some of the measures used in these administrative settings have undergone testing for comprehension, accuracy, and feasibility (see, e.g., Steiger et al., 2017; Wilson et al., 2016). As such, the need for an assessment of how well the measures perform in population-based and administrative data collection settings is needed to create best practices.

Another dimension of age is determining the youngest age at which sexual orientation questions can be feasibly and reliably asked. Although other English-speaking countries have decided on age standards for asking about sexual orientation, the panel did not find conclusive evidence to support setting age standards, and, as noted above, were tasked with a focus on adults. Ongoing panels and survey research in the United States collect information from middle and high school students (e.g., Add Health; YRBSS) regarding their attractions, behaviors, and identities. Given these findings, the panel believes that youth may comprehend and respond to questions regarding their sexual orientation. However, in the absence of empirical evidence regarding our recommended measure with children and adolescents, the panel recommends further research to appropriately evaluate its performance across both settings (e.g., schools, health care) and age groups.

Inclusion and Potential Expansion of Identity Categories

There are a growing number of sexual orientation identity labels and increasing popularity in adopting some of these labels. Various factors, in addition to popularity of newer terminology, are relevant to how sexual orientation identity measures will perform in the general population, including whether there is evidence that these terms are understood consistently across the general population. Continual assessment of evolving language and prevalence of sexual orientation identity labels is required. While terms beyond the historical labels of "gay," "lesbian," "bisexual," and "heterosexual or straight" (such as "queer," "pansexual") have not been tested for this broad level of comprehension or standardized in federal and national population-based surveys, the panel supports revisiting the sexual orientation identity categories and testing their use in federal and national population-based surveys when there is sufficient evidence to do so. Ongoing testing examination of how additional response categories may affect the performance of the panel's recommended measure is warranted, as it may offer the necessary evidence to empirically determine whether different responses need to be integrated into population-based surveys and acknowledge the presence of diverse sexual orientations in our society to the public without negatively affecting the currently established measures.

The panel acknowledges the need for continued psychometric testing of the measure to incorporate changes in response category terminology, particularly as the social meaning of sexual orientation identity continues to evolve. The panel also recognizes that for surveys that are conducted in specific communities and age-specific surveys, a more expansive list of identity categories may be warranted. The panel made a distinction between population-based and administrative data collection and the collection of sexual orientation data in community settings. Our recommended measure may not capture the full range of different sexual orientation identities among sexual and gender minorities. While the recommended "I use a different term" may allow respondents to self-report their own identities, these descriptors may be hard to standardize and aggregate. As a result, community-based studies that focus on the diversity in those populations may require additional categories that are reflective of the language, race, ethnicity, culture, geography, and age of respondents.

The addition of a write-in option for "I use a different term" does not preclude the inclusion of additional response options that are more culturally or age tailored for specific populations or community-based LGBTQI+ surveys. In modes of administration in which follow-up prompts may be easily programmed, for example, the panel suggests opportunities that allow respondents to request a second, more detailed set of answer categories as a follow-up question for those who indicate they prefer an identity that does not appear on the list of responses provided. This method is currently being used in several federal studies (e.g., All of Us) and may help streamline the data collection and coding process. Additional research testing whether a second prompt may offer greater accuracy and performance across diverse populations is warranted.

Proxy Reporting

Self-reporting in surveys is preferred and aligns with the panel's principle to respect identity and autonomy. However, proxy reporting is used in various federal data collection efforts. Before sexual orientation is collected through proxy reporting, additional research is needed to test the accuracy and quality of the data reported; a proxy may not know how other household members self-identify. Testing is also needed on the associated sensitivity regarding confidentiality, that is, disclosing other household members' sexual orientation identity without their consent. Future evidence from experimental studies and other survey methodology techniques are needed to understand the acceptability of this approach and its accompanying sources of error (e.g., nonresponse rate, misclassification rates).

RECOMMENDATION 3: To further improve the quality and inclusivity of current measures of sexual orientation identity, the National Institutes of Health should fund and conduct research on the following topics:

- Alternate wording for the "straight" response option that performs equally well as, or better than, the existing recommendation for English- and non-English-speaking populations without using language that negates gay or lesbian identities. Such an assessment should include studies on whether the clarification "that is, not gay or lesbian" is still needed to ensure accurate comprehension among heterosexual populations.
- The ordering of response categories, including sorting response categories based on population prevalence.
- Guidelines for measures that capture other dimensions of sexual orientation, including sexual behavior and sexual attraction: in particular, standards for assessing asexual identities should be developed and tested.
- The utility of including sexual orientation identity response options that may be more prevalent in subsets of the LGBTQI+ population, such as "queer" and "questioning" or, in African American communities, "same gender loving."
- The performance of existing measures and identification of best practices for how to assess sexual minority status among adolescents, including whether sexual orientation identity is the most effective dimension to track (compared with attraction or behavior) when assessing disparities in well-being, the appropriate age at

which to begin asking sexual orientation questions, best practices for reflecting feelings about being unsure (i.e., questioning), and the range of response options.

- How reporting of sexual orientation identity is affected when reporting is done by proxy, such as when a single household respondent responds on behalf of all household members.

ANNEX:
SEXUAL ORIENTATION IDENTITY MEASURES
IN THE UNITED STATES AND OTHER
ENGLISH-SPEAKING COUNTRIES

This annex comprises two tables: Table 5A-1 shows all measures used in the United States to measure sexual orientation identity; Table 5A-2 does the same for other English-speaking countries.

TABLE 5A-1 Measures of Sexual Orientation Identity in the United States

Question	Response Options	Source(s)
Which of the following best represents how you think of yourself?	○ Gay; ○ Lesbian; ○ Straight, that is, not gay or lesbian, etc; ○ Bisexual; ○ None of these describe me, and I'd like to see additional options [see below]	All of Us (NIH)
[If "None of these describe me":] Are any of these a closer description of how you think of yourself?	○ Queer ○ Polysexual, omnisexual, sapiosexual or pansexual ○ Asexual ○ Two-Spirit ○ Have not figured out or are in the process of figuring out your sexuality ○ Mostly straight, but sometimes attracted to people of your own sex ○ Do not think of yourself as having sexuality ○ Do not use labels to identify yourself ○ Don't know the answer ○ No, I mean something else [free text:] ○ Prefer not to answer	
Do you consider yourself to be heterosexual or straight; homosexual or gay or lesbian; or bisexual?	○ Heterosexual or straight ○ Homosexual or gay or lesbian ○ Bisexual ○ Something else [free text]	American National Election Studies (ANES) Women Only

TABLE 5A-1 Continued

Question	Response Options	Source(s)
Do you consider yourself to be heterosexual or straight or homosexual or gay or bisexual?	○ Heterosexual or straight ○ Homosexual or gay ○ Bisexual ○ Something else [free text]	American National Election Studies (ANES) Men Only
Which of the following best represents how you think of yourself?	○ Gay; ○ Straight, that is, not gay; ○ Bisexual; ○ Something else; ○ I don't know; ○ Refused	Behavioral Risk Factor Surveillance System (BRFSS-CDC) National Crime Victimization Survey (NCVS-DOJ) National Health Interview Survey (NHIS-CDC) National Health and Nutrition Examination Survey (NHANES) Men Only
Which of the following best represents how you think of yourself?	○ Lesbian or gay; ○ Straight, that is, not lesbian or gay; ○ Bisexual; ○ Something else; ○ I don't know; ○ Refused	Behavioral Risk Factor Surveillance System (BRFSS-CDC) National Crime Victimization Survey (NCVS-DOJ) National Health Interview Survey (NHIS-CDC) National Health and Nutrition Examination Survey (NHANES) Women Only
Which one of the following do you consider yourself to be?	○ Straight/heterosexual; ○ Gay/lesbian; ○ Bisexual; ○ Prefer not to say; ○ Other; ○ No response	Center for Substance Abuse Treatment-Government Performance Results and Modernization Act (SAMHSA-CSAT-GPRA)
Do you, personally, identify as lesbian, gay, bisexual, or transgender?	○ Yes ○ No ○ Don't Know ○ Refused	Gallup Daily Tracking Poll

continued

TABLE 5A-1 Continued

Question	Response Options	Source(s)
Which of the following best describes you?	○ Gay, lesbian, or homosexual; ○ Bisexual; ○ Heterosexual or straight; ○ Don't know; ○ No answer; ○ Not applicable	General Social Survey
Next, we'd like to ask you a question about how you think of yourself. Do you consider yourself to be [lesbian/gay], straight, bisexual or something else?	○ Lesbian/Gay; ○ Straight; ○ Bisexual; ○ Something else; ○ Don't know; ○ Refused	Health and Retirement Study (HRS)
Do you think of yourself as straight or heterosexual; as gay, lesbian, or homosexual; or as bisexual?	○ Straight or heterosexual ○ Gay, lesbian, homosexual; ○ Bisexual; ○ Not sexual/celibate/none ○ Other, please specify	Health Center Patient Surveys (HCPS-HHS)
Now I will read a list of terms people sometimes use to describe how they think of themselves. Lesbian or gay, that is, homosexual Straight, that is, heterosexual Bisexual Don't know, or Another sexual orientation As I read the list again, please say 'Yes' when you hear the option that best describes how you think of yourself.	○ Lesbian or gay, that is, homosexual ○ Straight, that is, heterosexual ○ Bisexual ○ Don't know, or ○ Another sexual orientation	High School Longitudinal Study of 2009 (HSLS:09) CAPI or CATI interview
Do you think of yourself as:	○ Lesbian or gay, that is, homosexual ○ Straight, that is, heterosexual; ○ Bisexual; ○ Don't know; ○ Another sexual orientation	High School Longitudinal Study of 2009 (HSLS:09) Web-based interview

---

TABLE 5A-1 Continued

Question	Response Options	Source(s)
Do you think of yourself as...?	○ Lesbian or Gay; ○ Straight, that is, not Lesbian or Gay; ○ Bisexual; ○ Something else; ○ Respondent does not understand response options; ○ Don't Know/Not Sure; ○ Refused	National Adult Tobacco Survey (NATS-NCHS)
Which of the categories on the card best describes you?	○ Heterosexual (straight); ○ Gay or lesbian; ○ Bisexual; ○ Not sure	National Epidemiologic Survey of Alcohol and Related Conditions (NESARC)
Do you consider yourself to be:	○ Heterosexual or "straight" ○ Homosexual, gay, or lesbian ○ Bisexual ○ Don't know ○ Refused	National HIV Behavioral Surveillance (NHBS)
Which one category best describes your SEXUAL ORIENTATION now?	○ Lesbian; ○ Gay; ○ Bisexual; ○ Two Spirit; ○ Specific tribal identity (e.g., Nádleehí or Winkte, etc.) (Please describe_____) ○ Heterosexual; ○ Other: (Please describe _____)	National HONOR Project Study of LGBTQ+-Two Spirit American Indians and Alaska Natives (Cassels et al., 2010).
Do you consider yourself to be heterosexual or 'straight' or bisexual, or homosexual or gay?	○ "Straight," which is also called heterosexual; ○ Bisexual; ○ [If R is male:] Homosexual or gay; ○ [If R is not male:] Homosexual, gay, or lesbian; ○ Other (Don't Know)	National Inmate Study (Bureau of Justice Statistics)

continued

TABLE 5A-1 Continued

Question	Response Options	Source(s)
Do you think of yourself as lesbian or gay; straight, that is, not gay; bisexual; Something else?	○ Lesbian or gay ○ Straight, that is, not gay ○ Bisexual ○ Something else ○ Don't know ○ Refused	National Intimate Partner and Sexual Violence Survey (NISVS)
Please choose the description that best fits how you think about yourself:	○ 100% heterosexual (straight); ○ Mostly heterosexual (straight), but somewhat attracted to people of your own sex; ○ Bisexual that is, attracted to men and women equally; ○ Mostly homosexual (gay), but somewhat attracted to people of the opposite sex; ○ 100% homosexual (gay); ○ Not sexually attracted to either males or females; ○ Refused; ○ Don't know	National Longitudinal Study of Adolescent to Adult Health (Add Health) National Longitudinal Study of Adolescent and Adult Health (Add Health—SOGI-SES Supplement)
Which one of the following do you consider yourself to be?	○ Heterosexual, that is, straight; ○ [If R is female then Lesbian or] Gay; ○ Bisexual; ○ Don't Know; ○ Refused	National Survey of Drug Use and Health (NSDUH)
Do you think of yourself as...	○ Heterosexual or straight; ○ Homosexual or Gay [If R is female then Lesbian]; ○ Bisexual; ○ Something else; ○ Don't Know; ○ Refused	National Survey of Family Growth (NSFG)
Which of the following best represents how you think of yourself?	○ [If R is female then Lesbian or] Gay; ○ Straight, that is, not [If R is female then Lesbian or] Gay; ○ Bisexual; ○ Something else; ○ Refused; ○ Don't Know	National Survey of Older Americans Act Participants (NSOAAP)

TABLE 5A-1 Continued

Question	Response Options	Source(s)
Which of these best fits how you think of yourself?	○ Totally straight (heterosexual) ○ Mostly straight but kind of attracted to people of your own sex ○ Bisexual - that is, attracted to males and females equally ○ Mostly gay (homosexual) but kind of attracted to people of the opposite sex ○ Totally gay (homosexual) ○ Not sexually attracted to either males or females ○ Don't Know	National Survey of Youth in Custody (NSYC-2)
Do you consider yourself to be...	○ Straight ○ Lesbian or gay ○ Bisexual ○ Something else ○ Don't know ○ Refused	Population Assessment of Tobacco and Health (PATH)
Which of the following best describes you?	○ Heterosexual (straight); ○ Gay or Lesbian; ○ Bisexual; ○ Not sure; [Additional response options added in 2021] ○ I describe my sexual identity some other way ○ I am not sure about my sexual identity (questioning) ○ I do not know what this question is asking	Youth Risk Behavior Surveillance System (YRBSS)

TABLE 5A-2 Measures of Sexual Orientation Identity in Other English-Speaking Countries

Question	Answer Options	Source
How do you describe your sexual orientation? Please [tick/mark/select] one box:	○ Straight (heterosexual) ○ Gay or lesbian ○ Bisexual ○ I use a different term (please specify) ○ Don't know ○ Prefer not to answer	Australian Bureau of Statistics (2021)
What is your sexual orientation? Would you say you are:	○ Heterosexual ○ Lesbian or gay ○ Bisexual ○ Or please specify your sexual orientation (free-text)	Statistics Canada (2021)
Which of the following options best describes how you think of yourself?	○ Heterosexual or straight ○ Gay or lesbian ○ Bisexual ○ Other, please state ___ ○ Don't know ○ Prefer not to say	Stats New Zealand (2019)
Which of the following best describes your sexual orientation? This question is voluntary.	○ Straight or Heterosexual ○ Gay or Lesbian ○ Bisexual ○ Other sexual orientation (free-text)	United Kingdom: 2021 Census of England and Wales; 2022 Census of Scotland (Office of National Statistics, 2016)

6

Measuring Sex and Gender Identity

As noted in Part I of this report, existing measures tend to conflate the constructs of sex and gender, typically by asking a single question that attempts to reflect one or the other or perhaps some combination of the two. One of the principles guiding the panel's recommendations is to provide questions that use precise terminology and ensure construct validity by measuring what they say they are measuring. Key to that effort is distinguishing measures of "gender" from measures of "sex."

This chapter begins by discussing our use of relevant sex and gender terminology and establishing how the measures we focus on in this chapter relate to broader constructs. We then review existing approaches that incorporate varying measures of sex and gender and use differing strategies for enumerating transgender people. We then offer our recommendations for measurement practices that include both cisgender and transgender people and conclude with recommendations for future research.

CONCEPTS AND TERMINOLOGY

Measures of gender include questions about a person's gender identity, which reflects their internal understanding of their own gender, as well as questions about gender expression, which is how a person expresses their gender to others. Questions about gender identity can be designed with categorical responses, asking whether people identify as men, women, or another gender, such as nonbinary, or they can be gradational, asking people to place themselves on scales of femininity and masculinity (Lindqvist et al., 2021; Magliozzi et al., 2016). The latter approach draws on a long-standing line of research in psychology that demonstrates femininity and masculinity should not be seen as polar "opposites" because people can also be low on both scales, high on both scales, or somewhere in between (Bem, 1974).

Incorporating gender scales has to date been most common to measure gender (non)conformity in studies of health disparities (Hart et al., 2019) and to understand growing gender diversity among U.S. youth and young adults (Ho and Mussap, 2019; Johfre and Saperstein, 2019; Lowry et al., 2018; Wilson et al., 2017; Wylie et al., 2010). There also are recent efforts in survey research to combine traditional categorical approaches with gender scales to better represent diversity both within gender identity categories and among them (e.g., Alexander et al., 2021). However, such studies typically require multi-item modules that make them less feasible for use in general population surveys or administrative data systems. Furthermore, they are not intended to distinguish between transgender and cisgender people in order to provide representative estimates of the transgender population. Thus, in this chapter we focus our review of gender measures on the most promising measures of categorical gender identity that can identify transgender people and that have been used most frequently in general population assessments of adults.

Measures of sex can include self-reported items that reference a person's sex as it was assigned on their original birth certificate or as it is currently represented on their legal documents. These classifications in government records are only rough categorical proxies for more detailed and often continuous measures of sex traits, including aspects of anatomy (such as internal organs or external genitalia), physiology (such as hormone milieu), or genetics (such as chromosomes). Studies of sex traits show that human variation is not fully captured by a male–female binary distinction (Montañez, 2017). However, until recently, these were the only designations offered on most U.S. identity documents, including passports and driver's licenses (see Chapter 3).

Because of their ubiquity in many data systems, binary sex categories have often been used in general survey research and in administrative and health contexts to describe and explain differences that may have roots in biology, social norms, or some combination of the two.[1] Direct measures of sex traits better represent specific biological mechanisms that can produce observed sex differences, but such measures are not commonly used, even in health research and clinical settings (see Chapter 3). We consider sex trait measures further in Chapter 7, in the context of promising approaches to enumerate intersex populations. In keeping with the panel's recommendation to collect gender by default (see Chapter 2) that emphasizes the importance of measuring gender, we limit our review of sex measures to the role

---

[1] See https://genderedinnovations.stanford.edu/terms/overemphasizing.html.

a measure of sex assigned at birth can play as part of a broader strategy of improved gender measurement and the enumeration of both cisgender and transgender people.

As noted in Part I, the absence of construct validity in most measures of sex and gender also contributes to using inconsistent terminology to describe binary distinctions between females and males (sex terms) or men and women (gender terms), in both research reports and everyday speech. Many of the measures we review in this chapter use a combination of sex and gender terminology in their question wording and answer options that continues to conflate the two constructs. For example, the sex terms of female and male frequently appear as responses to questions about both sex assigned at birth and gender identity. The practice of using sex terms in gender identity questions makes it challenging to maintain consistent terminology in our discussion; it also raises concerns about construct validity for these items. Given our focus in this chapter on improving gender measurement to include transgender and cisgender people, when not discussing a specific measure that uses sex terms, we use the gender terms, men and women, especially when discussing the conceptual underpinnings of different measures and the interpretation of resulting data.

EVALUATION OF EXISTING MEASUREMENT APPROACHES

Currently, there are two types of transgender-inclusive measures of gender: one-step measures that attempt to identify transgender people using a single question and two-step measures that include a broader measure of gender identity and try to enumerate transgender and cisgender people. Two-step measures consist of a two-question sequence—commonly asking for sex assigned at birth and current gender, though other variations exist— that is intended to be used as a pair. When cross-tabulated, these two-step measures provide counts of cisgender women and men, transgender women and men, and people who identify using terms outside of the gender binary, such as nonbinary, genderqueer, and, for some American Indians and Alaska Natives (AIAN) populations who may identify as Two-Spirit or as their tribal or culturally linguistic-specific term.[2] We first review the two-step measurement approach and contrast it with existing one-step measures.

The two-step measurement approach started as a pair of questions, one about sex assigned at birth and the other about gender identity, used for screening purposes to identify transgender people in health research settings (Melendez et al., 2006; Kenagy, 2005). This design was quickly adopted for the purposes of public health research in LGBTQI+ community settings

---

[2]Such terms represent culturally distinct "third" or nonbinary gender identities, such as fa'afafine in Samoan, Māhūwahine in Native Hawaiian, or Nádleehi in Navajo/Diné.

(e.g., Sausa et al., 2009), before being tested more broadly as a way to identify both cisgender and transgender people among U.S. adults (Reisner et al., 2014; Tate et al., 2013). A two-step measure was first tested for use in a general population survey as part of the California Health Interview Survey (Grant et al., 2015), and similar versions have since been included on several federally sponsored national surveys, including the Census Bureau's high-profile Household Pulse Survey. The National Center for Health Statistics will also begin fielding a two-step measure on its flagship survey, the National Health Interview Survey, beginning in 2022. Table 6A-1 in the annex to this chapter provides information on two-step measures used in these and other surveys.

Although sex assigned at birth is an imperfect proxy for anatomical, genetic, and physiological sex traits, it has utility in health contexts—including survey research, clinical trials, public health surveillance, and medical settings—for purposes ranging from clinical decision support to exploring the role of sex traits in health status and the etiology of disease. In addition, asking for the sex assigned to someone at birth, instead of just a person's "sex," avoids problems inherent in assuming that sex is an absolute and static representation of sex traits by grounding the question in the experience of having been labeled with a sex, rather than identifying with it. As such, a two-step measure that includes sex assigned at birth is being collected for the National Institutes of Health's major precision medicine research initiative, the All of Us program,[3] as well as on national and local case report forms for surveillance of conditions such as HIV/AIDS[4] and COVID-19.[5] A two-step measure has also been incorporated in clinical data systems such as the U.S. Department of Veterans Affairs' electronic medical record (EMR)[6] and is reflected in standards for EMR terminology codified by the U.S. Office of the National Coordinator for Health Information Technology.[7]

In terms of construct validity, the two-step design is a clear improvement over previous "Are you male or female?" measures for several reasons. First, it clearly distinguishes between two key constructs—sex assigned at birth and gender identity—and measures each of them directly. Second,

---

[3]See https://www.phenxtoolkit.org/protocols/view/11801.

[4]See https://www.cdc.gov/hiv/pdf/guidelines/cdc-hiv-adult-confidential-case-report-form-2019.pdf.

[5]For example, see https://www.dhhs.nh.gov/dphs/cdcs/covid19/covid19-reporting-form.pdf. The GenderSci Lab at Harvard University notes, however, that many jurisdictions still do not collect data inclusive of transgender and nonbinary identities in COVID-19 case reports: https://www.genderscilab.org/blog/unknown-covid19-gendersex-reporting.

[6]See https://www.patientcare.va.gov/LGBT/docs/2022/Birth-Sex-Gender-Identity-FactSheet-for-Veterans-2022.pdf.

[7]See https://www.healthit.gov/isa/section/sex-birth-sexual-orientation-and-gender-identity.

it allows for enumeration of both cisgender and transgender people by recognizing that a person's gender identity can either differ from or be the same as the sex they were assigned at birth. Third, it offers gender identity responses that acknowledge a range of potential identities rather than constraining everyone to identify with binary categories, in line with the diversity of gender identity and expression that is well documented across cultures (Devun, 2021; LaFleur, 2021; Thorne et al., 2019; Snorton, 2017; Pruden and Edmo, 2016; Stryker, 2008; Fieland et al., 2007; Walters et al., 2006; Meyerowitz, 2002).

The two-step measurement approach also was designed to reflect the broadest definition of the transgender population, which categorizes as "transgender" any person whose gender identity is different from their sex assigned at birth, regardless of whether they identify with the word "transgender." This definition is often called "transgender experience" (e.g., Puckett et al., 2020) or "transgender history" (as in the Scottish census question, described below). Not everyone with transgender experience or history expressly identifies as "transgender": they may identify simply as men or women, or they may describe their gender identity using terms outside of the man/woman binary, such as genderqueer, genderfluid, gender-nonconforming, nonbinary, agender, bigender, or Two-Spirit.

In one study of a two-step measure that offered the gender identity responses of "male," "female," or "transgender," half of the respondents categorized as transgender were recorded as such because they selected a binary gender identity different from the sex that was assigned to them at birth; the other half chose the term "transgender" to describe their gender identity (Truman et al., 2019). Thus, people who explicitly endorse the term "transgender" to describe themselves are a subset of the larger group of people who have transgender experience. Most two-step designs account for this key distinction by measuring both sex assigned at birth and gender identity so that transgender people can be identified either directly by their gender identity response or indirectly by providing different responses for the two items.

A variety of one-step measures have also been used to try to identify transgender people. A common one-step approach simply adds "transgender" as a response option to a binary sex or gender question, resulting in a measure such as, "Are you male, female, or transgender?"[8] This type of measure substantially underperforms in identifying people with transgender experience, because many of such respondents select female or male to describe themselves (Schilt and Bratter, 2015; Tate et al., 2013). One study conducted in a clinical setting found that the proportions of transgender men and women nearly doubled when a two-step measure was used rather

---

[8] See https://www.cms.gov/files/document/sgm-clearinghouse-nis-updated.pdf.

than a single question that required respondents to choose whether to use the term "transgender" to identify themselves (Tordoff et al., 2019; for similar results among youth, see Kidd et al., 2021). A second variation on a one-step measure, such as one used by the Gallup Poll, includes "transgender" alongside "gay," "lesbian," and "bisexual" responses to attempt to count the collective LGBT population. Both approaches are problematic, for two reasons: (1) they fail to account for people with transgender experience who do not use the term "transgender" to describe themselves, and (2) they conflate transgender experience with either gender identity or sexual orientation, which are different constructs (Grant et al., 2015).

Another approach to identifying transgender people asks, "Do you consider yourself transgender?" with yes or no response options. A version of this question has been used on the Behavioral Risk Factor Surveillance System (BRFSS) since 2014 (Flores et al., 2016; Conron et al., 2012).[9] If used as a stand-alone measure of the transgender population, however, questions like this may not count all men and women with transgender experience because, as noted above, not all people with transgender experience identify as transgender. The one-step approach also does not work well in some survey modes: Using a single item on an online general population survey—with or without providing respondents with a definition of transgender—results in a much higher estimate of people who identify as transgender than is found in other surveys with interviewer-assisted modes (Saperstein and Westbrook, 2021). The "Do you consider yourself transgender?" question also had low test-retest reliability relative to subsequent responses for the same individuals on both a two-step measure and another similar one-step transgender identity question (Saperstein and Westbrook, 2021). Together, these findings suggest a higher rate of "false positives" for this question format in an online self-completion context. Due to the low prevalence of transgender people in the population, even a small number of errors among cisgender people would have an outsized effect on population estimates for transgender people.

Our review of existing one-step approaches underscores two major challenges for enumerating transgender populations: (1) devising a measure that is inclusive not only of people who identify explicitly as transgender but also people with transgender experience; and (2) avoiding false positives from cisgender respondents who do not understand the question. The two-step design minimizes both types of measurement error by using question

---

[9]The BRFSS measure includes a follow-up question for people who answer yes to allow for more detailed responses of transgender male-to-female; female-to-male; and transgender, gender nonconforming. Since 2019, it has also included a question about sex assigned at birth as an optional item. See https://www.cdc.gov/brfss/data_documentation/pdf/BRFSS-SOGI-Stat-Brief-508.pdf.

wording and answer options that make it easier for cisgender people to provide appropriate responses and by accounting for both transgender identity and transgender experience.

Figure 6-1 illustrates this distinction by showing how a two-step approach provides a more comprehensive count of the broader universe of transgender people than existing single-item alternatives. As discussed above, the population of people who identify as transgender either in response to a single question (such as "Are you male, female, or transgender?") or on the gender identity item of the most common two-step measure are a subset of the people who would answer "yes" to the question "Do you consider yourself transgender?" Both sets of people who endorse a transgender identity on single-item measures are, in turn, a subset of the people who would be categorized as transgender based on their responses to a two-step measure that includes both the sex assigned at birth and gender identity questions. Although this two-step measure can also miss some transgender people if, for example, they prefer not to answer the question about sex assigned at birth and do not identify explicitly as transgender on the second step, the two-step approach provides better conceptual and empirical fit to the task of enumerating transgender people than one-step measures that are currently in use.

Importantly, the two-step approach also enumerates cisgender people, including separate counts for cisgender men and cisgender women. Even in the absence of the type of false positives described above, a stand-alone item, such as "Do you consider yourself transgender?," does not provide a count of cisgender people because the people who answer "no" can be a combination of cisgender people and some people with transgender experience. The question "Are you male, female, or transgender?" also fails to count cisgender people because the male and female responses can be selected by both cisgender people and people with transgender experience. In essence, accounting for the difference between sex assigned at birth and gender identity is a key component to being able to measure gender for both cisgender and transgender people.

The panel acknowledges that space on forms and survey questionnaires, as well as respondents' time, are not infinite and that, all else equal, a single-item measure would be preferable to reduce both costs and respondent burden. However, given the evidence, we cannot endorse existing single-item approaches to measuring gender or identifying transgender people.

Evidence of Two-Step Measure Performance in the United States

Over the past decade, the two-step measurement approach has been tested extensively and used in the United States among both transgender and cisgender people and English-speaking adults of all ages (Interagency

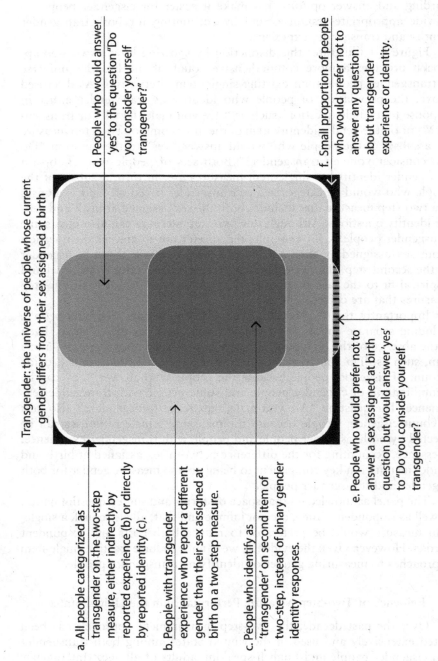

d. People who would answer 'yes' to the question "Do you consider yourself transgender?"

f. Small proportion of people who would prefer not to answer any question about transgender experience or identity.

Transgender: the universe of people whose current gender differs from their sex assigned at birth

a. All people categorized as transgender on the two-step measure, either indirectly by reported experience (b) or directly by reported identity (c).

b. People with transgender experience who report a different gender than their sex assigned at birth on a two-step measure.

c. People who identify as 'transgender' on second item of two-step, instead of binary gender identity responses.

e. People who would prefer not to answer a sex assigned at birth question but would answer 'yes' to "Do you consider yourself transgender?"

FIGURE 6-1 Conceptual and empirical distinctions in transgender population measurement.

Technical Working Group on Sexual Orientation and Gender Identity Items in the Household Pulse Survey, 2021; Saperstein and Westbrook, 2021; Suen et al., 2020; Burgess et al., 2019; Holzberg et al., 2019; Smith and Son, 2019; Truman et al., 2019; Haider et al., 2018; Federal Interagency Working Group, 2016a, 2016b; Lombardi and Banik, 2016; Deutsch and Buchholz, 2015; Grant et al., 2015; Reisner et al., 2015). Research to date has focused on the use of a two-step measure in general population surveys and in health contexts and has established that adults generally do not find questions about their sex assigned at birth or gender identity particularly sensitive or difficult to answer.

In terms of overall feasibility, a randomized multisite trial of adding sexual orientation and gender identity questions to patient intake forms in several Midwestern medical clinics found that 82 percent of the middle-aged and older adults surveyed endorsed the importance of collecting gender identity data, and just 3 percent expressed discomfort with the sexual orientation and gender identity questions they were asked; the same proportion expressed discomfort with other questions not about sexual orientation and gender identity (Rullo et al., 2018). Similarly, research finds considerably more positive than negative feedback from respondents who answered a two-step measure in online general population surveys (Medeiros et al., 2020). The two-step approach is designed primarily for self-completion, though behavior coding has also demonstrated its ease of use in interviewer-assisted telephone surveys (Jans et al., 2015). Previous research on the feasibility of the two-step measure for proxy reporting in the United States also suggests it will perform as well as reporting of other demographic characteristics in such contexts (Holzberg et al., 2019).

The two-step design performs as well or better than other standard demographic items on measures of nonresponse and test-retest reliability. As noted above, a two-step measure has been implemented in several federally sponsored national surveys, including the National Crime Victimization Survey (starting in 2016), the General Social Survey (starting in 2018), and the Household Pulse Survey (beginning in August 2021). Strong evidence of this measure's feasibility, across all such surveys, has been consistently low nonresponse rates, generally on the order of 1 percent per item. Table 6-1 shows the nonresponse rates and the prevalence rates for the transgender population in national samples of U.S. adults. For example, Truman et al. (2019) reported a combined item nonresponse of 1.3 percent for both sex assigned at birth and gender identity in the 2016 National Crime Victimization Survey (NCVS). Nonresponse rates in the General Social Survey (GSS) are lower for each item, and the combined nonresponse dropped from 0.9 to 0.3 percent between 2018 and 2020. Nonresponse rates in other large national studies with nonprobability samples are similar, with a 1.3 percent nonresponse rate for sex assigned at birth in the All of Us program, and

TABLE 6-1 Item Nonresponse Rates and Transgender Population Prevalence for Two-Step Measures

Measure	2016 NCVS	2018 GSS	2020 GSS	2021 Pulse
Item Nonresponse Percentage				
Sex Assigned at Birth	–	0.9	0.3	–
Gender Identity	–	0.6	0.1	1.6
Combined	1.3	0.9	0.3	–
Transgender Prevalence Rate				
Transgender Identity Alone	–	0.1	0.3	0.3
Transgender Experience	0.1	0.5	0.7	0.4

NOTES: Transgender experience responses include people who selected a binary gender that differed from their sex assigned at birth and people who selected a transgender identity regardless of their sex assigned at birth. Respondents who selected the residual gender identity option (e.g., "none of these") are not included in the estimates shown because their specific identities either were not collected or not publicly available; they may or may not correspond to nonbinary identities. Those represent an additional 0.18% of responses in the National Crime Victimization Survey (NCVS), 0.07% of responses in the 2018 GSS, 0.39% for the 2020 GSS and 1.1% for Pulse. The Pulse Survey is a nonprobability sample and should not be interpreted as providing nationally representative population estimates. The Census Bureau imputes missing sex assigned at birth in Pulse data (see Jesdale 2021a). Because of this, nonresponse rates are not available for this survey and the transgender calculation removes cases with imputed sex assigned at birth which otherwise produces an outsized number of respondents with transgender experience (Conron and O'Neill 2021). NCVS does not report transgender identity responses alone, though they note that 51.7% of respondents with transgender experience were coded as such because they selected "transgender" as their identity (Truman et al., 2019). Nonresponse rates calculated by committee members from publicly accessible online data tools for the General Social Survey (GSS) and detailed data tables for the U.S. Census Pulse Survey.
SOURCES: Data from NCVS (Truman et al., 2019), GSS (Davern et al., 2021), and U.S. Census Pulse Survey (U.S. Census Bureau, 2021).

a 1.6 percent nonresponse rate for gender identity in the Household Pulse Survey. These studies indicate that, as measured by item nonresponse, sex assigned at birth and gender identity are an order of magnitude less sensitive that other common questions, such as personal earnings and household income (Saperstein and Westbrook, 2021; Grant et al., 2015).

When general population surveys began testing the two-step approach, concerns were raised that the inclusion of questions about sex assigned at birth or gender identity would negatively affect overall survey completion because of the perceived sensitivity of the questions or because the presence of nonbinary response options would offend significant numbers of respondents. This concern prompted many surveys to include their two-step measures toward the end of the questionnaire to minimize breakoffs (where respondents stop answering entirely and fail to complete the rest of the survey). More recently, however, some surveys have begun placing the two-step measure either toward the beginning or in the middle of the questionnaire, with other demographic questions. For example, the GSS changed the placement of the two-step measure between its 2018 and 2020 waves and, as noted above, item nonresponse declined in 2020, when the questions were asked with other demographic items midway through the survey.[10] In the Household Pulse Survey, sex assigned at birth and gender identity are included as the sixth and seventh questions overall (between questions about education and marital status and questions about sexual orientation and household size).[11] These developments in overall survey placement, along with consistently low item nonresponse, underscore both the feasibility and acceptability of implementing a two-step gender measure in the United States.

There is also emerging evidence on test-retest reliability for the two-step approach. For example, stability rates were 99.4 percent for sex assigned at birth and 98.7 percent for gender identity responses between the 2018 and 2020 GSS (Saperstein, 2022). These stability rates are higher than previous studies have found for self-identified race, ethnicity, and religion, and they are comparable to stability rates for reported country of birth and inter-viewer-classified sex and gender (see Smith and Son, 2011). The panel is not aware of any research that directly compares the reliability of self-reported sex assigned at birth with the official designation on an original birth cer-tificate. However, responses for sex assigned at birth generally would not be expected to change over time, except in rare cases where someone found out as an adult that their sex was recorded differently than they had previ-ously been told. Responses to gender identity are expected to be fluid over the life course, but for an as-yet-unknown proportion of people. Including repeated measures of gender identity in longitudinal surveys would help clarify the degree of fluidity researchers can expect and provide appropriate recognition that a person's gender identity can change over time. At present, however, it appears that relatively few respondents are likely to change their reported gender identity, even over the span of several years.

There are other areas of two-step measure performance that would benefit from further study, and there is notable variation in the specific question wording and answer options used both among general population surveys and between survey research and clinical contexts. We discuss these outstanding issues and the challenges they raise for measurement in detail below. However, the panel recognizes that the same could be said for many demographic items already in regular use, and we do not believe it is appropriate to hold questions about sex assigned at birth or gender identity to higher testing and performance standards than have been used for other items before their widespread adoption. We conclude that there is sufficient evidence in the United States to support using a two-step approach to measuring gender for general population enumeration and research among English-speaking adults, as well as in health contexts, including medical settings, clinical trials, and public health surveillance.

Comparison with Other English-Speaking Countries

Although the United States has built up a strong evidence base in support of using a two-step measure of gender in assessments of the general adult population, it lags other English-speaking countries in implementing such measures in the census and other flagship national surveys, such as the American Community Survey. For example, in 2021 both Canada (Statistics Canada, 2021) and the United Kingdom (Office of National Statistics, 2021) implemented two-step approaches to measuring sex assigned at birth and gender identity in their national censuses. Australia debuted a nonbinary sex question for its 2021 count (Australia Bureau of Statistics, 2020) and published updated national standards in January 2021 that recommended the two-step approach (Australian Bureau of Statistics, 2021). New Zealand also revised its national statistical standard in 2021 to include a two-step measure (Stats NZ, 2021) and has announced it will be implementing new questions for its next census in 2023.[12]

Canada replaced the existing binary sex question on its census form with one that specifies sex assigned at birth and added a second question about current gender. The answer options for the sex assigned at birth component are male and female, while the responses for the current gender component are male, female, and a free-text option. The second question also specifies that current gender may be different from what is indicated on legal documents. Results from the 2021 Canadian census have yet to be released, but a 2019 content test of the same items found that 0.07 percent of the population provided a nonbinary gender identity,

---

[12]Other countries have also revised their censuses to provide nonbinary sex or gender categories. Nepal was the first to do so, in 2011, and India (2011) and Pakistan (2017) followed. However, these countries have not released counts of nonbinary residents, citing privacy concerns (United Nations Economic Commission for Europe, 2019), and their censuses rely more on enumerators than does the U.S. census, which likely results in the undercounting of nonbinary people.

with a total transgender population estimate of 0.35 percent. This result was comparable to the estimated transgender population from the 2018 Survey of Safety in Public and Private Spaces, 0.24 percent, which was Canada's first national survey to use a two-step measure. In the 2019 test, the combined rate of nonresponse and invalid responses to the new gender identity question was 0.10 percent on electronic questionnaires. On paper questionnaires, nonresponse rose to 1 percent for sex assigned at birth and 8 percent for current gender, with most of the latter concentrated among people over the age of 70.

The 2021 census of England and Wales also used a two-question approach but adopted a different format. After its pretesting, the Office of National Statistics (ONS) recommended the existing sex question remain largely unchanged, except for reversing the answer options so female is listed before male and adding a note that a gender identity question would follow later in the questionnaire. The new gender identity question asked: "Is the gender you identify with the same as your sex registered at birth?" The responses offered were yes and no; for those who responded "no," a free-text field asked for their current gender. Although this question uses different wording than other two-step approaches, it similarly aims to account for both transgender identity and transgender experience. Reporting for sex was mandatory by law but reporting gender identity was voluntary and limited to ages 16 and up. Results from this census are not yet available.

Overall, measurement recommendations across these countries are quite similar. They all are either testing or actively using a two-step gender measure that references sex assigned at birth and gender identity, and they all affirm the importance of providing inclusive counts of both cisgender and transgender people in national statistics. They also all endorse the principle that gender should be the default construct for data collection rather than sex (or sex assigned at birth) alone. Two key points of divergence are whether to offer a nonbinary response to sex assigned at birth and how best to account for both transgender identity and transgender experience.

In terms of implementing a nonbinary measure of sex, to date, only Australia added "non-binary sex" as a third response option for its 2021 census. Both Canada and the United Kingdom opted to retain binary male/female responses, while New Zealand continued to recommend binary responses but noted in the text of its revised standards that offering the option "Another term" with a write-in line may be necessary to account for birth registrations "that are neither male nor female." As discussed in the next chapter, both Australia and New Zealand also provide optional questions on variation in sex characteristics in their revised national standards to better account for intersex populations. No country includes "intersex" as a response option for sex assigned at birth.

Recommendations and practices also diverge on how to provide inclusive measures of the transgender population. Australia explicitly recommends against using a single-item transgender identity question and also discourages including "transgender" as a response option in a general gender question, in both cases citing concerns about data quality. As part of its precensus planning for England and Wales, the United Kingdom's ONS reported testing several question formats to gauge transgender identity and experience: it found that nonresponse was higher with a question that used the term "transgender" (5%, compared with 1% for a question that did not use the term) and that a much lower percentage of respondents deemed it an "acceptable" question to ask (71%, compared with 90% for the two-step measure). Despite this, Scotland is planning to include a combined transgender identity and experience question as the second step in its 2022 census after finding that respondents found it acceptable in their pretesting. Scotland's new census form[13] asks first, "What is your sex?" with female and male response options, and then asks, "Do you consider yourself to be trans, or have a trans history?" with no and yes as response options. For those who respond "yes," a free-text field is offered for them to "describe your trans status (for example, non-binary, trans man, trans woman)." In settings where it is important to identify transgender people but where privacy protections are deemed inadequate for collecting data on sex assigned at birth, New Zealand endorses asking "Do you consider yourself to be transgender?" in addition to a gender identity question that offers the answer options of female, male, and a free-text field for another gender.

The panel carefully considered the range of recommendations offered by these countries along with evidence on item performance, when available. As in the United States, there is overall support for a two-step measurement approach, but considerable variation in the specific format of the two items. With results from the latest census rounds in these countries still pending, we could not factor in the new measures' performance in those important and high-profile contexts. Given the absence of that evidence, along with variation among countries in the changes that are allowed to sex/gender markers and in options for nonbinary registration in government documents, as well as potential differences in the specific gender terminology locally deemed "acceptable," the panel gave more weight to the results of testing the two-step measures conducted in the United States. However, when relevant to the rationale for our recommended measures, we include comparisons to these countries' approaches in our discussion below.

---

[13]See https://www.scotlandscensus.gov.uk/media/fxonlo0d/scotlands-census-2022-question-set-version-v4-0-09-09-2021.pdf.

CONCLUSIONS AND RECOMMENDATIONS

In this section we present our recommended two-step question for gender identity that makes it possible to identify those with transgender experience, followed by a discussion of considerations for the recommended measure. The subsequent two sections separately discuss the two components of the measure: sex assigned at birth and gender identity.

RECOMMENDATION 4: The panel recommends that the National Institutes of Health use the following pair of questions assessing sex assigned at birth and gender identity:

Q1: What sex were you assigned at birth, on your original birth certificate?
O   Female
O   Male
(Don't know)
(Prefer not to answer)

Q2: What is your current gender? [Mark only one]
O   Female
O   Male
O   Transgender
O   [If respondent is AIAN:] Two-Spirit
O   I use a different term: [free text]
(Don't know)
(Prefer not to answer)

Overall Measure Considerations

In keeping with our recommendation to collect gender by default, this two-step gender measure, which allows respondents to report both binary and nonbinary gender identities and can identify both cisgender and transgender people, can replace existing standalone questions that measure either sex or gender. This two-step measure is best included with other demographic measures, such as race, ethnicity, and age, given the demonstrated acceptability of answering these questions among the general population, as indicated by the very low rates of nonresponse noted above. In addition to the issue of placement with demographic questions, other general considerations about this measure include maintaining the questions as a pair, how to address skip patterns, the order in which to present the two components, and whether to include a confirmation question. Below, we discuss each of these considerations in turn and provide a summary in Table 6-2.

The two-step measure is designed to be presented in sequence and used in tandem to produce counts for both transgender and cisgender people. For cisgender people, the count will include cisgender men (male at birth, male current gender) and cisgender women (female at birth, female current gender). For people with transgender experience, the count will include transgender men (female at birth, male current gender) and transgender women (male at birth, female current gender),[14] transgender-identified people (who report any sex at birth and expressly choose to identify using the term "transgender") and people with other nonbinary gender identities who report any sex at birth and select either Two-Spirit or "I use a different term"[15] to write in a different gender identity.

In analyzing the responses to the two-step measure, we advise that data from the two-step measure not be collapsed to report counts of females, males, and transgender people (leaving the cisgender categories unmarked), but data for each item can also be analyzed separately to examine disparities along different dimensions, such as for all people who were assigned male at birth or all people who selected "female" for their current gender. However, we recommend that the questions are always asked as a pair: we do not recommend collecting sex assigned at birth as a standalone item in any data collection context.

We note that some data collections routinely use a single question with female/male response options to drive skip patterns: for example, the American Community Survey skips a question about recent births for people who are reported as male. In such cases, we suggest substituting sex assigned at birth responses to program skip logics.[16] In cases for which detailed information on physical sex traits is needed (such as some health surveys or clinical settings), sex assigned at birth alone may not be adequate to drive survey skip patterns, and other methods, such as an organ inventory, may be more appropriate (see Chapter 3).

In general population surveys, the two-step measure typically has been

---

[14]We remind readers that we use the gender terms *cisgender man* and *cisgender woman* and *transgender man* and *transgender women* to reflect that the underlying concept being measured is gender, even when some gender identity answer options are provided using the sex terminology, *female* and *male*.

[15]Analysts cannot not assume that all write-in responses for "I use a different term" will represent nonbinary gender identities. Write-ins need to be examined to determine whether responses represent nonbinary identities, are consistent with existing binary categories (and can be recoded accordingly), or need to be treated as (uncodable) missing data. The latter may include "protest" write-ins or other off-topic responses (see Jaroszewski et al., 2018; Saperstein and Westbrook, 2021).

[16]Jans et al. (2015) offer sample wording for transition text by the California Health Interview Survey in its interviewer script before a section of the survey on prostate screening: "These next questions may be relevant to you because you were assigned male at birth. If not, please let me know and I will skip them."

ordered with sex assigned at birth asked first, followed by gender identity. This represents a chronological order from past to present and helps to provide context for the second question for cisgender people who may not be used to thinking about gender as an identity. Smaller-scale cognitive interview studies among transgender people have reported that some respondents expressed concerns about the question order, and suggested the opposite order—with gender identity first—because it conveys more respect for self-identification (e.g., Lombardi and Banik, 2016). There is evidence from several small split-panel studies that varying the question order did not yield significantly different response distributions (Amaya, 2020; Sanderson and Immerwahr, 2019 as cited in Federal Committee on Statistical Methodology, 2020; Saperstein and Westbrook, 2021). Previous research has also suggested that ensuring the two items are presented on the same page, especially in online formats, may resolve ordering concerns for some (Bauer et al., 2017). However, there is insufficient evidence to demonstrate that switching the order avoids issues of sensitivity, as other transgender people may find it offensive when sex assigned at birth is asked as the second step because it could be seen as a check on gender identity. Thus, the panel's recommendation follows the question ordering with sex assigned at birth first and gender identity second because it has been used successfully in both general population surveys and health contexts; however, further research on this point is warranted.

Several general population surveys, including the NCVS and the Household Pulse Survey, follow the two-step measure with a confirmation question to reduce false positive responses. The exact wording of the confirmation question varies, but it typically asks: "Just to confirm, you said you were assigned [X] at birth and you currently identify as [Y], is that correct?" It is intended to reduce false positives by giving people who gave differing responses to sex assigned at birth and current gender a chance to revise their responses. The panel suggests including a follow-up confirmation question in automated data collections. However, other than cost-effectiveness, there is insufficient evidence that supports the practice of asking a confirmation question only of people who will be categorized as transgender because they gave different answers to the two components (while ignoring potential false negatives). For this topic, too, future research is warranted to consider the unequal survey burden this practice places on an already marginalized population.

Considerations for Component of Sex Assigned at Birth

Specific formatting considerations for the sex assigned at birth question in our recommended measure include the wording of the question stem, the wording and ordering of response options, and whether to include a free-text option.

120

TABLE 6-2 Summary of Findings on Recommended Two-Step Gender Measure and Evaluation Criteria

Question Stem	Question Responses	Evaluation Criteria	Evaluation
Which of the following best represents how you think of yourself?	• Gay; • Straight, that is, not gay; • Bisexual; • I use a different term (Don't know) (Prefer not to answer)	Previous use in population-based data collection	• Close versions of this have been used in: the Behavioral Risk Factor Surveillance System (BRFSS) (since 2014), the National Crime Victimization Survey (NCVS) (since 2016), the National Health Interview Survey (NHIS) (since 2013), and the National Health and Nutrition Examination Survey (since 2013) • Close versions used in electronic medical records (EMR) in health systems following a 2015 final rule by the Office of the National Coordinator for Health Information Technology (ONC) • Recommended by the Federal Interagency Working Group on Improving Measurement of Sexual Orientation and Gender Identity in Federal Surveys (2016)
		Conceptual fit	• Measures sexual orientation identity only (i.e., does not conflate identity with attraction and/or behavior) • Clearly distinguished people with varying sexual orientation identities and broadly between sexual minority and sexual majority populations, while allowing for enumeration of those who do not use any of the listed labels • Allows for culturally specific identification for Indigenous populations; response category needs to be explicitly included only in automated data collection where racial identity is collected and respondent endorses AIAN [American Indian and Alaska Native] identity
		Testing: comprehension and validity	• Debriefing interviews, targeted interviews, cognitive interviewing, and focus groups (Holzberg et al., 2019; Truman et al., 2019; Martinez et al., 2017; Michaels et al., 2017; Wilson et al., 2016; Ridolfo, Miller, and Maitland, 2012; Miller and Ryan, 2011; Austin et al., 2007; Miller, 2001) • Acceptability studies in clinical settings (Rullo et al., 2018; Ruben et al., 2017; Cahill et al., 2014) • Behavior coding and split-sample question format experiments in telephone interviews (West and McCabe, 2021; Dahlhamer et al., 2019; Michaels et al., 2017)

Populations included in testing	• Sexual minority and heterosexual/straight identified • Spanish and English speakers • U.S. general population, including racially diverse samples, urban and rural residents, and ages 12–85
Testing: errors and nonresponse	• Testing options with expanded response list to existing list (Meyer et al., 2019) • Testing response rate and willingness to be asked sexual orientation questions in the census (Bates, García Trejo, and Vines, 2019; Truman et al., 2019; Ruben et al., 2017; Saewyc et al., 2004) • Nonresponse rates on the BRFSS (2020), NCVS (2017), NHIS (2019), General Social Survey (2018) ≤3%
Adjustments to previously tested item included in recommended measure	• Removed "something else" and replaced with open-text and wording of "I use a different term" • Include Two-Spirit category in automated data collection where racial identity is collected and AIAN is indicated
Weaknesses and challenges	• Narrow set of responses that do not reflect current culture and terms used by many sexual minorities (e.g., queer, Two-Spirit) • Write-in sexual orientation identity field will have to be cleaned and coded for reporting; newer terms not listed (e.g., pansexual) also may grow in popularity and need to be assessed for inclusion as explicit options • Does not provide a clear option to indicate lack of sureness about a label that describes them (i.e., questioning) • Though testing showed a need for the "that is, not gay" phrase among some heterosexual respondents, it is not clear this is still needed; also, as written, it is a conceptually inaccurate description of what it means to be "straight" and has implications for the definition of bisexual • Response options are not presented in order of prevalence or other common ordering (e.g., alphabetical)

Our recommended question includes a reference to "your original birth certificate" in the question stem. This wording is not universal across general population surveys that have asked questions on sex assigned at birth and is not used in the All of Us Program, in particular. The panel considered the merits of including this reference and concluded it helps to clarify the question, particularly for people who may have changed the sex designation on their original birth certificate (see, e.g., Miller, Wilson, and Ryan, 2021). Being explicit that the question is asking for sex assignment on a specific government record also helps to distinguish it from the second step self-identification question about current gender.

We recommend that only two categories—female and male—be offered for sex assigned at birth, as they are the only options available on original birth certificates in the United States. We recognize that some U.S. measures of sex assigned at birth include a third category of intersex (e.g., All of Us and the 2018 GSS); however, intersex is not currently an available designation at the time of birth in the United States. It is standard practice in the United States for children born with intersex variations to be assigned either male or female at or shortly after birth, and the majority of adults with intersex variations identify as male or female (Shteyler, 2021; Rosenwohl-Mack et al., 2020; Almasri et al., 2018; Lee et al., 2006).[17] At present, "X" designations and other nonbinary sex markers are only available in a subset of states on a case-by-case basis by petition (see Chapter 3). Thus, for now, offering just two sex responses is consistent with current U.S. vital statistics practice for original birth certificates.

For responses to the question on sex at birth, many surveys list male first and female second. However, this ordering has little justification and lacks consistent scientific rationale. Current best practices recommend randomizing response options for survey items, but this is generally emphasized for other purposes, such as when listing candidates on ballots or when varying which end of an agree–disagree scale appears first. There is no existing body of evidence that explicitly tests response ordering for demographic questions, though it is common practice to order nominal response categories either alphabetically or by expected population size to help respondents make sense of otherwise unordered lists. Listing female first fits both criteria. This response order is currently being used by the All of Us program, following pretesting (Cronin et al., 2019). It was also used in the 2018 GSS, following a survey experiment that randomly varied the answer order in an online sample of U.S. adults (Saperstein et al., 2019). The ONS also opted to change the answer order for the 2021 census of England and Wales after extensive testing, prompted by focus-group respondents highlighting inconsistent response ordering across questionnaire

---

[17]See also Courtney Finlayson's 2021 public testimony to the panel.

items (Office for National Statistics, 2021). Consequently, our recommendation lists female first, with a caveat that optimal answer option ordering for all demographic questions would benefit from further empirical study.

Under the panel's guiding principle of allowing respondents the autonomy to self-identify, we generally recommend offering open-ended write-in response options for identity questions. However, "sex assigned at birth, on your original birth certificate" asks respondents to report what was recorded on an official government record; therefore, our recommendation does not include a free-text option to provide other responses. However, our recommendation does include the option for people to say they do not know what sex they were assigned at birth or to decline to answer. Whether these responses should be provided explicitly depends on the context. Signaling that people have the right to opt-out of responding is especially important in settings in which voluntary consent has not been established and responses could be individually identifying (such as employment records and college or grant applications). In such settings, and in line with our guiding principle affirming autonomy, our recommendation uses the wording "prefer to not answer" rather that such alternatives as "decline to state" or "refused." For data collections where respondents can easily skip over items if they do not wish to answer, it is not necessary to provide an explicit "prefer not to answer" response.

Specific Considerations for the Component of Current Gender

As for the component of sex assigned at birth, specific considerations for the current gender component of the recommended measure include the wording of the question stem, the wording and ordering of response options, and whether to include a free-text option. Other considerations related to implementing the gender identity measure, such as whether to allow for multiple responses, are covered in the section below on recommended research areas.

In considering the wording on gender, the panel considered other approaches, such as "How do you describe yourself" or "Do you consider yourself to be...." We concluded it was important to include the word "gender," given the guiding principle of using precise terminology. The recommended question stem also contains the qualifier "current," which is used in several surveys using the two-step method, including the NCVS, GSS, and the National Longitudinal Study of Adolescent to Adult Health (Add Health), and helps to convey that the response can change over time.

Other surveys specify gender identity in the question stem (the National Intimate Partner and Sexual Violence Survey) or offer additional text noting that "gender is how you feel inside" (High School Longitudinal Study of 2009) or that current gender "may be different from sex assigned at birth and may be different from what is indicated on legal documents" (2021 Canadian census). The panel appreciates the specificity of these items, but incorporating lengthy definitional text in the question wording adds cognitive burden, which can reduce respondent comprehension (Yan and Tourangeau, 2008; Holbrook et al., 2006; Knauper et al., 1997). Such clarifications could be provided instead in telephone interviewer scripts or incorporated as information help boxes in automated data collection. The panel also weighed concerns that using subjective language, such as "consider yourself to be," might inadvertently minimize gender identity by implying it is less factual than sex assigned at birth. This concern, combined with the goal of limiting both questionnaire space and cognitive burden, made the simple and straightforward wording of "What is your current gender?" most appealing among the existing alternatives.

The panel's recommended question uses female and male answer options, which is intended to keep the response categories consistent between sex assigned at birth and current gender. Several U.S. surveys have opted to offer gender terms instead (All of Us and the 2018 GSS), and Australia recommends offering both (female and woman, male and man). The U.S. surveys that include gender terms did so after extensive pretesting, though the panel is not aware of published evidence that directly compares either respondent comprehension of the two types of response labels or overall item performance. In the absence of other evidence, the panel's recommendation of female/male terminology is in keeping with response options that are used by the majority of current two-step measures. As we note below, further research on this issue is needed given concerns about conceptual conflation and construct validity.

The panel's recommended answer options for current gender include "transgender," based in part on research conducted using the 2016 NCVS, which showed that including a transgender category as an answer option in the second step is necessary to fully enumerate the transgender population in the United States (Truman et al., 2019). The panel considered measures that used a "nonbinary" response either in addition to, or instead of, a "transgender" response option, but decided against recommending this, given the absence of any published evidence of testing a "nonbinary" answer option in general population surveys of adults. This, too, is a subject for future research. Overall, given the impossibility of providing a truly exhaustive list, the panel preferred a shorter list of responses that is augmented with a write-in option for those who do not wish to identify with these listed responses.

The panel does not recommend including more detailed subcategories of transgender experience or identity (e.g., transgender male/man or transgender female/woman),[18] particularly in general population surveys, for several reasons. First, even in large-scale surveys, the sample sizes for these responses are likely to be small and, for data privacy reasons, would need to be aggregated for reporting, especially at lower levels of geography, to ensure the confidentiality of individuals' information. Second, regardless of data collection setting, the panel decided it was inconsistent to label some responses as intended only for transgender men and women while leaving the "female" and "male" responses, presumably intended for cisgender people, unmarked (i.e., they are not labeled equivalently as "cisgender woman" or "cisgender man"). Such a formulation would recognize transgender men and women, but it would incorrectly imply that they cannot (or should not) identify with existing binary categories. Furthermore, the specific wording of these response options is inconsistent across the data collection systems that do use them, and the various sex and gender terms may not be universally understood (e.g., some people might interpret "transgender man/male" to mean a transgender woman who was assigned male at birth). Finally, if respondents want to specify that they use such terms as "transgender woman," "transgender man," or any other, they can do so through the write-in response.

The panel's recommended wording, "I use a different term," as the lead-in response to the write-in option follows Australia's recommendation and is in keeping with the guiding principle of allowing respondents to self-identify. The panel concluded that this wording is better and more affirming than other options typically used in the United States, such as "Something else," "Other," or "None of these," which can have negative and dehumanizing connotations for populations not reflected in a response list. The New Zealand standards recommend "Another gender (please state)," which also offers a more neutral alternative for the write-in response.

Finally, as with sexual orientation, the panel's recommendation includes the Two-Spirit category in general population surveys, provided they collect racial identification data prior to gender identity and can be automated to ensure that this response option is available only to AIAN respondents. When this is not possible, respondents who want to identify explicitly as Two-Spirit can write in that response. We note that the Indian Health Service recommends using a two-step measure with the inclusion of a Two-Spirit response option, as well as a write-in gender response option in its strategic plan for gender-affirming care (NPAIHB 2020). In addition, in the only national study of people who identify as AIAN LGBTQI+ Two-Spirit, 28 percent of the sample identified their gender as Two-Spirit and not as female, male, or transgender (HONOR Project; Cassels et al.,

---

[18]We note that such detailed response options are common practice in electronic medical records.

2010). Although small sample sizes may prohibit detailed analysis of these responses in most general population surveys (which are not designed to oversample AIAN respondents[19]), the panel concluded that the aims of signaling inclusion and explicitly acknowledging Indigenous identities were paramount. Accurate AIAN data, inclusive of gender representation, are crucial as policy makers need national datasets to shape funding allocations and develop policy interventions in order to specifically serve AIAN communities as mandated by federal law.

RECOMMENDED RESEARCH AREAS

The panel's recommended two-step gender measure is the result of a review of currently available evidence. We concluded there is sufficient evidence to support asking for sex assigned at birth and current gender as part of a two-step approach to gender measurement for general population enumeration and research among English-speaking adults, as well as in health contexts, including medical settings, clinical trials, and public health surveillance. We also identified a number of potential challenges to even the best existing measures. Although the two-step approach is the strongest option available for a gender measure that identifies both transgender and cisgender respondents, additional research is needed to address concerns expressed by transgender people, scholars, and other stakeholders about some aspects of its operationalization to date (see, e.g., Glick et al., 2018). In addition to the issues already noted above, these include the following concerns:

- whether the sex assigned at birth component should be replaced with a question about transgender identity in nonresearch and nonhealth administrative settings;
- whether the current gender question should be measured as "mark all that apply";
- the need to reevaluate and expand answer options over time, particularly with regard to nonbinary responses; and
- the need for further assessment of item performance across all survey modes, including proxy reporting, in languages other than English, for all major U.S. racial and ethnic populations, and among youth.

---

[19]The National Congress of American Indians (2021) issued a report decrying inadequate federal data collection strategies stating that the state of current data collection methods leads to invisibility of AIANs in national studies. The report called for oversampling of AIAN populations for large-scale studies of the general U.S. population not only to ensure accurate data, but also to meet federal mandates and trust responsibilities to AIAN communities and populations.

In this section we briefly review these additional considerations and offer recommendations for future research.

Alternative Measures to Sex Assigned at Birth

Sex assigned at birth has specific uses in large population surveys and health-related contexts, both for enumerating transgender and cisgender populations and for guiding clinical research and practice. In other contexts, however, collecting information about sex assigned at birth may be considered invasive or unnecessary, particularly when it is directly associated with an identifiable individual and not covered by privacy laws, such as the Health Insurance Portability and Accountability Act (HIPAA). These settings may include employee records, beneficiary files for services unrelated to health care or health insurance coverage, and applications for employment or credit and other services. In these circumstances, it may be inappropriate to ask transgender people to disclose their sex assigned at birth, but still important to distinguish between transgender and cisgender people in order to ensure access to appropriate services and to monitor disparate treatment.

As noted above, the New Zealand statistical standards recommend a modified two-step measure that first asks about gender identity broadly (with the answer options "male"; "female"; and "another gender, please state") and then asks the yes/no question "Do you consider yourself transgender?" for circumstances where respondent privacy cannot be assured or where it is otherwise undesirable or unnecessary to ask about sex assigned at birth (Stats NZ, 2021). A similar option is currently being used on the employment application form for the Biden Administration.[20] Other alternatives to using sex assigned at birth to enumerate transgender people could include a modified two-step approach that combines a current gender question with a second question like those used in either the Scottish census or the census of England and Wales: "Do you consider yourself to be trans, or have a trans history?" "Is the gender you identify with the same as your sex registered at birth?" Both of these have the potential to offer more inclusive counts of the transgender population because they more explicitly include people with transgender experience who do not identify with the term "transgender."

More research is needed to identify circumstances in which collecting data on sex assigned at birth as part of a two-step gender measure is inadvisable and where alternative question designs may be preferable (see, e.g., Alpert et al., 2021). Alternative measures that do not rely on sex assigned at birth may also become necessary, more broadly, if sex designation is moved

---

[20] See https://www.whitehouse.gov/get-involved/join-us/.

below the line of demarcation on original birth certificates (see Shteyler, Clarke, and Adashi, 2020). If that occurs, a person's sex assigned at birth would become available only for research purposes, and future generations would not see such designations on their birth certificates.

Another topic that needs research is assessment of the performance and acceptability of the recommended two-step measure in comparison with alternative approaches on enrollment forms for nonhealth-related services and programs. Such research needs to cover different domains, such as employment, education, social services, business services, and criminal justice, where concerns about identifiability and disclosure may be different. As noted above, the transgender populations identified using different measurement approaches cannot be assumed to be identical or directly comparable: people who might be classified as transgender using the panel's recommended two-step method may not endorse a transgender identity on an alternative measure. Considerations of when to use different approaches require assessment of the relative importance of generating more complete counts of the transgender population and respect for individual privacy around either sex assigned at birth or transgender experience.

Allowing Multiple Response Options

Our recommended current gender question is "mark only one," which aligns with most of the gender identity measures used in federally sponsored surveys (see Appendix A). Allowing for only one response greatly simplifies coding, classification, and tabulation. However, the panel recognizes a conceptual limitation in the recommended measure for transgender people who identify with binary gender categories but who also want to indicate that they would use the term "transgender" to describe themselves (Miller, Wilson, and Ryan, 2021). The panel's recommended measure requires a forced choice between endorsing a binary gender identity and a transgender identity. Although there is no evidence that this forced choice decreases the feasibility of fully enumerating the transgender population in the United States, the panel recognizes the tension caused by the misalignment between the construct conceptualization and a forced-choice measurement of gender identity.

Some large-scale surveys, such as All of Us, allow respondents to select more than one answer option for their current gender. Allowing multiple responses for gender identity is also a feature of New Zealand's revised national standard. Slight alterations to the recommended question wording, such as "Which of the following best describes your current gender?," could also be considered for surveys that want to retain the ease of analysis of the "mark only one" option while acknowledging that the existing responses are not mutually exclusive. Alternatively, surveys could address the conceptual misalignment directly by offering forced-choice response options that are mutually exclusive (at least at a given time), such as "man," "woman," "nonbinary," and "I use a different term." Testing of these options would further improve the construct validity of the recommended current gender item.

Incorporating Nonbinary Responses

As noted above, the panel considered including "nonbinary" as a current gender response option, either in addition to or instead of "transgender." Current research shows that "nonbinary" and other similar labels are selected almost as frequently as "transgender" in samples of LGBTQI+ populations, and the response has been offered explicitly in a range of contexts (e.g., Tordoff et al., 2019), particularly among youth (Vivienne et al., 2021). Nonetheless, no systematic research has demonstrated that the category "nonbinary" is a commonly agreed upon term to represent nonbinary identities across cultures and age groups in the United States, and there is no published evidence to date that it performs well among cisgender people (i.e., that it does not increase false positives, other errors, or nonresponse rates). In addition, "nonbinary" and other similar terms include a range of identities that can reflect resistance to binary gender identities rather than endorsing a transgender identity per se, and thus these terms may be used by people who are or are not transgender (see, e.g., Wilson and Meyer, 2021; Thorne et al., 2019; Streed, McCarthy, and Haas, 2018).

In this respect, it is important to note that the panel makes a distinction between a current gender question for use in the general population and the collection of gender identity in LGBTQI+ community settings because the recommended measure may not capture the full range of gender identities in the LGBTQI+ population. Also, while the recommended write-in option may allow respondents to self-report their identities in their own words, these descriptors may be harder to standardize and aggregate, and efforts to do so may result in representing respondents in ways they did not intend (e.g., recategorizing someone who writes in "woman of trans experience" into the "transgender" category). As a result, community-based studies focused on the diversity in LGBTQI+ populations may require additional categories that are reflective of language, race and ethnicity, tribal affiliation, region, and age.

We note that a nonbinary response option for sex assigned at birth, in addition to female and male, may need to be considered in the future. As noted above and discussed in more detail in Part I, there have been rapid changes to state laws regarding amendments to birth certificates and other legal identity documents over the past few years, and more than a dozen states currently allow adults—or parents of newborns—to change a birth certificate classification to nonbinary. It is unclear how many parents may have filed these amendments in the states that allow them. Nevertheless, some current toddlers are being raised with a nonbinary sex at birth or no marker at all (Newberry, 2019), which will have implications not only for how parents report them on current surveys, but also how they will report themselves in the future.

Overall, the answer options for both aspects of this measure may need to be periodically revisited in light of new developments. These developments may include not only changes in federal and state laws related to identity documents and the collection of vital statistics, but also changes in the pattern and prevalence of write-in gender identities. Studies of new gender identities as they emerge, particularly in LGBTQI+ populations (e.g., Vivienne et al., 2021; Frohard-Dourlent et al., 2017), will also aid in coding and classifying write-in responses in ways that most accurately reflect respondent intent.

Proxy Reporting

Although self-reporting in surveys is preferred and in keeping with the panel's principle to respect identity and autonomy, many U.S. official statistics are derived from surveys that depend on a single household respondent to provide proxy responses for other household members. Examples include the decennial census, the American Community Survey, and the Current Population Survey. These surveys are the source for high-profile statistics, including the unemployment rate and Congressional reapportionment. Other English-speaking countries, including Canada, England, and Wales have collected gender identity using proxy reporting in their censuses, but little quantitative research has been conducted on proxy reporting of gender identity or transgender experience in the United States.

In 2016, the federal interagency work group on measures of sexual orientation and gender identity listed proxy testing among its highest research agenda priorities (Federal Interagency Working Group, 2016c). Several recent feasibility studies (Holzberg et al., 2019; Kuhne et al., 2019; Ortman et al., 2017) indicate both sexual orientation and gender identity can be successfully collected by proxy. However, there is no evidence on this issue among nationally representative probability samples. More research is needed using pilot tests, methods panels, and other small-scale quantitative experiments to understand the measurement error properties and best practices for collecting both sexual orientation and gender identity by proxy.

Expanding Research on General Population Surveys

Testing for the two-step gender measure has largely focused on general acceptance of the questions, understanding of response options, and item performance among the general population of English-speaking adults. However, testing has been either more limited or not done at all in other populations. The needed research includes testing of translations and nonresponse in languages beyond Spanish and examining response invariance and preferred answer options across people of all races and ethnic backgrounds, regardless of their native language.

Spanish speakers were included in cognitive interviews for the two-step approach, and the questions in federally sponsored national surveys have been offered in both English and Spanish. Collectively, the results indicate that questions about gender identity tend to perform better among Spanish speakers than questions about sexual orientation, both in terms of overall comprehension and item nonresponse. For example, even when older Spanish-speaking cisgender adults were unfamiliar with the term "transgender," they were still able to find an appropriate response for their gender identity and report it without difficulty (Michaels et al., 2017).

There have been few studies of comprehension testing in languages other than Spanish, and a commonly cited challenge for setting international standards for two-step data collection is the absence of words distinguishing between "sex" and "gender" in some languages (United Nations Economic Commission for Europe, 2019). The California Health Interview Survey translated its two-step measure into Spanish, Vietnamese, Korean, Cantonese, Mandarin, and Tagalog, but small cell sizes for languages other than Spanish restrict detailed analysis of the results. Sanderson and Immerwahr (2019 as cited in Federal Committee on Statistical Methodology, 2020) analyzed nonresponse for the five non-English languages included in their 2018 survey of New Yorkers and found the highest rates of nonresponse among Russian speakers (2.6% for gender identity, 0.9% for sex assigned at birth) and the lowest rates among Bengali and Haitian Creole speakers (0% on either item); Spanish speakers fell somewhere in between (1.7% for gender identity and 0.8% for sex assigned at birth) and were most notable for being the only linguistic minorities who identified as transgender. In contrast, Canada reported finding a lower proportion of nonbinary individuals from French-language questionnaires than English-language questionnaires in its 2019 content test, despite qualitative pretests showing the concepts were understood by French-speaking nonbinary people. Thus, translation and cultural equivalency remain open questions for research, particularly for the specific combination of question wording and answer options included in the panel's recommended current gender question.

Evaluating Best Practices for Gender Identity Measures Among Youth

As noted above, the panel found insufficient evidence to support setting age standards for asking about current gender. The other countries we considered tended to set age minimums on their gender identity items, recommending they be asked only of people ages 16 and older. When explicitly justified, this was noted as being determined by the age of majority or when someone was legally considered an adult for the purposes of consent and was similar to age minimums for asking about sexual orientation. In the United States, some studies have asked gender identity questions of younger children. For example, in 2017, the Centers for Disease Control and Prevention piloted a single-item question to identify transgender students on the Youth Risk Behavior Survey (YRBS), which samples both middle and high school students (see Johns et al., 2019). Cognitive interviews indicated the item performed well, and it is now included among the YRBS optional question list for use along with a binary sex question. In 2019, a two-step measure was also tested in clinical settings among adolescents aged 12 to 18; in this pilot test, clinics that used the two-step measure identified six times more adolescents as transgender or gender diverse (1.3% at the pilot clinics and 0.2% at other clinics), and less than 2 percent of adolescents found the question confusing, offensive, or uncomfortable (Lau et al., 2021). This study, along with a pilot of the two-step approach among youth in foster care (Wilson et al., 2016), suggests younger children can understand and answer questions about their gender identity; however, for younger respondents, some answer options may need to be altered to include "boy" and "girl" alongside either male or man and female or woman. Further research is needed to appropriately adapt gender measures for children and adolescents.

> RECOMMENDATION 5: To improve the quality and inclusivity of the recommended two-step gender measure—sex assigned at birth and current gender—the National Institutes of Health should fund and conduct research on the following topics:
>
> - Explicit tests of the use of terminology for sex (female/male) and gender (woman/man) for current gender responses, along with optimal answer option ordering, and the utility of a confirmation question. Testing should also confirm optimal ordering of the two-step components in both survey research and in other settings.
> - Alternative two-step gender measures that offer an inclusive count of both cisgender and transgender people for use in contexts where the privacy and confidentiality of sex assigned at birth responses cannot be assured or where specific information on sex assigned at

birth is unnecessary but identifying transgender people for the purposes of service delivery or monitoring disparities is still desirable.

- Assessment of the inclusion of "nonbinary" as an answer option either instead of or in addition to "transgender" and of the utility of allowing multiple gender identity responses.
- Periodic reevaluation of write-in gender identity responses and how they change over time and may vary in different settings (e.g., among LGBTQI+ samples in comparison with general population samples and in clinical settings in comparison with surveys), as well as periodic reevaluation of listed response options.
- Evaluation of the utility of including a nonbinary response when asking about sex assigned at birth, particularly if nonbinary sex markers on birth certificates become more widely available, and consideration of how nonbinary gender identities should be counted in terms of cisgender or transgender status.
- Expanded testing of the recommended two-step gender measure beyond general population assessments of English-speaking adults, including updated translations and studies of response equivalence, as well as further testing among youth and in settings where a single respondent replies for all household members.

ANNEX:
EXAMPLES OF TWO-STEP GENDER MEASURES

Table 6A-1 details examples of two-step gender measures in national and international surveys.

TABLE 6A-1 Examples of Two-Step Gender Measures in National and International Surveys

First Item Stem	First Item Response Options	Second Item Stem	Second Item Response Options	Source(s)
What is your gender?	○ Male ○ Female ○ Other, specify	What sex were you assigned at birth, on your original birth certificate?	○ Male ○ Female	Add Health (Wave V)
What was your biological sex assigned at birth?	○ Female ○ Male ○ Intersex ○ None of these	What terms best express how you describe your gender identity? (Check all that apply)	☐ Woman ☐ Man ☐ Non-binary ☐ Transgender ☐ Another term	All of Us Program
Do you think of yourself as:	○ Male ○ Female ○ Transgender man/trans man/female-to-male (FTM) ○ Transgender women/ trans woman/male-to-female (MTF) ○ Genderqueer, gender noncon-forming, neither exclusively male or female ○ Additional gender category (or other), please specify	What sex was originally listed on your birth certificate?	○ Male ○ Female	CDC Recommendations (2020)

TABLE 6A-1 Continued

First Item Stem	First Item Response Options	Second Item Stem	Second Item Response Options	Source(s)
What sex were you assigned at birth? (For example, on your birth certificate.)	○ Female ○ Male ○ Intersex	What is your current gender?	○ Woman ○ Man ○ Transgender ○ A gender not listed here [free text]	GSS (2018)
What sex were you assigned at birth, on your original birth certificate?	○ Male ○ Female	What is your current gender identity? (Check all that apply)	☐ Male ☐ Female ☐ Trans male/trans man ☐ Trans female/trans woman ☐ Genderqueer/gender nonconforming ☐ Different identity (please state)	The GenIUSS Group (2014, Promising GI measure)
What sex were you assigned at birth (what the doctor put on your birth certificate)? (select one)	○ Male ○ Female	What is your gender? Your gender is how you feel inside and can be the same or different than your biological or birth sex. (check all that apply)	☐ Male ☐ Female ☐ Transgender male-to-female ☐ Transgender female-to-male ☐ Genderqueer or gender nonconforming, or some other gender ☐ You are not sure	HSLS:09 (2016 follow-up)
What sex were you at birth?	○ Male ○ Female	Do you currently consider yourself to be:	○ Male ○ Female	NATS
What sex were you assigned at birth, on your original birth certificate?	○ Male ○ Female	Do you currently describe yourself as...?	○ Male ○ Female ○ Transgender ○ None of these	NCVS, U.S. Census Pulse Survey
What was your sex at birth?	○ Male ○ Female ○ Intersex/ambiguous	Do you consider yourself to be:	○ Male ○ Female ○ Transgender	NHIVBS

continued

TABLE 6A-1 Continued

First Item Stem	First Item Response Options	Second Item Stem	Second Item Response Options	Source(s)
First, I'd like to confirm your gender. What sex were you assigned at birth, on your original birth certificate?	○ Male ○ Female [If needed: We have to know your sex in order to direct you to the right questions.]	How do you describe your gender identity?	○ Male ○ Female ○ Male-to-female transgender (MTF) ○ Female-to-male transgender (FTM) ○ Other gender identity, specify	NISVS
What sex were you assigned at birth, on your original birth certificate?	○ Female ○ Male	How do you describe yourself?	○ Female ○ Male ○ Transgender ○ Do not identify as female, male, or transgender	NORC recommendations for CMS (2017)
What sex were you assigned at birth, on your original birth certificate?	○ Male ○ Female	How do you currently describe your gender? (Check the ONE that best applies to you)	○ Male ○ Female ○ Genderqueer/gender nonconforming ○ Transgender female-to-male ⊙ Transgender male-to-female ○ Something else, please specify	START
Is the person:	○ Male ○ Female ○ Non-binary sex	How [do/does] [you/Person's name/they] describe [your/their] gender? Gender refers to current gender, which may be different to sex recorded at birth and may be different to what is indicated on legal documents. Please [tick/mark/select] one box	○ Man or male ○ Woman or Female ○ Non-binary ○ [I/They] use a different term (please specify) ○ Prefer not to answer	Australia Sex: Census (2021) Gender identity: Recommendations (January 2021)

TABLE 6A-1 Continued

First Item Stem	First Item Response Options	Second Item Stem	Second Item Response Options	Source(s)
What was this person's sex at birth? Sex refers to sex assigned at birth.	◯ Male ◯ Female	What is this person's gender? Refers to current gender which may be different from sex assigned at birth and may be different from what is indicated on legal documents.	◯ Male ◯ Female ◯ Or please specify this person's gender	Canada Census (2021)
What is your sex? A question about gender identity will follow later on in the questionnaire.	◯ Female ◯ Male	Is the gender you identify with the same as your sex registered at birth?	◯ Yes ◯ No ◯ [if no] Enter gender identity	England and Wales Census (2021)
What was your sex at birth? (for example what was recorded on your birth certificate)	◯ Male ◯ Female	What is your gender?	◯ Male ◯ Female ◯ Another gender (Please state)	New Zealand Recommendations (April 2021)
What is your sex?	◯ Female ◯ Male	Do you consider yourself to be trans, or have a trans history?	◯ No ◯ Yes ◯ [if yes] Please describe your trans status (for example, non-binary, trans man, trans woman)	Scotland Census (2021)

NOTES: Add Health, National Longitudinal Study of Adolescent to Adult Health; CDC, Centers for Disease Control and Prevention; GSS, General Social Survey; HSLS:09, High School Longitudinal Study of 2009; NATS, National Adult Tobacco Survey; NCVS, National Crime Victimization Survey; NHIVBS, National HIV Behavioral Surveillance System; NISVS, National Intimate Partner and Sexual Violence Survey; NORC, National Opinion Research Center; START, Survey of Today's Adolescent Relationships and Transitions.

7

Measuring Intersex/
DSD Populations

The measurement of intersex status—also known as differences in sex development (DSD)—is complicated by the unique experiences of intersex populations and a limited research base. As discussed in Part I, intersex variations are highly heterogeneous and can involve any sex trait. Most people with intersex traits are born with genitals that appear to be male or female and are therefore assigned either male or female at birth. Often, they are not identified as having an intersex variation until later in life, at times in adolescence or adulthood, if at all.

EVALUATION OF MEASURES

Background: History and Care

Unlike sexual identity and gender identity, which have been studied extensively for more than a decade and for which measures have been used, research on intersex people and people with differences in sex development is in its infancy. The clinical identification and treatment of intersex/ DSD people have changed substantially over the past century (Reis, 2012), often in ways that have repercussions for data collection practices. In the early 20th century, intersex variations that were not associated with genital difference were not readily identified by clinicians. Infants who were born with genital difference were often perceived as a shameful aberration. These factors led to the invisibility of intersex bodies—a result of both ignorance and concealment (Reis, 2012). By the 1950s, medicine's advances enabled clinicians to diagnose and surgically alter intersex bodies.

Stigma, however, persisted in the application of psychological theories of gender development, which held that a binary gender could be assigned and enforced through social learning. Standard practice for intersex management was surgical alteration in infancy and binary gender assignment (Karkazis, 2008). Concealment was prioritized under the assumption that any perceived uncertainty about sex could introduce gender uncertainty and expose a child to social stigma (Reis, 2012). This model was also applied to intersex children without genital difference. Because the focus of these interventions was on early childhood development, parents were at the center of protecting information and decision making (Lee et al., 2006).

This model of care persisted for several decades. By the 1990s, however, intersex advocacy organizations had begun to underscore the internalized stigma that this systematic concealment caused in intersex/DSD persons[1] (Davis, 2015). In 2006, the standard of care shifted toward recommending increased engagement of children in decision making and routine disclosure of medical information to children, although parents continued to play important roles in receiving and understanding medical information, and medical practice continues to be informed by parents' needs and concerns (Mulkey, Streed, and Chubak, 2021). At the same time that standards of care began to shift, a new system of nomenclature was proposed, using an umbrella term of "disorders of sex development" rather than specific intersex variations and replacing a more confusing system referring to different forms of hermaphroditism (Lee et al., 2006). Diagnostic technology and research continue to evolve, and some people do not know their specific intersex variation or learn in adolescent or adulthood that their diagnosis was incorrect.

Most people with intersex variations born before the early 2000s are likely to have learned about their intersex status as adults, and may have incomplete knowledge of their anatomy, medical treatment, and surgical history (Grimstad et al., 2021). Some adults may be aware of their intersex status but have never received a formal medical diagnosis. The history of silence and erasure of intersex status means that many intersex adults may be reluctant to disclose their intersex status because they were taught that it is confidential or because they fear stigma or discrimination. However, in one study based on a convenience sample of those who self-identified as intersex or had a DSD diagnosis, all of the participants endorsed the inclusion of a measure of intersex status in survey research (Tamar-Mattis et al., 2018).

The evolution in the identification and treatment of intersex people has meant that language preferences vary considerably in this population: some people prefer medicalized language, such as having a difference or disorder

---

[1]For example, the Intersex Society of North America founded in the mid-1990s: see https://isna.org/faq/history/.

of sex development, an intersex condition, or a specific diagnosis, while others prefer to describe themselves as being intersex and avoid terms that appear to be medicalizing (Rosenwohl-Mack et al., 2020; Tamar-Mattis et al., 2018). Although research has been limited, it appears that these preferences can be specific to either clinical or social contexts and that multiple terms may be acceptable to respondents (Johnson et al., 2017). For example, disorder of sex development is actively eschewed by many advocacy groups, and the support group for congenital adrenal hyperplasia does not use any DSD or intersex language.[2] Even among physicians and researchers there remains disagreement as to which variations "count" as intersex or DSD (Jenkins and Short, 2017).

The Use of Sex Assigned at Birth to Measure Intersex Status

As noted above, when a child is born with genital difference, the process of assigning gender at birth is highly complex. Current medical standards of care recommend identifying a binary gender with which the child is most likely to identify, with the understanding that this may shift over time. Though families are encouraged to maintain openness to their children's gender exploration and diversity, very few choose to raise a child as nonbinary.

Also, as noted in Chapter 3, it is only recently that some states have legally permitted a nonbinary designation to be included on birth certificates. Although some intersex adults have amended their birth certificates to the nonbinary category (Reuters, 2019; O'Hara, 2016), it is not known how many people have chosen to do so or how many families of intersex infants have chosen this designation at birth. Additionally, some people have cautioned against reflexively identifying intersex infants as an indeterminate or third gender, arguing that this reinforces the "otherness" of intersex children as well as the gender binary (Asia Pacific Forum of National Human Rights Institutions, 2016; Council of Europe Commissioner of Human Rights, 2015). However, because intersex status is viewed as a "medical condition," it has traditionally been easier for people with intersex traits to amend their birth certificates to another binary sex designation than it has been for transgender people to do so.

CONCLUSION 2: Intersex status is an important component of demographic status, private medical information, and an aspect of identity. Although there are barriers to disclosure, people appear to want to disclose their status. Because of historical, legal, and medical factors, almost no person in the United States is assigned intersex at birth.

---

[2]See https://www.livingwithcah.com/.

Therefore, it is inappropriate to assess intersex status primarily with an "intersex" response option for sex assigned at birth; however, when sex assigned at birth is asked, it may be appropriate to include "prefer not to answer" or "do not know" options.

RECOMMENDATION 6: When the National Institutes of Health seeks to identify people with intersex traits or differences of sex development in clinical, survey, research, and administrative settings, they should do so by using a standalone measure that asks respondents to report their intersex status. They should not do so by adding "intersex" as a third response category to a binary measure of sex.

Measures That Have Been Used

Each of the unique aspects of intersex populations, particularly when layered with evolving societal understandings of sex and gender, can affect the context and questions used to identify people with intersex traits. Unfortunately, very few data are available to guide recommendations on best practices for the specific language to use to measure intersex status. A number of recommendations for questions have been either offered by or developed in collaboration with members of intersex communities: see Table 7A-1 in the annex to this chapter.

A 2018 online, anonymous survey of a convenience sample of 111 adults who self-identified as being intersex or having a diagnosis of a DSD involved cognitive testing of the first single-item measure recommended by the Gender Identity in the U.S. Surveillance Group (GenIUSS) (Tamar-Mattis et al., 2018, p. 321):

> Have you ever been diagnosed by a medical doctor with an intersex condition or a "Difference of Sex Development (DSD)" or were you born with (or developed naturally in puberty) genitals, reproductive organs, and/ or chromosomal patterns that do not fit standard definitions of male or female?

Nearly all of the respondents, 96.4 percent, reported having been diagnosed with a DSD, 18.0 percent identified as intersex, and 72 percent endorsed the measure as important and straightforward. All of the respondents agreed with including an intersex measure in survey research. Qualitative analysis found that some participants found the question to be overly medicalizing, which may exclude respondents who have not had access to care or a diagnosis, and others expressed concern with the use of DSD language.

Importantly, survey recruitment was through Facebook advertisements and posts to community support and advocacy forums. Respondents were predominantly White (83.8%), educated (63.9% with a bachelor's degree or graduate education), and assigned female at birth (72.1%). Only 36.9 percent identified with their sex assigned at birth. Additionally, the study provided a list of intersex variations from which to choose, and there was an uneven distribution of specific variations. Consequently, these results may not generalize to other diagnostic groups or clinical settings, and they indicate a need for further research. Moreover, because the study population was comprised of only those who identified as intersex or had been diagnosed with a DSD, it could not assess the degree to which this measure generates "false positives"—people who are not intersex but respond that they are.

A 2020 community-based participatory survey of 179 respondents that was also conducted online and recruited from intersex support and advocacy groups used a similar question to confirm that participants had intersex variations, as well as another question regarding specific intersex variation (Rosenwohl-Mack et al., 2020, S2 p. 1):

> Some people are assigned male or female at birth but are born with traits including sexual anatomy, reproductive organs, and/or chromosome patterns that may not fit the typical definition of male or female. These traits may be known as variations or differences of sex development (DSD) or intersex.
>
> Have you ever been diagnosed by a medical doctor or other health professional with an intersex condition or a "Difference of Sex Development (DSD)" or were you born with (or developed naturally in puberty) genitals, reproductive organs, and/or chromosomal patterns that do not fit standard definitions of male or female?

Among this sample, over 10 percent of the respondents had no confirmed intersex diagnosis, and nearly 50 percent reported two or more intersex diagnoses. These respondents were also asked to report their sex assigned at birth and gender identity: 3.7 percent responded "not sure" to their sex assigned at birth, 63.4 percent reported intersex as their gender identity, and 15.8 percent identified as transgender. Again, the sample was predominantly White (72.8%), educated (60.9% with a bachelor's or higher degree), and assigned female at birth (66.3%). For those who reported their specific intersex variation, complete androgen insensitivity syndrome was relatively overrepresented as the most common variation (19.1%), and classic congenital adrenal hyperplasia was relatively underrepresented (5.7%).[3]

A 2020 survey conducted by the Center for American Progress (2021) included an intersex status question that simplified the first GenIUSS question listed above: "Have you ever been diagnosed by a medical doctor with an intersex condition?" The initial sample of self-identified LGBT adults was selected from a national, probability panel of U.S. households held by AmeriSpeak and was supplemented with respondents from a nonprobability opt-in online panel of respondents. Of 1,528 participants, 4.9 percent answered that they had been diagnosed with an intersex condition. The nonresponse rate was 0.9 percent. This sample was somewhat more diverse than the previous studies with respect to both race and ethnicity (59% White, 12% Black, 18% Hispanic, and 4% Asian) and education (34% with a bachelor's or higher degree). The result of the 4.9 percent figure is far higher than usual estimates of intersex prevalence, but it was not possible to determine whether this was due to the overrepresentation of LGBT respondents or misreporting because there was no follow-up question to assess specific intersex variations or the rate of false positives.

The 2020 Pennsylvania LGBT Health Needs Assessment,[4] a biannual community-based survey using convenience sampling that was conducted in a partnership between the Pennsylvania Department of Health and the Bradbury-Sullivan LGBT Community Center, included an intersex status question. This question was also based on a simplified version of the first GenIUSS question: "Were you born intersex, or with a variation of sex characteristics or sex development?" This question does not rely on medical verification of intersex status, and this study was novel in its use in a larger sample (N = 6,582) and broader LGBT community setting. The "yes" rate was 1.7 percent, which is the highest estimate of intersex prevalence in the academic literature. However, as with the Center for American Progress study, there was no follow-up question to assess specific intersex variation or the rate of false positives. The question had a 0.29 percent nonresponse rate. Respondents were predominantly White (83.8%) and educated (56.6% held a bachelor's or higher degrees). Of note, 27 percent of respondents identified as transgender, nonbinary, genderqueer, or gender fluid.

---

[3]In the general population, complete androgen insensitivity syndrome is less common (1 in 20,000) than classical congenital adrenal hyperplasia (1 in 15,000) (Therrell et al., 1998). If infants with intersex traits occur in 1 in 2,000 births, this suggests that roughly 10 percent of those with intersex traits should have complete androgen insensitivity syndrome and roughly 13 percent should have classical congenital adrenal hyperplasia.

[4]See https://www.pacancercoalition.org/images/pdf/LGBTQ_resources/2020_pa_lgbtq_full_report_final_public_distribution.pdf.

RECOMMENDATION: INTERSEX STATUS MEASURES

Available research on specific language is too limited for the panel to offer definitive recommendations on the exact terminology to use in the measurement of intersex status. Only one known study has involved cognitive interviewing; its sample included only intersex-identified adults, and it did not include adults without intersex variations or parents of children with or without intersex variations. While nonresponse rates are reported in the small number of existing studies, these studies lack assessments of sensitivity and specificity. Because most standard measures of validity were unavailable, we therefore evaluated potential questions by considering the following elements (when present): any available scientific evidence of construct validity and item response metrics; application in population-based samples; ease of administration and clarity of understanding; recommendations of U.S. intersex-led policy and advocacy organizations; and consistency with the panel's principles for data collection.

The panel also valued an intersex status question as one that accurately assesses a person's naturally developed sex variation rather than gender identity, while acknowledging that people with sex variations may also assert intersex as a gender identity (Rosenwohl-Mack et al., 2020). The panel acknowledges the problems associated with grounding an intersex status question in medical diagnosis and experience, especially for a population known to have experienced traumatic medical treatment.

In summary, there is very little evidence regarding the language or impact of measurement of intersex status in research, clinical, and administrative settings. Thus, our recommendation is a limited one. However, based on the available research, historical context, and community recommendations, there are three questions that appear to have the strongest grounding in evidence, which we offer as options.

Option 1:
Have you ever been diagnosed by a medical doctor or other health professional with an intersex condition or a difference of sex development (DSD) or were you born with (or developed naturally in puberty) genitals, reproductive organs, or chromosomal patterns that do not fit standard definitions of male or female?

Option 2:
Were you born with a variation in your physical sex characteristics? (This is sometimes called being intersex or having a difference in sex development, or DSD.)

Option 3:
Have you ever been diagnosed by a medical doctor with an intersex condition or a difference of sex development?

All three questions offer the same response options:
○ Yes
○ No
(Don't know)
(Prefer not to answer)

Of these three options, the panel prefers option 1 because it is the only measure that has been tested among intersex populations, although it is long and potentially cumbersome to administer. Both options 2 and 3 are modified versions of GenIUSS group recommendations and effectively divide into two parts the questions that were tested in intersex communities. A version of each bifurcation was tested in population-based surveys of the Center for American Progress and Pennsylvania LGBT Health Needs Assessment: while positive responses rates varied substantially in ways that were difficult to assess given differences among the survey populations, nonresponse rates for both questions were low. We note that there is no research that examines proxy reporting of intersex status, such as by parents or caregivers of young children, nor has any testing of questions on intersex status been conducted using minors as respondents.

In some situations, it might be necessary to identify the respondent's specific intersex variation. InterACT Advocates for Intersex Youth has provided a list of variations that are often considered by medical providers and community members to be intersex: see the list in Annex 7-2 to this chapter.

> CONCLUSION 3: Based on the best available evidence, community guidance, and expert opinion, intersex status can be measured using the following question:

Have you ever been diagnosed by a medical doctor or other health professional with an intersex condition or a difference of sex development (DSD) or were you born with (or developed naturally in puberty) genitals, reproductive organs, or chromosomal patterns that do not fit standard definitions of male or female?
○ Yes
○ No
(Don't know)
(Prefer not to answer)

If identification of specific intersex variations is needed, as in a clinical care or research, a list of intersex variations can be provided.

RECOMMENDED RESEARCH AREAS

In light of the many unresolved issues and questions regarding the measurement of people with intersex characteristics, the panel offers recommendations for research.

RECOMMENDATION 7: To improve the quality and inclusivity of current measures of intersex status, the National Institutes of Health should fund and conduct research on the following topics:

- The use of a single-item intersex/DSD status question.
- The quality of the three measures of intersex/DSD status that were identified by the panel as having the strongest grounding in evidence to determine which measure most effectively identifies the intersex/DSD population in a range of settings.
- The effects of including definitions and examples of terms used in intersex status questions, such as "intersex," "DSD," and specific intersex variations.
- The prevalence of "intersex" as a gender identity both among people with known intersex variations and people without intersex variations.
- The effects of proxy reporting of intersex/DSD status, particularly of parents reporting their children's status.

ANNEX 7-1:
MEASURES OF INTERSEX STATUS

Table 7A-1 shows measures for intersex status that have been recommended by bodies in the United States and other English-speaking countries.

TABLE 7A-1 Measures of Intersex Status in the United States and Other English-Speaking Nations

Question	Response Options	Source (Notes)
Were you born with a variation of sex characteristics (sometimes called "intersex" or 'DSD')?	◯ Yes ◯ No ◯ Don't know ◯ Prefer not to answer	Australian Bureau of Statistics (2021) (Only recommended for self-report)
Some people are assigned male or female at birth, but are born with sexual anatomy, reproductive organs, and/or chromosome patterns that do not fit the typical definition of male or female. This physical condition is known as intersex. Are you intersex?	◯ Yes, an Intersex man ◯ Yes, an Intersex woman ◯ Yes, an Intersex person, gender non-conforming ◯ No	The GenIUSS Group (2014)
Have you ever been diagnosed by a medical doctor with an intersex condition or a "Difference of Sex Development," or were you born with (or developed naturally in puberty) genitals, reproductive organs, and/or chromosomal patterns that do not fit standard definitions of male or female?	◯ Yes ◯ No	The GenIUSS Group (2014)
Were you born with a variation in your physical sex characteristics? (This is sometimes called being intersex or having a difference in sex development, or DSD)?	◯ No ◯ Yes, my chromosomes, genitals, reproductive organs, or hormone functions were observed to be different from the typical female/male binary at birth and/or I have been diagnosed with intersex variation or Difference of Sex Development ◯ I don't know	The Fenway Institute/ InterACT (2020)

TABLE 7A-1 Continued

Question	Response Options	Source (Notes)
Some people are born with bodies that are a little different from what we think of as standard "male" or "female" bodies. For example, some people have genitals that don't look exactly like most other penises or vaginas, or they might have reproductive organs that aren't what we'd expect based on how their body looks. This is called being intersex. Are you intersex?	○ Yes, I am intersex ○ No, I am not intersex ○ I do not know if I am intersex ○ I do not know what this question is asking	The Fenway Institute/InterACT (2020) (Modification for youth respondents)
Some people are labeled male or female at birth, but are born with physical differences in sex anatomy, reproductive organs, chromosomes, and/or hormone function that do not fit typical expectations. These differences are known as variations in sex characteristics, differences in sex development, intersex traits, or sometimes by specific medical terms (like Congenital Adrenal Hyperplasia or Androgen Insensitivity Syndrome). Were you born with any of these physical differences?	○ Yes ○ No ○ I don't know	The Fenway Institute/InterACT (2020)
Were you born with a variation of sex characteristics (otherwise known as an intersex variation)?	○ Yes ○ No ○ Don't know ○ Prefer not to say	Statistics New Zealand (2021) (Recommends including a definition of what variations of sex characteristics means and including a list of common conditions [where possible].)

ANNEX 7-2:
CONDITIONS CLASSIFIED AS INTERSEX OR
DIFFERENCES IN SEX DEVELOPMENT

This annex lists the varieties of intersex conditions that are often specified by medical providers and groups that represent affected people (The Fenway Institute/InterACT, 2020).

5-Alpha reductase deficiency (5-ARD)
17-Beta-hydroxysteroid dehydrogenase deficiency
Aphallia
Bladder exstrophy
Classic Congenital Adrenal Hyperplasia (Classic CAH)
Clitoromegaly (large clitoris)
Complete Androgen Insensitivity Syndrome (CAIS)
Cryptorchidism (undescended testicle/s)
de la Chapelle (XX Male) syndrome
Epispadias
Fraser Syndrome
Gonadal dysgenesis (partial or complete)
Hypospadias
Jacobs/XYY Syndrome
Kallmann Syndrome
Klinefelter Syndrome
Late Onset Congenital Adrenal Hyperplasia (late onset CAH)
Leydig Cell Hypoplasia
Micropenis
Mosaicism involving 'sex' chromosomes
MRKH (Mullerian agenesis; vaginal agenesis; congenital absence of vagina)
Mullerian (Duct) aplasia
Ovo-testes (formerly 'true hermaphroditism')
Partial Androgen Insensitivity Syndrome (PAIS)
Persistent Mullerian Duct Syndrome
Polycystic Ovary Syndrome (PCOS)/Hyperandrogenism
Progestin Induced Virilization
Swyer Syndrome
Triple-X Syndrome (XXX)
Turner Syndrome (TS, one X chromosome)
XXY/47
XY/XO Mosaicism
XY-Turner Syndrome
Another variation [free text]
Unknown

References

Adair, C. (2019). Licensing Citizenship: Anti-Blackness, Identification Documents, and Transgender Studies. *American Quarterly*, 71(2), 569-594.

Alexander, A. C., Bolzendahl, C., and Wängnerud, L. (2021). Beyond the binary: new approaches to measuring gender in political science research. *European Journal of Politics and Gender*, 4(1), 7-9.

Almasri, J., Zaiem, F., Rodriguez-Gutierrez, R., Tamhane, S.U., Iqbal, A.M., Prokop, L.J., Speiser, P., Baskin, L., Bancos I., and Murad, M.H. (2018). Genital reconstructive surgery in females with congenital adrenal hyperplasia: A systematic review and meta-analysis. *Journal of Clinical Endocrinology and Metabolism*, 103(11), 4089-4096.

Alpert, A.B., Ruddick, R., and Manzano, C. (2021). Rethinking sex-assigned-at-birth questions. *BMJ*, 373: n1261. doi: 10.1136/bmj.n1261.

Amaya, A., (2020). Adapting how we ask about the gender of our survey respondents. Pew Research Center. Available: https://medium.com/pew-research-center-decoded/adapting-how-we-ask-about-the-gender-of-our-survey-respondents-77b0cb7367c0.

American Medical Association. (2021). AMA announced policies adopted on final day of Special Meeting. American Medical Association Press Release, June 16, 2021. https://www.ama-assn.org/press-center/press-releases/ama-announced-policies-adopted-final-day-special-meeting.

American Psychiatric Association. (2013). Diagnostic and Statistical Manual of Mental Disorders (DSM-5), Fifth edition.

Annandale, E., and Hunt, K. (1990). Masculinity, femininity and sex: an exploration of their relative contribution to explaining gender differences in health. *Sociology of Health & Illness*, 12(1), 24-46.

Antonio, M., Lau, F., Davison, K., Devor, A., Queen, R., and Courtney, K. (2022). Toward an inclusive digital health system for sexual and gender minorities in Canada. *Journal of the American Medical Informatics Association*, 29(2, February), 379-384. Available: https://doi.org/10.1093/jamia/ocab183.

Aragon, S.R., Poteat, V.P., Espelage, D.L., and Koenig, B.W. (2014). The Influence of Peer Victimization on Educational Outcomes for LGBTQ and Non-LGBTQ High School Students. *The Journal of LGBT Youth*, 11(1), 1-19.

Ashley, F. (2021). Recommendations for institutional and governmental management of gender information. *New York University Review of Law & Social Change*, 44(4), 489-528.

Asia Pacific Forum of National Human Rights Institutions. (2016). *Promoting and Protecting Human Rights: Sexual Orientation, Gender Identity and Sex Characteristics*. Asia Pacific Forum of National Human Rights Institutions Resource Manual. Available: https://www.asiapacificforum.net/resources/manual-sogi-and-sex-charactersitics/.

Aultman, B. (2014). Cisgender. *Transgender Studies Quarterly*, 1(1-2), 61-62. Available: doi: 10.1215/23289252-2399614.

Austin, S.B., Conron, K., Patel, A., and Freedner, N. (2007). Making sense of sexual orientation measures: Findings from a cognitive processing study with adolescents on health survey questions. *Journal of LGBT Health Research*, 3(1), 55-65. Available: doi: 10.1300/j463v03n01_07. PMID: 18029316.

Australian Bureau of Statistics. (2021). *Standard for Sex, Gender, Variations of Sex Characteristics and Sexual Orientation Variables*. Available: https://www.abs.gov.au/statistics/standards/standard-sex-gender-variations-sex-characteristics-and-sexual-orientation-variables/latest-release.

Australian Bureau of Statistics. (2020). 2021 Census topics and data release plan. Available: https://www.abs.gov.au/statistics/research/2021-census-topics-and-data-release-plan#topics-included-in-the-2021-census.

Babu, R., and Shah, U. (2021). Gender identity disorder (GID) in adolescents and adults with differences of sex development (DSD): A systematic review and meta-analysis. *Journal of Pediatric Urology*, 17(1), 39-47.

Badgett, M. (Ed.). (2009). *Best Practices for Asking Questions about Sexual Orientation on Surveys*. The Williams Institute, University of California at Los Angeles. Available: https://escholarship.org/uc/item/706057d5.

Bajko, M.S. (2021). California to collect LGBTQ violent death data under bill signed by Newsom. *Bay Area Reporter* (September 16). Available: https://www.ebar.com/news/latest_news/308938.

Baker, K.E., Streed, C.G., and Durso, L.E. (2021). Ensuring that LGBTQI+ people count—Collecting data on sexual orientation, gender identity, and intersex status. *New England Journal of Medicine*, 384, 1184-1186. Available: DOI: 10.1056/NEJMp2032447.

Barsigian, L.L., Hammack, P.L., Morrow, Q.J., Wilson, B.D.M., and Russell, S.T. (2020). Narratives of gender, sexuality, and community in three generations of genderqueer sexual minorities. *Psychology of Sexual Orientation and Gender Diversity*. Available: https://doi.org/10.1037/sgd0000384.

Bates, N., García Trejo, Y.A. and Vines, M. (2019). Are sexual minorities hard-to-survey? Insights from the 2020 Census Barriers, Attitudes, and Motivators Study (CBAMS) Survey. *Journal of Official Statistics*, 35(4), 709-729. Available: https://doi.org/10.2478/jos-2019-0030.

Bauer, G.R., Braimoh, J., Scheim, A.I., and Dharma, C. (2017). Transgender-inclusive measures of sex/gender for population surveys: Mixed-methods evaluation and recommendations. *PloS One*, 12(5), e0178043. Available: https://doi.org/10.1371/journal.pone.0178043.

Beemyn, G. (2015). Coloring Outside the Lines of Gender and Sexuality: The Struggle of Nonbinary Students to Be Recognized. *The Educational Forum*, 79, 4, 359-361.

Beimer, P.B., Groves, R.M., Lyberg, L.E., Mathiowetz, N.A., and Sudman, S. (1991). *Measurement Errors in Surveys*. New York: John Wiley and Sons, Inc.

Beischel, W.J., Schudson, Z.C., and van Anders, S.M. (2021). Visualizing gender/sex diversity via sexual configurations theory. *Psychology of Sexual Orientation and Gender Diversity*, 8(1), 1-13. https://doi.org/10.1037/sgd0000449.

Bem, S.L. (1974). The measurement of psychological androgyny. *Journal of consulting and clinical psychology*, 42(2), 155.

Bi, S., Cook, S.C., and Chin, M.H. (2021). Improving the care of LGBTQ people of color: Lessons from the voices of patients. *AFT Health Care*, 2(2), 22-30, 40. Available: https://www.aft.org/hc/fall2021/bi_cook_chin.

Bird, C.E., and Rieker, P.P. (1999). Gender matters: An integrated model for understanding men's and women's health. *Social Science and Medicine*, 48(6), 745-755.

Blackless, M., Charuvastra, A., Derryck, A., Fausto-Sterling, A., Lauzanne, K., and Lee, E. (2000). How sexually dimorphic are we? Review and synthesis. *American Journal of Human Biology*, 12(2), 151-166.

Bonvicini, K.A. (2017). LGBT healthcare disparities: What progress have we made? *Patient Education and Counseling*, 100(12), 2357-2361.

Brinkley-Rubinstein, L., Peterson, M., Zaller, N.D., and Wohl, D.A. (2019). Best practices for identifying men who have sex with men for corrections-based pre-exposure prophylaxis provision. *Health & Justice*, 7. Available: https://doi.org/10.1186/s40352-019-0088-7.

Brooks, H., Llewellyn, D., Nadarzynski, T., Castilho Pelloso, F., De Souza Guilherme, F., Pollard, A., and Jones, C.J. (2018). *British Journal of General Practice*, 68(668), e187-e196. Available: DOI: 10.3399/bjgp18X694841.

Burgess, C., Kauth, M.R., Klemt, C., Shanawani, H., and Shipherd, J.C. (2019). Evolving Sex and Gender in Electronic Health Records. *Federal practitioner: for the health care professionals of the VA, DoD, and PHS*, 36(6), 271-277.

BusinessTech Staff. (2021). *New ID system planned for South Africa*. Available: https://businesstech.co.za/news/government/534602/new-id-system-planned-for-south-africa/.

Caceres, B.A., Streed, Jr., C.G., Corliss, H.L., Lloyd-Jones, D.M., Matthews, P.A., Mukherjee, M., Poteat, T., Rosendale, N., Ross, L.M., and on behalf of the American Heart Association Council on Cardiovascular and Stroke Nursing; Council on Hypertension; Council on Lifestyle and Cardiometabolic Health; Council on Peripheral Vascular Disease; and Stroke Council. (2020). Assessing and addressing cardiovascular health in LGBTQ adults: A scientific statement from the American Heart Association. *Circulation*, 142(19), e321-e332. Available: https://doi.org/10.1161/CIR.0000000000000914.

Cahill, S., Singal, R., Grasso, C., King, D., Mayer, K., Baker, K., and Makadon, H. (2014). Do ask, do tell: High levels of acceptability by patients of routine collection of sexual orientation and gender identity data in four diverse American community health centers. *PLOS One*, 9(9), 1-8.

California Legislative Assembly. (2021). *AB-1094 Sexual Orientation and Gender Identity Data Collection Pilot Project*. Chapter 177. Reg. Sess. 2021-2022. Available: https://leginfo.legislature.ca.gov/faces/billNavClient.xhtml?bill_id=202120220AB1094.

California Legislative Assembly. (2015). *AB-959 Lesbian, Gay, Bisexual, and Transgender Disparities Reduction Act*. Chapter 565. Reg. Sess. 2015-2016. Available: https://leginfo.legislature.ca.gov/faces/billNavClient.xhtml?bill_id=201520160AB959.

Callis, A.S. (2014). Bisexual, pansexual, queer: Non-binary identities and the sexual borderlands. *Sexualities*. 17(1-2), 63-80. Available: doi:10.1177/1363460713511094.

Campanelli, P.C., Martin, E.A., and Rothgeb, J.M. (1991). The use of respondent and interviewer debriefing studies as a way to study response error in survey data. *The Statistician*, 40(3), 253-264. Available: https://doi.org/10.2307/2348278.

Cassels, S., Pearson, C.R., Walters, K.L., Simoni, J.M., and Morris, M. (2010). Sexual partner concurrency and sexual risk among gay, lesbian, bisexual, and transgender American Indian/Alaska Natives. *Sexually Transmitted Diseases*, 12, 1-7. Available: PMID: 20051930. ISSN: 1537-4521.

Center for American Progress. (2021). Key Issues Facing People with Intersex Traits. Available: https://www.americanprogress.org/article/key-issues-facing-people-intersex-traits/.

Centers for Disease Control and Prevention. (2021). Behavioral Risk Factor Surveillance System LLCP 2020 Codebook Report. Available: www.cdc.gov/brfss/annual_data/2020/pdf/codebook20_llcp-v2-508.pdf.

Centers for Medicare and Medicaid Services' Innovation Center. (2021). *Innovation Center Strategy Refresh*. Available at: https://innovation.cms.gov/strategic-direction-whitepaper.

Chin, M.H. (2021). New Horizons - Addressing healthcare disparities in endocrine disease: bias, science, and patient care. *Journal of Clinical Endocrinology & Metabolism*. Available: doi: 10.1210/clinem/dgab229.

Chin, M.H. (2020). Advancing health equity in patient safety: A reckoning, challenge, and opportunity. *BMJ Quality and Safety*. Available: doi: 10.1136/bmjqs-2020-012599.

Clayton, J.A. (2018). Applying the new SABV (sex as a biological variable) policy to research and clinical care. *Physiology and Behavior*, 187(1), 2-5.

Clayton, J.A., and Tannenbaum, C. (2016). Reporting sex, gender, or both in clinical research? *JAMA*, 316(18): 1863-1864. Available: doi:10.1001/jama.2016.16405.

Cohen, D. (2011). The Stubborn Persistence of Sex Segregation. *Columbia Journal of Gender and Law*, 20(1), 51-140.

Coleman, E. (1987). Assessment of sexual orientation. *Journal of Homosexuality*, 14(1-2), 9-24. Available: doi: 10.1300/J082v14n01_02.

Conference of European Statisticians. (2017). *In-Depth Review of Measuring Gender Identity*. United Nations Economic and Social Council. Available: https://unece.org/sites/default/files/2021-01/In-depth%20review%20of%20Measuring%20Gender%20Identity%20for%20bureau.pdf.

Connolly, M., and Jacobs, B. (2020). Counting American Indians and Alaska Natives in the US Census. *Statistical Journal of the IAOS*, 36, 201-210.

Conron, K.J., and O'Neill, K.K. (2021). *Food Insufficiency among Transgender Adults During the COVID-19 Pandemic*. Williams Institute. Available: https://williamsinstitute.law.ucla.edu/publications/trans-food-insufficiency-covid/.

Conron, K.J., Scott, G., Stowell, G.S., and Landers, S.J. (2012). Transgender Health in Massachusetts: Results from a Household Probability Sample of Adults. *American Journal of Public Health*, 102(1), 118-122.

Converse, J.M., and Presser, S. (1989). *Survey Questions: Handcrafting the Standardized Questionnaire*. Newbury Park, CA: Sage Publications.

Cook, S.C., Gunter, K.E., and Lopez, F.Y. (2017). Establishing effective health care partnerships with sexual and gender minority patients: Recommendations for obstetrician gynecologists. *Seminars in Reproductive Medicine*, 35(5), 397-407.

Cooper, K.C., Wilson, B.D.M., and Choi, S.K. (2017). *Los Angeles County LGBTQ Youth Preparedness Scan*. Williams Institute. Available: https://williamsinstitute.law.ucla.edu/wp-content/uploads/LACo-Youth-Prepare-Scan-Feb-2017.pdf.

Council of Europe Commissioner of Human Rights. (2015). *Human Rights and Intersex People*. Council of Europe Commissioner of Human Rights Issue Paper F-67075. Available: https://rm.coe.int/16806da5d4.

Crenshaw, K. (1989). Demarginalizing the intersection of race and sex: A Black feminist critique of antidiscrimination doctrine, feminist theory and antiracist politics. *University of Chicago Legal Forum*, 1989(1), Article 8. Available: http://chicagounbound.uchicago.edu/uclf/vol1989/iss1/8.

Crenshaw, K. (2017). *On Intersectionality: Essential Writings*. New York: The New Press.

Cronin, R.M., Jerome, R.N., Mapes, B., Andrade, R., Johnston, R., Ayala, J., Schlundt, D., Bonnet, K., Kripalani, S., Goggins, K., Wallston, K.A., Couper, M.P., Elliott, M.R., Harris, P., Begale, M., Munoz, F., Lopez-Class, M., Cella, D., Condon, D., AuYoung, M., Mazor, K.M., Mikita, S., Manganiello, M., Borselli, N., Fowler, S., Rutter, J.L., Denny, J.C., Karlson, E.W., Ahmedani, B.K., and O'Donnell, C. (2019). Development of the Initial Surveys for the All of Us Research Program. *Epidemiology*, 30(4), 597-608.

Dahlhamer, J.M., Galinsky, A.M., and Joestl, S.S. (2019). Asking about sexual identity on the National Health Interview Survey: Does mode matter? *Journal of Official Statistics*, 35(4), 807-833. Available: doi: 10.2478/jos-2019-0034. PMID: 32565608; PMCID: PMC7304855.

Dahlhamer, J.M., Galinsky, A.M., Joestl, S.S., and Ward, B.W. (2014). Sexual orientation in the 2013 National Health Interview Survey: A quality assessment. *Vital Health Statistics*, 2(169), 1-32.

Davern, M., Bautista, R., Freese, J., Morgan, S.L., and Smith, T.W. (2021). General Social Surveys, 1972-2021 cross-section. Davern, M. (Principal Investigator). Chicago, IL: NORC at the University of Chicago. Available: gssdataexplorer.norc.org.

Davis, G. (2015). *Contesting intersex: The dubious diagnosis.* New York: New York University Press.

Davis, J.L. (2019). Refusing (Mis)recognition: Navigating multiple marginalization in the U.S. Two-Spirit movement. *Review of International American Studies*, 1, 65-86. Available: https://www.ceeol.com/search/article-detail?id=901658.

DeMaio, T.J., Bates, N., and O'Connell, M. (2013). Exploring measurement error in reporting of same-sex couples. *Public Opinion Quarterly*, 77(SI): 145-158.

DeMeester, R.H., Lopez, F.Y., Moore, J.E., Cook, S.C., and Chin, M.H. (2016). A model of organizational context and shared decision making: Application to LGBT racial and ethnic minority patients. *Journal of General Internal Medicine*, 31, 651-662. Available: doi: 10.1007/s11606-016-3608-3.

Desimone, L.M., and La Floch, K.C. (2004). Are we asking the right questions? Using cognitive interviews to improve surveys in education research. *Educational Evaluation and Policy Analysis*, 26(1), 1-22.

Devun, L. (2021). *The Shape of Sex: Nonbinary Gender from Genesis to the Renaissance.* New York: Columbia University Press.

Deutsch, M.B., and Buchholz, D. (2015). Electronic health records and transgender patients—practical recommendations for the collection of gender identity data. *Journal of General Internal Medicine*, 30(6), 843-847. Available: https://doi.org/10.1007/s11606-014-3148-7.

Diamond, L.M. (2003). What does sexual orientation orient? A biobehavioral model distinguishing romantic love and sexual desire. *Psychological Review*, 110(1), 173-192. Available: https://doi.org/10.1037/0033-295X.110.1.173.

Dillbary, J.S., and Edwards, G. (2019). An Empirical Analysis of Sexual Orientation Discrimination. *The University of Chicago Law Review*, 86(1), 1-76. Available: https://www.jstor.org/stable/26554392.

Dorak, M.T., and Karpuzoglu, E. (2012). Gender differences in cancer susceptibility: An inadequately addressed issue. *Frontiers in Genetics*, 28. Available: https://doi.org/10.3389/fgene.2012.00268.

Drydakis, N. (2022). Sexual orientation and earnings: A meta-analysis 2012–2020. *Journal Population Economics*, 35, 409-440. Available: https://doi.org/10.1007/s00148-021-00862-1.

Dy, C.J., LaMont, L.E., Ton, Q.V., and Lane, J.M. (2011). Sex and gender considerations in male patients with osteoporosis. *Clinical Orthopaedics and Related Research*, 469(7): 1906-1912. Available: doi: 10.1007/s11999-011-1849-3.

Ecker, J., Aubry, T., and Sylvestre, J. (2019). A review of the literature on LGBTQ adults who experience homelessness. *Journal of Homosexuality*, 66(3), 297-323. Available: https://doi.org/10.1080/00918369.2017.1413277.

Eisenberg, M.E., Kelly, E.D., McRee, A.L., Brady, S.S., and Barnes, A.J. (2019). Homelessness experiences and gender identity in a population-based sample of adolescents. *Preventive medicine reports*, 16, 100986. Available: https://doi.org/10.1016/j.pmedr.2019.100986.

Eliason, M.J., and Streed, C.G. (2017). Choosing "something else" as a sexual identity: Evaluating response options on the National Health Interview Survey. *LGBT Health*, 4(5), 376-379. Available: doi: 10.1089/lgbt.2016.0206.

Ellis, R., Virgile, M., Holzberg, J.L., Nelson, D.V., Edgar, J., Phipps, P., and Kaplan, T. (2018). *Assessing the Feasibility of Asking About Sexual Orientation and Gender Identity in the Current Population Survey: Results from Cognitive Interviews*. Research and Methodology Directorate, Center for Survey Measurement Study Series (Survey Methodology #2018-06), U.S. Census Bureau. Available: http://www.census.gov/content/dam/Census/library/working-papers/2018/adrm/rsm2018-06.pdf.

Epps, G. (2018). How birth certificates are being weaponized against trans people. *The Atlantic* (June 8). Available: https://www.theatlantic.com/ideas/archive/2018/06/how-birth-certificates-are-being-weaponized-once-again/562361/.

Erhardt, C.L. (1962). Race or color on vital records: Why confidential? *American Journal of Public Health*, 52(4), 666-670.

Federal Committee on Statistical Methodology. (2021). *Why Do Federal Agencies Ask About Sexual Orientation and Gender Identity on Surveys?* Available: https://nces.ed.gov/FCSM/pdf/FCSM_21_01_062221.pdf.

Federal Committee on Statistical Methodology. (2020). *Updates on Terminology of Sexual Orientation and Gender Identity Survey Measures*. FCSM-20-03 (August 2020). Available: https://nces.ed.gov/FCSM/pdf/FCSM_SOGI_Terminology_FY20_Report_FINAL.pdf.

Federal Interagency Working Group on Improving Measurement of Sexual Orientation and Gender Identity in Federal Surveys. (2016a). *Current Measures of Sexual Orientation and Gender Identity in Federal Surveys*. August White Paper. Available: https://nces.ed.gov/FCSM/pdf/buda5.pdf.

Federal Interagency Working Group on Improving Measurement of Sexual Orientation and Gender Identity in Federal Surveys. (2016b). *Evaluations of Sexual Orientation and Gender Identity Survey Measures: What Have We Learned?* September White Paper. Available: https://nces.ed.gov/FCSM/pdf/Evaluations_of_SOGI_Questions_20160923.pdf.

Federal Interagency Working Group on Improving Measurement of Sexual Orientation and Gender Identity in Federal Surveys. (2016c). *Toward a Research Agenda for Measuring Sexual Orientation and Gender Identity in Federal Surveys: Findings, Recommendations, and Next Steps*. October White Paper. Available: https://nces.ed.gov/FCSM/pdf/SOGI_Research_Agenda_Final_Report_20161020.pdf.

Fenton, K.A, Johnson, A.M., McManus, S., and Erens, B. (2001). Measuring sexual behaviour: methodological challenges in survey research. *Sexually Transmitted Infections*, 77(2), 84-92. Available: doi: 10.1136/sti.77.2.84.

The Fenway Institute/InterACT. (2020). *Intersex Data Collection: Your Guide to Question Design*. Available: https://interactadvocates.org/intersex-data-collection/.

Fieland, K.C., Walters, K.L., and Simoni, J.M. (2007). Determinants of health among two-spirit American Indians and Alaska Natives. In I.H. Meyer and M.E. Northridge (Eds.) *The Health of Sexual Minorities: Public Health Perspectives on Lesbian, Gay, Bisexual, and Transgender Populations* (pp. 268-300). Springer: Kluwer Academic Publishers.

Fielding, S. (2020). US Trans and non-binary people hit by voting barriers. *The Guardian*, June 16.

Finlayson, C. (2021). Sex Designation for Individuals with DSD. Public Workshop for the Committee on Measuring Sex, Gender Identity, and Sexual Orientation. (July 19), Washington, DC: National Academies of Sciences, Engineering, and Medicine.

Flatt, J.D., Cicero, E., Kittle, K.R., and Brennan-Ing, M. (2022). Recommendations for advancing research with sexual and gender minority older adults, *The Journals of Gerontology: Series B*, 77(1), 1-9. Available: https://doi.org/10.1093/geronb/gbab127.

Flores, A.R., Herman, J.L., Gates, G.J., and Brown, T.N.T. (2016). *How Many Adults Identify as Transgender in the United States?* Williams Institute. Available: http://williamsinstitute.law.ucla.edu/wp-content/uploads/How-Many-Adults-Identify-as-Transgender-in-the-United-States.pdf.

Fredriksen-Goldsen, K.I. and Hudson, R. (2018). Shifting social context in the lives of LGBTQ older adults. *Public Policy & Aging Report*, 28(1), 24-28.

Fredriksen-Goldsen, K.I., and Kim, H.-J. (2015). Count me in: Response to sexual orientation measures among older adults. *Research on Aging*, 37(5), 464-480. Available: doi:10.1177/0164027514542109.

Frohard-Dourlent, H., Dobson, S., Clark, B.A., Doull, M., and Saewyc, E.M. (2017). "I would have preferred more options": Accounting for non-binary youth in health research. *Nursing inquiry*, 24(1). Available: https://doi.org/10.1111/nin.12150.

Galupo, M.P., Davis, K.S., Grynkiewicz, A.L., and Mitchell, R.C. (2014). Conceptualization of sexual orientation identity among sexual minorities: Patterns across sexual and gender identity. *Journal of Bisexuality*, 14(3-4), 433-456. Available: doi: 10.1080/15299716.2014.933466.

Galupo, M.P., Ramirez, J.L., and Pulice-Farrow, L. (2017). "Regardless of their gender": Descriptions of sexual identity among bisexual, pansexual, and queer identified individuals. *Journal of Bisexuality*, 17(1), 108-124. Available: DOI: 10.1080/15299716.2016.1228491.

Gender Identity in U.S. Surveillance. (2014). *Best Practices for Asking Questions to Identify Transgender and Other Gender Minority Respondents on Population-Based Surveys*. J.L. Herman (Ed.). Los Angeles: The Williams Institute. Available: https://williamsinstitute. law.ucla.edu/wp-content/uploads/Survey-Measures-Trans-GenIUSS-Sep-2014.pdf.

Glick, J.L., Lopez, A., Pollock, M., and Theall, K.P. (2019). "Housing insecurity seems to almost go hand in hand with being trans": Housing stress among transgender and gender non-conforming individuals in New Orleans. *Journal of Urban Health: Bulletin of the New York Academy of Medicine*, 96(5), 751-759. Available: https://doi.org/10.1007/s11524-019-00384-y.

Glick, J.L., Theall, K., Andrinopoulos, K., and Kendall, C. (2018). For data's sake: dilemmas in the measurement of gender minorities. *Culture, health & sexuality*, 20(12), 1362-1377. Available: https://doi.org/10.1080/13691058.2018.1437220.

Goldberg, S.K., Rothblum, E.D., Russell, S.T., and Meyer, I.H. (2020). Exploring the Q in LGBTQ: Demographic characteristic and sexuality of queer people in a U.S. representative sample of sexual minorities. *Psychology of Sexual Orientation and Gender Diversity*, 7(1), 101-112. Available: https://doi.org/10.1037/sgd0000359.

Gonzales, G., and Henning-Smith, C. (2017). Barriers to care among transgender and gender nonconforming adults. *The Milbank Quarterly*, 95(4), 726-748. Available: https://doi.org/10.1111/1468-0009.12297.

González Cabrera, C. (2021). *Argentina Recognizes Non-Binary Identities*. Human Rights Watch Dispatches (July 22). Available: https://www.hrw.org/news/2021/07/22/argentina-recognizes-non-binary-identities.

Grant, D., Jans, M., Park, R., Ponce, N., Kil, J., Gates, G., Wilson, B.D.M., and Herman, J.L. (2015). *Putting the "T" in LGBT: A pilot test of questions to identify transgender people in the California Health Interview Survey*. The American Association of Public Opinion Researchers Annual Meeting, Hollywood, Florida. Available: http://www.asasrms.org/Proceedings/y2015/files/234234.pdf?msclkid=9ac120d8ab3f11ecb1142b298434c890.

Grasso, C., Goldhammer, H., Thompson, J., and Keuroghlian, A.S. (2021). Optimizing gender-affirming medical care through anatomical inventories, clinical decision support, and population health management in electronic health record systems. *Journal of the American Medical Informatics Association*, 28(11), 2531-2535. Available: doi: 10.1093/jamia/ocab080.

Grimstad, F., Kremen, J., Streed, Jr., C.R., and Dalke, K. (2021). The health care of adults with differences in sex development or intersex traits is changing: Time to prepare clinicians and health systems. *LGBT Health*, 8, 7. Available: https://doi.org/10.1089/lgbt.2021.0018.

Groves, R.M., Fowler, F.J., Couper, M.P., Lepkowski, J.M., Singer, E., and Tourangeau, R. (2009). *Survey Methodology*. Hoboken, NJ: John Wiley and Sons, Inc.

Guyan, K. (2022). Straightwashing: The cleaning and analysis of queer data. In *Queer Data: Using Gender, Sex and Sexuality Data for Action*. London, UK: Bloomsbury Academic Bloomsbury Publishing.

Haas, A.P., Lane, A.D., Blosnich, J.R., Butcher, B.A., and Mortali, M.G. (2019). Collecting sexual orientation and gender identity information at death. *American Journal of Public Health*, 109(2), 255-259. Available: doi: 10.2105/AJPH.2018.304829.

Haider, A., Adler, R.R., Schneider, E., Leitz, T.U., Ranjit, A., Ta, C., Levine, A., Harfouch, O., Pelaez, D., Kodadek, L., Vail, L., Snyder, C., German, D., Peterson, S., Schuur, J.D., and Lau, B.D. (2018). Assessment of patient-centered approaches to collect sexual orientation and gender identity information in the emergency department: The EQUALITY Study *JAMA Network Open*, 1, e186506. Available: https://pubmed.ncbi.nlm.nih.gov/30646332/.

Hahn, R.A., Wetterhall, S.F., and Gay, G.A. (2002). The recording of demographic information on death certificates: A national survey of funeral directors. *Public Health Reports*, 117 (1), 37-43. Available: https://doi.org/10.1093/phr/117.1.37.

Hall, J., Jao, L., Di Placido, C., and Manikis, R. (2021). "Deep questions for a Saturday morning": An investigation of the Australian and Canadian general public's definitions of gender. *Social Science Quarterly*, 102(4), 1866-1881.

Hankivsky, O., Springer, K.W., and Hunting, G. (2018). Beyond sex and gender difference in funding and reporting of health research. *Research Integrity and Peer Review*, 3, 6. Available: https://doi.org/10.1186/s41073-018-0050-6.

Harawa, N.T., Brewer, R., Buckman, V., Ramani, S., Khanna, A., Fujimoto, K., and Schneider, J.A. (2018). HIV, sexually transmitted infection, and substance use continuum of care interventions among criminal justice-involved Black men who have sex with men: A systematic review. *American Journal of Public Health*, 108, e1_e9. Available: https://doi.org/10.2105/AJPH.2018.304698.

Harper, G.W., and Schneider, M. (2003). Oppression and discrimination among lesbian, gay, bisexual, and transgendered people and communities: A challenge for community psychology. *American Journal of Community Psychology*, 31, 243-252. Available: https://doi.org/10.1023/A:1023906620085.

Harris, K.M., Halpern, C.T., Whitsel, E., Hussey, J., Tabor, J., Entzel, P., and Udry, J.R. (2009). The National Longitudinal Study of Adolescent to Adult Health: Research design. Available: https://addhealth.cpc.unc.edu//documentation/study-design.

Hart, C.G., Saperstein, A., Magliozzi, D., and Westbrook, L. (2019). Gender and health: Beyond binary categorical measurement. *Journal of health and social behavior*, 60(1), 101-118.

Heidari, S., Babor, T.F., De Castro, P., Tort, S., and Curno, M. (2016). Sex and Gender Equity in Research: rationale for the SAGER guidelines and recommended use. *Research Integrity and Peer Review*, 1(2). Available: https://doi.org/10.1186/s41073-016-0007-6.

Ho, F., and Mussap, A.J. (2019). The Gender Identity Scale: Adapting the Gender Unicorn to measure gender identity. *Psychology of Sexual Orientation and Gender Diversity,* 6(2), 217-231. Available: https://doi.org/10.1037/sgd0000322.

Holbrook, A., Ik, C.Y., and Johnson, T. (2006). The impact of question and respondent characteristics on comprehension and mapping difficulties. *Public Opinion Quarterly,* 70, 565-595.

Holzberg, J., Ellis, R., Kaplan, R., Virgile, M., and Edgar, J. (2019). Can they and will they? Exploring proxy response of sexual orientation and gender identity in the Current Population Survey. *Journal of Official Statistics,* 35(4), 885-911. Available: https://doi.org/10.2478/jos-2019-0037.

Holzer, L. (2018). Non-binary gender registration models in Europe: Report on third gender marker or no gender marker options. ILGA-Europe. Available: https://www.ilga-europe.org/resources/ilga-europe-reports-and-other-materials/non-binary-gender-registration-models-europe.

Indian Health Service. (2020). *Trans and Gender-Affirming care in IHS/Tribal/Urban Facilities: 2020 Strategic Vision and Action Plan.* Available: https://www.npaihb.org/wp-content/uploads/2021/05/Trans-and-Gender-Affirming-Care-2020-Strategic-Vision-and-Action-Plan_vClickable-v2.pdf.

InterACT. (n.d.). InterACT Statement on Intersex Terminology. Available: https://interactadvocates.org/interact-statement-on-intersex-terminology/.

Interagency Technical Working Group on Sexual Orientation and Gender Identity Items in the Household Pulse Survey. (2021). *Report and Recommendations.* U.S. Office of Management. Available: https://omb.report/icr/202106-0607-003/doc/112605500.

Irvine, A., and Canfield, A. (2016). The overrepresentation of lesbian, gay, bisexual, questioning, gender nonconforming and transgender youth within the child welfare to juvenile justice crossover population. *Journal of Gender, Social Policy & the Law,* 24(2), Article 2. Available: http://digitalcommons.wcl.american.edu/jgspl/vol24/iss2/2.

Ivankovich, M.B., Leichliter, J.S., and Douglas, J.M. (2013). Measurement of sexual health in the U.S.: An inventory of nationally representative surveys and surveillance systems. *Public Health Reports,* 128(2 supp), 62-72. Available: https://doi.org/10.1177%2F00333549131282S107.

Jacobs, S.E., Thomas, W., and Lang, S. (1997). Navajo cultural constructions of gender and sexuality. In *Two-Spirit People: Native American Gender Identity, Sexuality, and Spirituality* (pp. 156-173). Urbana: University of Illinois Press.

James, S.E., Herman, J.L., Rankin, S., Keisling, M., Mottet, L., and Anafi, M. (2016). *The Report of the 2015 U.S. Transgender Survey.* Washington, DC: National Center for Transgender Equality.

Jans, M., Grant, D., Park, R., Kil, J., Viana, J., Zahnd, E., Wilson, B.D.M., and Herman, J.L. (2015). Using verbal paradata monitoring and behavior coding to pilot test gender identity questions in the California Health Interview Survey: The role of qualitative and quantitative feedback. Available: http://www.asasrms.org/Proceedings/y2015/files/234238.pdf.

Jaroszewski, S., Lottridge, D., Haimson, O.L. and Quehl, K. (2018). "Genderfluid" or "attack helicopter": responsible HCI research practice with non-binary gender variation in online communities, proceedings of the CHI Conference on Human Factors in Computing Systems, Montreal, Canada. Available: https://dl.acm.org/doi/10.1145/3173574.3173881.

Jenkins, T.M., and Short, S.E. (2017). Negotiating intersex: A case for revising the theory of social diagnosis. *Social Science & Medicine,* 175, 91-98. Available: http://dx.doi.org/10.1016/j.socscimed.2016.12.047.

Jesdale, B.M. (2021a). *Influence of Imputed Sex of Birth on Gender Minority Populations in the Household Pulse Survey (The AGENID=2 Memo).* National LGBT Cancer Network. Available: https://cancer-network.org/resources/counting-gender-minority-populations-in-the-household-pulse-survey/

Jesdale, B.M. (2021b). Sources of missing sexual orientation and gender identity data in the Behavioral Risk Factor Surveillance System. *American Journal of Preventive Medicine*, 61(2), 281-290. Available: https://doi.org/10.1016/j.amepre.2021.02.027.

Johfre, S.S., and Saperstein, A. (2019). Racial and gender identities. In *State of the Union: The Poverty and Inequality Report* (Stanford Center on Poverty and Inequality, Ed.). Special issue, *Pathways*. Available: https://inequality.stanford.edu/sites/default/files/Pathways_SOTU_2019_RaceGender.pdf.

Johns, M.M., Lowry, R., Andrzejewski, J., Barrios, L.C., Demissie, Z., McManus, T., Rasberry, C.N., Robin, L., and Underwood, J.M. (2019). Transgender identity and experiences of violence victimization, substance use, suicide risk, and sexual risk behaviors among high school students—19 states and large urban school districts, 2017. *Morbidity and Mortality Weekly Report*, 68, 67-71. Available: doi: http://dx.doi.org/10.15585/mmwr.mm6803a3.

Johnson, E.K., Rosoklija, I., Finlayson, C., Chen, D., Yerkes, E.G., Madona, M.B., Holl, J.L., Baratz, A.B., David, G., and Cheng, E.Y. (2017). Attitudes towards "disorders of sex development" nomenclature among affected individuals. *Journal of Pediatric Urology*. 13(6), e601-e608. Available: https://pubmed.ncbi.nlm.nih.gov/28545802/.

Jones, J. (2021). *LGBT identification rises to 5.6% in latest US estimate*. Gallup. Available: https://news.gallup.com/poll/329708/lgbt-identification-rises-latest-estimate.aspx.

Jourian, T.J. (2015). Evolving nature of sexual orientation and gender identity. *New Directions for Student Services*, 2015(152), 11-23. Available: https://doi.org/10.1002/SS.20142.

Karkazis, K. (2008). *Fixing sex: Intersex, medical authority, and lived experience*. Durham, NC: Duke University Press.

Kelley, A., Piccione, C., Fisher, A., Matt, K., Andreini, M., and Bingham, D. (2019). Survey Development: Community Involvement in the Design and Implementation Process. *Journal of Public Health Management and Practice*, 25, S77-S83. Available: https://doi.org/10.1097/PHH.0000000000001016.

Kenagy, G.P. (2005). Transgender health: Findings from two needs assessment studies in Philadelphia. *Health & Social Work*, 30(1), 19-26.

Keuroghlian, A. (2021). Electronic health records as an equity tool for LGBTQIA+ people. *Nature Medicine*, 27, 2071-2073.

Kidd, K.M., Sequeira, G.M., Douglas, C., Paglisotti, T., Inwards-Breland, D.J., Miller, E., and Coulter, R.W.S. (2021). Prevalence of gender-diverse youth in an urban school district. *Pediatrics*, 147(6). Available: https://doi.org/10.1542/peds.2020-049823.

Kim, Y.S., and Kim, N. (2018). Sex-Gender Differences in Irritable Bowel Syndrome. *Journal of Neurogastroenterology and Motility*, 24, 544-558. Available: https://doi.org/10.5056/jnm18082.

Knauper, B., Belli, R.F., Hill, D.H., and Herzog, A.R. (1997). Question difficulty and respondents' cognitive ability: The effect on data quality. *Journal of Official Statistics*, 13, 181-199.

Knutson, D., Koch, J.M., Arthur, T., Mitchell, T.A., and Martyr, M.A. (2016). "Trans broken arm": Health care stories from transgender people in rural areas. *Journal of Research on Women and Gender*, 7(1), pp. 30-46.

Krosnick, J. (1999). Survey research. *Annual Review of Psychology*, 50, pp. 537-567.

Krosnick, J.A., and Alwin, D. (1987). An evaluation of a cognitive theory of response-order effects in survey measurement. *Public Opinion Quarterly*, 51(2), 201-219.

Krueger, R.A. (1994). *Focus groups: A practical guide for applied research*. Thousand Oaks, CA: Sage.

Kuhne, S., Kroh, M., and Richter, D. (2019). Comparing self-reported and partnership-inferred sexual orientation in household surveys. *Journal of Official Statistics*, 35(4), 777-805.

LaFleur, G. (2021). *Trans Historical: Gender Plurality Before the Modern.* Ithaca, NY: Cornell University Press.

Lagos, D. (2018). Looking at population health beyond "male" and "female": Implications of transgender identity and gender nonconformity for population health. *Demography*, 55(6), 2097-2117. Available: https://doi.org/10.1007/s13524-018-0714-3.

Lassiter, J.M. (2014). Extracting dirt from water: A strengths-based approach to religion for African American same-gender-loving men. *Journal of Religion and Health*, 53, 178-189. Available: https://doi.org/10.1007/s10943-012-9668-8.

Lau, J.S., Kline-Simon, A., Sterling, S., Hojilla, J.C., and Hartman, L. (2021). Screening for Gender Identity in Adolescent Well Visits: Is It Feasible and Acceptable? *Journal of Adolescent Health*, 68, 6, pp. 1089-1095. Available: https://doi.org/10.1016/j.jadohealth.2020.07.031.

Laumann, E., Gagnon, J.H., Michael, R.T., and Michaels, S. (1994). *The Social Organization of Sexuality: Sexual Practices in the United States.* Chicago: University of Chicago Press.

Lee, P.A., Houk, C.P., Ahmed, S.F., and Hughes, I.A., and International Consensus Conference on Intersex organized by the Lawson Wilkins Pediatric Endocrine Society and the European Society for Paediatric Endocrinology. (2006). *Consensus statement on management of intersex disorders. Pediatrics*, 118(2), e488-e500.

Lee, S., Fredriksen-Goldsen, K.I., McClain, C., Kim, H.-J., and Suzer-Gurtekin, Z.T. (2018). Are sexual minorities less likely to participate in surveys? An examination of proxy nonresponse measures and associated biases with sexual orientation in a population-based health survey. *Field Method*, 30(3), 208-224. Available: doi: 10.1177/1525822X18777736.

Lindqvist, A., Sendén. M.G., and Renström E.A. (2021). What is gender, anyway: a review of the options for operationalising gender, *Psychology & Sexuality*, 12(4), 332-344. Available: DOI: 10.1080/19419899.2020.1729844.

Lombardi, E., and Banik, S. (2016). The utility of the two-step gender measure within trans and cis populations. *Sexuality Research and Social Policy*, 13(3), 288-296.

Lowry, R., Johns, M.M., Gordon, A.R., Austin, S.B., Robin, L.E., and Kann, L.K. (2018). Nonconforming gender expression and associated mental distress and substance use among high school students. *JAMA Pediatrics*, 172(11), 1020-1028.

Magliozzi, D., Saperstein, A., and Westbrook, L. (2016). Scaling up: Representing gender diversity in survey research. *Socius.* Available: https://doi.org/10.1177/2378023116664352.

Maier, M.B. (2019). Parental gender designations on children's birth certificates: The need for a modifiable form. *DePaul Journal of Women, Gender and Law*, 8, 1.

Malatino, H., and Stoltzfus-Brown, L. (2020). *Best Practices for Gender Inclusion in Research.* Available: https://covidupdates.la.psu.edu/wp-content/uploads/sites/9/Gender-Inclusion-in-Research.pdf.

Mallory, C., and Sears, B. (2016). *Evidence of Housing Discrimination Based on Sexual Orientation and Gender Identity: An Analysis of Complaints Filed with State Enforcement Agencies, 2008-2014.* Williams Institute. Available: https://williamsinstitute.law.ucla.edu/publications/lgbt-housing-discrimination-us/.

Marksamer, J., and Tobin, H.J. (2014). *Standing with LGBT Prisoners: An Advocate's Guide to Ending Abuse and Combating Imprisonment.* Report of the National Center for Transgender Equality, Washington, D.C. Available: https://transequality.org/sites/default/files/docs/resources/JailPrisons_Resource_FINAL.pdf.

Martinez, M., Henderson, A., Luck, J., and Davis, M.C. (2017). *Cognitive Pretesting of the NCVS Survey Supplement Victimization Survey.* U.S. Census Bureau, Center for Survey Measurement. Available: https://www.census.gov/library/working-papers/2017/adrm/rsm2017-03.html.

Matsuno, E., and Budge, S.L. (2017). Non-binary/genderqueer identities: A critical review of the literature. *Current Sexual Health Reports*, 9, 116-120.

Mays, V.M., and Cochran, S.D. (2019). Challenges and opportunities for modernizing the national violent death reporting system. *American Journal of Public Health*, 109(2), 192-194. Available: DOI: 10.2105/AJPH.2018.304891.

McCall, G.J. (2003). The me and the not-me: Positive and negative poles of identity. In P.J. Burke, T.J. Owens, R.T. Sherpe, and P.A. Thoits (Eds.), *Advances in Identity Theory and Research* (pp. 11-25). New York: Kluwer Academic/Plenum Publishers.

McDonnell, D., Goldman, A., and Koumjian, K. (2020). *Asking Sexual Orientation and Identity Questions in a Respectful and Inclusive Way.* Available: https://harderco.com/asking-sexual-orientation-and-identity-questions-in-a-respectful-and-inclusive-way/.

Medeiros, M., Forest, B., and Ohberg, P. (2020). The case for non-binary gender questions in surveys, *PS: Political Science & Politics*, 53(1): 128-35.

Medicare and Medicaid Programs. (2015). *Electronic Health Record Incentive Program-Stage 3 and Modifications to Meaningful Use in 2015 Through 2017.* (October 16, 2015). Rule 80 FR 62761, 62761-62955. Available: https://www.federalregister.gov/documents/2015/10/16/2015-25595/medicare-and-medicaid-programs-electronic-health-record-incentive-program-stage-3-and-modifications.

Melendez, R.M., Exner, T.A., Ehrhardt, A.A., Dodge, B., Remien, R.H., Rotheram-Borus, J.-J., Lightfoot, M., Hong, D., and the National Institute of Mental Health Healthy Living Project Team. (2006). Health and health care among male-to-female transgender persons who are HIV positive. *American Journal of Public Health*, 96(6), 1034-1037. Available: https://doi.org/10.2105/AJPH.2004.042010.

Meyer, I.H., Luo, F., Wilson, B.D.M., and Stone, D.M. (2019). Sexual orientation enumeration in state antibullying statutes in the United States: Associations with bullying, suicidal ideation, and suicide attempts among youth. *LGBT Health*, 6(1), 9-14. Available: http://doi.org/10.1089/lgbt.2018.0194.

Meyer, I.H., Marken, S., Auter, Z., Wilson, B.D.M., and Conron, K. (2019). *Asking About Sexual Orientation in a National General Population Survey: Do Expanded Response Options Improve Survey Performance with Sexual Minority Respondents?* Annual Meeting of the American Association of Public Opinion Researchers, May 16-19, Toronto, Canada.

Meyer, I., Flores, A., Stemple, L., Romero, A., Wilson, B.D.M., and Herman, J. (2016). Incarceration rates and traits of sexual minorities in the United States: National Inmate Survey, 2011–2012. *American Journal of Public Health*, 107(2), 267-273. Available: https://pubmed.ncbi.nlm.nih.gov/27997242/.

Meyer, I.H., Rossano, L., Ellis, J.M., and Bradford, J. (2002). A brief telephone interview to identify lesbian and bisexual women in random digit dialing sampling. *The Journal of Sex Research*, 39(2), 139-144. Available: DOI: 10.1080/00224490209552133.

Meyerowitz, J.J. (2002). *How sex changed: A history of transsexuality in the United States.* Cambridge, Mass: Harvard University Press.

Michaels, S., Milesi, C., Stern, M., Viox, M.H., Morrison, H., Guerino, P., Dragon, C.N., and Haffer, S.C. (2017). Improving measures of sexual and gender identity in English and Spanish to identify LGBT older adults in surveys. *LGBT Health*, 4(6), 412-418. Available: https://doi.org/10.1089/lgbt.2016.0168.

Miller, K. (2001). *Cognitive testing of the NHANES sexual orientation questions.* Q-Bank. Available: http://www.cdc.gov/qbank.

Miller, L.R., and Grollman, E.A. (2015). The social costs of gender nonconformity for transgender adults: Implications for discrimination and health. *Sociological Forum*, 30(3), 809-831.

Miller, L., Leeth, E.A., Johnson, E.K., Rosoklija, I., Chen, D., Aufox, S.A., and Finlayson, C. (2018). Attitudes toward 'disorders of sex development' nomenclature among physicians, genetic counselors, and mental health clinicians. *Journal of Pediatric Urology*, 14(5), 418 e411-418 e417. Available: doi:10.1016/j.jpurol.2018.08.009.

Miller, K., and Ryan, J.M. (2011). *Design, development and testing of the NHIS sexual identity question.* Hyattsville, MD: National Center for Health Statistics.

Miller, K., Willson, S., and Ryan, V. (2021). *An Initial Cognitive Evaluation of a 2-Step Gender Identity Measure.* National Center for Health Statistics, Questionnaire Design Research Laboratory. Available: https://wwwn.cdc.gov/QBank/Report.aspx?1219.

Montañez, A. (2017). Beyond XX and XY. *Scientific American, 317*(3), 50-51. Available: doi:10.1038/scientificamerican0917-50.

Moore, M. (2018). Collecting qualitative data on less visible and marginalized populations. In *Other, Please Specify: _____ : Queer Methods in Sociology,* D. Compton, R. Meadow, and K. Schilt. Berkeley, CA: University of California Press.

Morris, B.J. (2009). *History of Lesbian, Gay, Bisexual and Transgender Social Movements.* Available: https://www.apa.org/pi/lgbt/resources/history.

Morrison, T., Dinno, A., and Salmon, T. (2021). The erasure of intersex, transgender, nonbinary, and agender experiences through misuse of sex and gender in health research. *American Journal of Epidemiology,* 190(12), 2712-2717. Available: doi: 10.1093/aje/kwab221.

Mortality Disparities in American Communities. (2017). Mortality Disparities in American Communities Analysis File Reference Manual, Version 1.0 (May 30, 2017). https://www.census.gov/content/dam/Census/about/about-the-bureau/adrm/MDAC/MDAC%20Reference%20Manual%20V1_6_21_17.pdf.

Mulkey, N., Streed, Jr., C.G., and Chubak, B.M. (2021). A call to update standard of care for children with differences in sex development. *AMA Journal of Ethics,* 23(7), E550-E556.

National Academies of Sciences, Engineering, and Medicine. (2020). *Understanding the Well-Being of LGBTQI+ Populations.* Washington, D.C.: National Academies Press.

National Academies of Sciences, Engineering, and Medicine. (2018). *Sexual Harassment of Women: Climate, Culture, and Consequences in Academic Sciences, Engineering, and Medicine.* Washington, D.C.: National Academies Press.

National Center for Health Statistics. (2021). 2020 National Health Interview Survey: Codebook for sample adult file. Available: https://ftp.cdc.gov/pub/Health_Statistics/NCHS/Dataset_Documentation/NHIS/2020/adult-codebook.pdf.

National Center for Health Statistics. (2016). The validity of race and Hispanic-origin reporting on death certificates in the United States: An update. *Vital and Health Statistics Reports,* Series 2, Number 172. https://www.cdc.gov/nchs/data/series/sr_02/sr02_172.pdf.

National Center for Health Statistics. (2003a). *Medical Examiners' and Coroners' Handbook on Death Registration and Fetal Death Reporting.* (2003 Revision). DHHS Publication Number (PHS) 2003-1110. Available: https://www.cdc.gov/nchs/data/misc/hb_me.pdf.

National Center for Health Statistics. (2003b). *Physician's Handbook on Medical Certification on Death.* (2003 Revision). DHHS Publication Number (PHS) 2003-1108. Available: https://www.cdc.gov/nchs/data/misc/hb_cod.pdf.

National Congress of American Indians. (2021). Data Disaggregation and the Asterisk Nation. NCAI Policy Research Center. https://www.ncai.org/policy-research-center/research-data/data.

National Institutes of Health. (2015). *Consideration of Sex as a Biological Variable in NIH-funded Research.* Companion Reference to Notice Number NOT-OD-15-102. Available: https://orwh.od.nih.gov/sites/orwh/files/docs/NOT-OD-15-102_Guidance.pdf.

National Longitudinal Mortality Study. (2014). Variable Reference Manual for the National Longitudinal Mortality Study Extract and Analysis Files Version 4.0 (July 1, 2014). U.S. Census Bureau: Washington, DC. https://www.census.gov/content/dam/Census/about/about-the-bureau/adrm/MDAC/NLMS%20Reference%20Manual%20Version.pdf.

National Public Radio, Robert Wood Johnson Foundation, and the Harvard T.H. Chan School of Public Health. (2017). Discrimination in America: Experiences and Views of LGBTQ Americans. Available: https://www.rwjf.org/content/dam/farm/reports/surveys_and_polls/2017/rwjf441734.

National Research Council. (2009). *Vital Statistics: Summary of a Workshop*. Washington, DC: The National Academies Press.

Newberry, L. (2019). These L.A. parents don't want to assign a gender to their baby, so the government did it for them. *Los Angeles Times*, September 25. Available: https://www.latimes.com/california/story/2019-09-24/gender-neutral-non-binary-baby.

Office of Management and Budget. (1997). Revisions to the Standards for the Classification of Federal Data on Race and Ethnicity. *Federal Register*, 62, 210, 58782-58790.

Office of National Statistics. (2021). *Sex and Gender Identity Question Development for Census 2021*. Available: https://www.ons.gov.uk/census/censustransformationprogramme/questiondevelopment/sexandgenderidentityquestiondevelopmentforcensus2021.

Office of National Statistics. (2016). *Sexual Identity Guidance and Project: Guidance for Users of Statistics and Organisations that Wish to Collect Data on Sexual Identity*. Available: https://www.ons.gov.uk/methodology/classificationsandstandards/sexualidentityguidanceandprojectdocumentation.

O'Hara, M.E. (2016). *Nation's First Known Intersex Birth Certificate Issued in NYC. NBC News* (December 29). Available: https://www.nbcnews.com/feature/nbc-out/nation-s-first-known-intersex-birth-certificate-issued-nyc-n701186.

Olson, K. (2010). An examination of questionnaire evaluation by expert reviewers. *Field Methods*, 22(4), 295-318. Available: https://doi.org/10.1177/1525822X10379795.

O'Neill, K., Wilson, B.D.M., and Herman, J.L. (2020). *Homeless Shelter Access among Transgender Adults Findings from the 2015 US Transgender Survey*. Los Angeles, CA: Williams Institute.

Ongena, Y., and Dijkstra, W. (2006). Methods of behavior coding survey interviews. *Journal of Official Statistics*, 22(3), 419-451.

Ortman, J., Bates, N., Brown, A., and Sawyer, R.C. (2017). *Optimizing Self and Proxy Response to Survey Questions on Sexual Orientation and Gender Identity*. Presentation at the 2017 Population Association of America Conference. Chicago, IL, USA.

Pachankis, J.E., and Bränström, R. (2018). Hidden from happiness: Structural stigma, sexual orientation concealment, and life satisfaction across 28 countries. *Journal of Consulting and Clinical Psychology*, 86(5), 403-415. Available: http://dx.doi.org/10.1037/ccp0000299.

Pachankis, J.E., Mahon, C.P., Jackson, S.D., Fetzner, B.K., and Bränström, R. (2020). Sexual orientation concealment and mental health: A conceptual and meta-analytic review. *Psychological Bulletin*, 146(10), 831-871. Available: https://doi.org/10.1037/bul0000271.

Patterson, J.G., Jabson, J.M., and Bowen, D.J. (2017). Measuring sexual and gender minority populations in health surveillance. *LGBT Health*, 4(2), 82-105. Available: DOI: 10.1089/lgbt.2016.0026.

Peek, M.E., Lopez, F.Y., Williams, H.S., Xu, L.J., McNulty, M.C., Acree, M.E., and Schneider, J.A. (2016). Development of a conceptual framework for understanding shared decision making among African-American LGBT patients and their clinicians. *Journal of General Internal Medicine*, 31(6), 677-687.

Pember, M.A. (2016). 'Two-Spirit' Tradition Far from Ubiquitous among Tribes. rewire news group. Available: https://rewirenewsgroup.com/article/2016/10/13/Two-Spirit-tradition-far-ubiquitous-among-tribes/.

Pryzgoda, J., and Chrisler, J.C. (2000). Definitions of gender and sex: The subtleties of meaning. *Sex Roles*, 43(7/8), 553-569.

Presser, S., Couper, M.P., Lessler, J.T., Martin, E., Martin, J., Rothgeb, J.M., and Singer, E. (2004). Methods for testing and evaluating survey questions. *Public Opinion Quarterly*, 1(68), 109-130.

Pruden, H., and Edmo, S. (2016). Two-Spirit people: Sex, gender & sexuality in historic and contemporary native America. *National Congress of American Indians Policy Research Center*. Available: https://www.ncai.org/policy-research-center/initiatives/Pruden-Edmo_TwoSpiritPeople.pdf.

Puckett, J.A., Brown, N.C., Dunn, T., Mustanski, B., and Newcomb, M.E. (2020). Perspectives from transgender and gender diverse people on how to ask about gender. *LGBT Health*, 7(6), 305-311.

Quinan, C.L., and Bresser, N. (2020). Gender at the border: Global responses to gender-diverse subjectivities and nonbinary registration practices. *Global Perspectives*, 1(1).

Reis, E. (2021). How intersex erasure sustained the sex and gender binary: A history. Public Workshop for the Committee on Measuring Sex, Gender Identity, and Sexual Orientation. (July 19). Washington, DC: National Academies of Sciences, Engineering, and Medicine.

Reis, E. (2012). *Bodies in Doubt: An American History of Intersex*. Baltimore, MD: Johns Hopkins University Press.

Reisner, S.L., Conron, K.J., Scout, Baker, K., Herman, J.L., Lombardi, E., Greytak, E.A., Gill, A.M., and Matthews, A.K. (2015). "Counting" transgender and gender-nonconforming adults in health research: Recommendations from the Gender Identity in US Surveillance Group. *Transgender Studies Quarterly*, 2, 34-57.

Reisner, S.L., Conron, K.J., Tardiff, L.A., Jarvi, S., Gordon, A.R., and Austin, S.B. (2014). Monitoring the health of transgender and other gender minority populations: Validity of natal sex and gender identity survey items in a U.S. national cohort of young adults. *BMC Public Health*, 14, 1224. Available: https://doi.org/10.1186/1471-2458-14-1224.

Reisner, S.L., and Hughto, J.M.W. (2019). Comparing the health of non-binary and binary transgender adults in a statewide non-probability sample. *PLoS ONE*, 14(8), e0221583. Available: https://doi.org/10.1371/journal.pone.0221583.

Remafedi, G., Resnick, M., Blum, R., and Harris, L. (1992). Demography of sexual orientation in adolescents. *Pediatrics*, 89(4), 714-721. Available: https://doi.org/10.1542/peds.89.4.714.

Reuters. (2021). *U.S. Issues First Passport with 'X' Gender Marker*. Reuters Press Service (October 27). Available: https://www.reuters.com/world/us/us-issues-first-passport-with-x-gender-marker-2021-10-27/.

Reuters. (2019). *Nonbinary? Intersex? 11 U.S. States Issuing Third Gender IDs*. Reuters Press Service (January 31). Available: https://www.reuters.com/article/us-us-lgbt-lawmaking/nonbinary-intersex-11-u-s-states-issuing-third-gender-ids-idUSKCN1PP2N7.

Richards, C., Bouman, W.P., and Barker, M.-J. (2017). *Genderqueer and Non-Binary Genders*. London, UK: Palgrave McMillan.

Ridolfo, H., Miller, K., and Maitland, A. (2012). Measuring sexual identity using survey questionnaires: How valid are our measures? *Sexuality Research & Social Policy: A Journal of the NSRC*, 9(2), 113-124. Available: https://doi.org/10.1007/s13178-011-0074-x.

Robinson, M. (2020). Two-Spirit identity in a time of gender fluidity. *Journal of Homosexuality*, 67(12), 1675-1690.

Romero, A.P., Goldberg, S.K., and Vasquez, L.A. (2020). *LGBT People and Housing Affordability, Discrimination, and Homelessness*. Williams Institute. Available: https://escholarship.org/content/qt3cb5b8zj/qt3cb5b8zj.pdf.

Rosenwohl-Mack, A., Tamar-Mattis, S., Baratz, A.B., Dalke, K.B., Ittelson, A., Zieselman, K., and Flatt, J.D. (2020). A national study on the physical and mental health of intersex adults in the U.S. *PLoS One*, 15(10), e0240088.

Rothblum, E.D., Krueger, E.A., Kittle, K.R., and Meyer, I.H. (2020). Asexual and non-asexual respondents from a U.S. population-based study of sexual minorities. *Archives of Sexual Behavior*, 49, 757-767. Available: https://doi.org/10.1007/s10508-019-01485-0.

Ruben, M.A., Blosnich, J.R., Dichter, M.E., Luscri, L., and Shipherd, J.C. (2017). Will veterans answer sexual orientation and gender identity questions? *Medical Care*, 55(Suppl 9 Suppl 2). S85-S89. Available: doi: 10.1097/MLR.0000000000000744.

Rubin, G. (1984). Thinking sex: Notes for a radical theory of the politics of sexuality. In *Pleasure and Danger: Exploring Female Sexuality*, C.S. Vance, Ed., pp. 267-319. Boston: Routledge and Kegan Paul.

Rullo, J.E., Foxen, J.L., Griffin, J.M., Geske, J.R., Gonzalez, C.A., Faubion, S.S., and van Ryn, M. (2018). Patient acceptance of sexual orientation and gender identity questions on intake forms in outpatient clinics: a pragmatic randomized multisite trial. *Health Services Research*, 53(5), 3790-3808. Available: doi: 10.1111/1475-6773.12843.

Russomanno, J., and Jabson Tree, J.M. (2020). Food insecurity and food pantry use among transgender and gender non-conforming people in the Southeast United States. *BMC Public Health*, 20, 590. Available: https://doi.org/10.1186/s12889-020-08684-8.

Saewyc, E.M., Bauer, G.R., Skay, C.L., Bearinger, L.H., Resnick, M.D., Reis, E., and Murphy A. (2004). Measuring sexual orientation in adolescent health surveys: Evaluation of eight school-based surveys. Journal of Adolescent Health, 35(4), 345.e1-15. Available: doi: 10.1016/j.jadohealth.2004.06.002.

Sahota, P. (2007). Research Regulation in American Indian/Alaska Native Communities: Policy and Practice Considerations NCAI Policy Research Center. Available: https://www.ncai.org/policy-research-center/initiatives/Research_Regulation_in_AI_AN_Communities_-_Policy_and_Practice.pdf.

San Francisco Human Services Agency. (2020). *Collection of Sexual Orientation and Gender Identity Data: FY19-20 Annual Report*. Available: https://www.sfhsa.org/sites/default/files/Report_SOGI%20FY19-20.pdf.

Sanderson, M., and S. Immerwahr. (2019). New York City Community Health Survey: SOGI Measurement. PowerPoint presented at SOGI Measurement Interagency Workgroup, Washington, DC, on June 4, 2019.

Saperstein, A. (2022). Stability of Two-Step Sex and Gender Responses in U.S. Panel Data. Population Association of America Annual Meeting, Atlanta, GA.

Saperstein, A., and Westbrook, L. (2021). Categorical and gradational: Alternative survey measures of sex and gender. *European Journal of Politics and Gender*, 4(1), 11-30.

Saperstein, A., Westbrook, L., Magliozzi, D., and Hart, C. (2019). *Alternative Gender Measures Survey: User's Guide and Codebook*. Stanford, CA: Clayman Institute for Gender Research. Available: https://www.openicpsr.org/openicpsr/project/109542/version/V1/view.

Sausa, L.A., Sevelius, J., Keatley, J., Iñiguez, J.R., and Reyes, M. (2009). *Policy Recommendations for Inclusive Data Collection of Trans People in HIV Prevention, Care & Services*. Center of Excellence for Transgender HIV Prevention: University of California, San Francisco. Available: https://prevention.ucsf.edu/transhealth/education/data-recs-long.

Scheim, A.I., and Bauer, G.R. (2014). Sex and gender diversity among transgender persons in Ontario, Canada: Results from a respondent-driven sampling survey. *The Journal of Sex Research*, 52, 1, 1-14. Available: https://doi.org/10.1080/00224499.2014.893553.

Schilt, K., and Bratter, J. (2015). From multiracial to transgender? Assessing attitudes toward expanding gender options on the US census. *Transgender Studies Quarterly*, 2(1), 77-100.

Schudson, Z.C., Beischel, W.J., and van Anders, S.M. (2019). Individual variation in gender/sex category definitions. *Psychology of Sexual Orientation and Gender Diversity*, 6(4), 448-460. Available: https://doi.org/10.1037/sgd0000346.

Scotland's Census. (2021). *Scotland's Census 2022 Question Set.* Available: https://www. scotlandscensus.gov.uk/documents/scotland-s-census-2022-question-set/.

Sell, R.L. (1997). Defining and measuring sexual orientation: A review. *Archives of Sexual Behavior,* 26, 643-658. Available: https://doi.org/10.1023/A:1024528427013.

Sell, R.L., and Krims, E.I. (2021). Structural Transphobia, Homophobia, and Biphobia in Public Health Practice: The Example of COVID-19 Surveillance. *American Journal of Public Health,* 111(9), 1620-1626. Available: https://pubmed.ncbi.nlm.nih.gov/34111944/.

Sexual Minority Assessment Research Team. (2009). *Best Practices for Asking Questions About Sexual Orientation on Surveys.* Los Angeles: The Williams Institute, UCLA School of Law. Available: https://williamsinstitute.law.ucla.edu/publications/smart-so-survey/.

Shannon, M. (2021). The labour market outcomes of transgender individuals. *Labour Economics.* Available: https://doi.org/10.1016/j.labeco.2021.102006.

Shteyler, V.M. (2021). *Medicolegal issues related to legal sex designations.* Public Workshop for the Committee on Measuring Sex, Gender Identity, and Sexual Orientation. (July 19). Washington, DC: National Academies of Sciences, Engineering, and Medicine.

Shteyler, V.M., Clarke, J.A., and Adashi, E.Y. (2020). Failed assignments—Rethinking sex designations on birth certificates. *New England Journal of Medicine,* 383(25). 2399-2401. Available: Available: DOI: 10.1056/NEJMp2025974.

Smet, M.-E., Scott, F.P., and McLennan, A.C. (2020). Discordant fetal sex on NIPT and ultrasound. *Prenatal Diagnosis,* 40(11), 1353-1365. Available: https://doi.org/10.1002/pd.5676.

Smith, T. W., and Son, J. (2019). Transgender and alternative gender measurement on the 2018 General Social Survey (GSS Methodology Report No. 129). Chicago, IL: NORC at the University of Chicago.

Smith, T., and Son, J. (2011). *An Analysis of Panel Attrition and Panel Change on the 2006-2008 General Social Survey Panel.* GSS Methodological Report No. 118. Available: http://gss.norc.org/Documents/reports/methodological-reports/MR118.pdf.

Snorton, C.R. (2017). *Black on Both Sides: A Racial History of Trans Identity.* Minneapolis, MN: University of Minnesota Press.

Springer, K.W., Stellman, J.M., and Jordan-Young, R.M. (2012). Beyond a catalogue of differences: A theoretical frame and good practice guidelines for researching sex/gender in human health. *Social Science & Medicine,* 74(11), 1817-1824.

Stall, R., Dodge, B., Bauermeister, J.A., Poteat, T., and Beyrer, C. (2020). *LGBTQ Health Research: Theory, Methods, Practice.* Baltimore, MD: Johns Hopkins University Press.

State Health Access Data Assistance Center. (2021). Collection of sexual orientation and gender identity (SOGI) data: Considerations for Medicaid and spotlight on Oregon. *State Health & Value Strategies Issue Brief.* Available: https://www.shvs.org/wp-content/uploads/2021/10/SOGI-Data-Collection-in-Medicaid_SHVS-Issue-Brief_Revised.pdf.

Statistics Canada. (2021). *2021 Census Fact Sheets: Updated Content for the 2021 Census of Population: Family and Demographic Concepts, and Activities of Daily Living.* Available: https://www12.statcan.gc.ca/census-recensement/2021/ref/98-20-0001/982000012020001-eng.pdf.

Statistics Canada. (2020). *Measurement of Sexual Orientation at Statistics Canada.* UNECE Virtual Meetings on Gender Statistics (October 14). Available: https://unece.org/fileadmin/DAM/stats/documents/ece/ces/ge.30/2020/mtg3/prokopenko_canada_eng.pdf.

Stats NZ. (2021). *Statistical Standard for Gender, Sex, and Variations of Sex Characteristics.* Available: https://www.stats.govt.nz/methods/statistical-standard-for-gender-sex-and-variations-of-sex-characteristics.

Stats NZ. (2019). *Statistical Standard for Sexual Identity.* Available: https://www.stats.govt.nz/assets/News/Sexual-identity-standard.pdf.

Steiger, D., Heaton, L., Behm, J., MacAllum, C., and Stroop, J. (2017). *Improving the Measurement of Sexual Orientation and Gender Identity among Youth*. American Association for Public Opinion Research Annual Meeting, (May 18-21), New Orleans, LA.

Streed, Jr., C.G., Beach, L.B., Caceres, B.A., Dowshen, N.L., Moreau, K.L., Mukherjee, M., Poteat, T., Radix, A., Reisner, S.L., Singh, V., and on behalf of the American Heart Association Council on Peripheral Vascular Disease; Council on Arteriosclerosis, Thrombosis and Vascular Biology; Council on Cardiovascular and Stroke Nursing; Council on Cardiovascular Radiology and Intervention; Council on Hypertension; and Stroke Council. (2021). Assessing and Addressing Cardiovascular Health in People Who Are Transgender and Gender Diverse: A Scientific Statement from the American Heart Association. *Circulation*, 144(6), e136-e148. Available: https://doi.org/10.1161/CIR.0000000000001003.

Streed, C.G., Grasso, C., and Mayer, K.H. (2020). Sexual orientation and gender identity data collection: Clinical and public health importance. *American Journal of Public Health*, 110(7), 991-993.

Streed, C.G., McCarthy, E.P., and Haas, J.S. (2018). Self-reported physical and mental health of gender nonconforming transgender adults in the United States. *LGBT Health*, 443-448. Available: doi: 10.1089/lgbt.2017.0275.

Stryker, S. (2008). *Transgender History*. Berkeley, CA: Seal Press.

Stuhlsatz, M.A.M., Buck Bracey, Z.E., and Donovan, B.M. (2020). Investigating conflation of sex and gender language in student writing about genetics. *Science & Education*, 29, 1567-1594. Available: https://doi.org/10.1007/s11191-020-00177-9.

Suen, L.W., Lunn, M.R., Seveliusn J.M., Flentje, A., Capriotti, M.R., Lubensky, M.E., Hunt, C., Weber, S., Bahati. M., Rescate, A., Dastur, Z., and Obedin-Maliver, J. (2022). Do ask, tell, and show: Contextual factors affecting sexual orientation and gender identity disclosure for sexual and gender minority people. *LGBT Health*. Available: doi: 10.1089/lgbt.2021.0159.

Suen, L.W., Lunn, M.R., Katuzny, K., Finn, S., Duncan, L., Sevelius, J., Flentje, A., Capriotti, M.R., Lubensky, M.E., Hunt, C., Weber, S., Bibbins-Domingo, K., and Obedin-Maliver, J. (2020). What sexual and gender minority people want researchers to know about sexual orientation and gender identity questions: A qualitative study. Archives of Sexual Behavior, 49, 2301–2318. Available: https://doi.org/10.1007/s10508-020-01810-y.

Tamar-Mattis, S., Gamarel, K.E., Kantor, A., Baratz, A., Tamar-Mattis, A., and Operario, D. (2018). Identifying and counting individuals with differences of sex development conditions in population health research. *LGBT Health*, 5(5), 320-324. Available: doi:10.1089/lgbt.2017.0180.

Tate, C.C., Ledbetter, J.N., and Youssef, C.P. (2013). A two-question method for assessing gender categories in the social and medical sciences. *Journal of Sex Research*, 50(8), 767-776. Available: 10.1080/00224499.2012.690110.

Therrell, B.L., Jr., Berenbaum, S.A., Manter-Kapanke, V., Simmank, J., Korman, K., Prentice, L., Gonzalez, J., and Gunn, S. (1998). Results of screening 1.9 million Texas newborns for 21-hydroxylase-deficient congenital adrenal hyperplasia. *Pediatrics*, 101(4 Pt 1), 583.

Thorne, N., Yip, A.K., Bouman, W.P., Marshall, E., and Arcelus, J. (2019). The terminology of identities between, outside and beyond the gender binary - A systematic review. *The International Journal of Transgenderism*, 20(2-3), 138-154. Available: https://doi.org/10.1080/15532739.2019.1640654.

Tolman, D.L., Diamond, L.M., Bauermeister, J.A., George, W.H., Pfaus, J.G., and Ward, L.M. (Eds.). (2014). *APA Handbook of Sexuality and Psychology*. Washington, DC: American Psychological Association.

Tomlinson, Y., and Baruch, M. (2013). *Framing Questions on Intersectionality*. U.S. Human Rights Network. Available: https://ushrnetwork.org/uploads/Resources/framing_questions_on_intersectionality_1.pdf.

Tordoff, D.M., Morgan, J., Dombrowski, J.C., Golden, M.R., and Barbee, L.A. (2019). Increased ascertainment of transgender and non-binary patients using a 2-step versus 1-step gender identity intake question in an STD clinic setting. *Sexually Transmitted Diseases*, 46(4), 254-259. Available: https://doi.org/10.1097/olq.0000000000000952.

Traglia, M., Bseiso D., Gusev, A., Adviento, B., Park, D.S., Mefford, J.A., Zaitlen. N., and Weiss, L.A. (2017). Genetic Mechanisms leading to sex differences across common diseases and anthropometric traits. *Genetics*, 205(2), 979-992. Available: https://dx.doi.org/10.1534%2Fgenetics.116.193623.

Truman, J., Morgan, R., Gilbert, T., and Vaghela, P. (2019). Measuring sexual orientation and gender identity in the National Crime Victimization Survey. *Journal of Official Statistics*, 35(4), 835-858. Available: 10.2478/jos-2019-0035.

United Nations Economic Commission for Europe. (2019). *In-Depth Review of Measuring Gender Identity*. Conference of European Statisticians, 67th plenary session. Available: https://unece.org/DAM/stats/documents/ece/ces/2019/ECE_CES_2019_19-G1910227E.pdf.

U.S. Census Bureau. (2021). Household Pulse Survey, Detailed Tables, Weeks 34-39. Available: https://www.census.gov/programs-surveys/household-pulse-survey/data.html.

U.S. Equal Employment Opportunity Commission. (2021). Protections Against Employment Discrimination Based on Sexual Orientation or Gender Identity. Available: https://www.eeoc.gov/laws/guidance/protections-against-employment-discrimination-based-sexual-orientation-or-gender.

U.S. Department of Health and Human Services-Office of Minority Health. (2013). *National Standards for Culturally and Linguistically Appropriate Services (CLAS) in Health and Health Care*. Document Citation 78 FR 58539. Document Number 2013-231-64. Available: https://www.federalregister.gov/documents/2013/09/24/2013-23164/national-standards-for-culturally-and-linguistically-appropriate-services-clas-in-health-and-health.

U.S. Department of Health and Human Services. (2013). National Standards for Culturally and Linguistically Appropriate Services (CLAS) in Health and Health Care. Office of Minority Health. Available: https://thinkculturalhealth.hhs.gov/clas.

U.S. Department of Justice. (2015). *Protecting the Rights of Lesbian, Gay, Bisexual, Transgender, and Intersex (LGBTI) Individuals*. Civil Rights Division. Available: https://www.ada.gov/hiv/lgbti_brochure.html.

U.S. Department of State. (2021). Need a Passport: Selecting Your Gender Marker. Available: https://travel.state.gov/content/travel/en/passports/need-passport/selecting-your-gender-marker.html.

van Anders, S.M. (2015). Beyond sexual orientation: Integrating gender/sex and diverse sexualities via sexual configurations theory. *Archives of Sexual Behavior*, 44, 1177-1213. Available: https://doi.org/10.1007/s10508-015-0490-8.

Vela, M.B., Erondu, A.I., Smith, N.A., Peek, M.E., Woodruff, J.N., and Chin, M.H. (2022). Eliminating explicit and implicit biases in health care: Evidence and research needs. *Annual Review of Public Health*. Available: doi: 10.1146/annurev-publhealth-052620-103528.

Vivienne, S., Hanckel, B., Byron, P., Robards, B., and Churchill, B. (2021). The social life of data: Strategies for categorizing fluid and multiple genders. *Journal of Gender Studies*, 1-15. Available: https://doi.org/10.1080/09589236.2021.2000852.

Walters, K.L., Evans-Campbell, T., Simoni, J.M., Ronquillo, T., and Bhuyan, R. (2006). "My spirit in my heart": Identity experiences and challenges among two-spirit American Indian women. *Journal of Lesbian Studies*, 10(1-2), 125-49. Available: PMID: 16873218. ISSN: 1089-4160.

Webb, M.C., Chaney, J.D., Chen, W.W., Dodd, V.J., Huang, I-C., and Sanders, S. (2015). Assessing specific sexual behavior: Instrument development and validation techniques. *Journal of Education and Social Science*, 2(2), 1-11.

West, B.T., and McCabe, S.E. (2021). Choices matter: How response options for survey questions about sexual identity affect population estimates of its association with alcohol, tobacco, and other drug use. *Field Methods*, 33(4), 335-354. Available: doi: 10.1177/1525822X21998516.

West, C., and Zimmerman, D.H. (1987). Doing gender. *Gender & Society*, 1(2), 125-151. Available: https://doi.org/10.1177/0891243287001002002.

Westbrook, L., and Saperstein, A. (2015). New categories are not enough: Rethinking the measurement of sex and gender in social surveys. *Gender & Society*, 29(4), 534-560.

Wilber, S. (2013). *Guidelines for Managing Information Related to the Sexual Orientation and Gender Identity and Expression of Children in Child Welfare Systems.* Available: https://cssr.berkeley.edu/cwscmsreports/documents/Information%20Guidelines%20P4.pdf.

Wilber, S., and Canfield, A. (2019). *SOGIE Data Collection in Public Systems of Care: A Practice Guide For Santa Clara County.* Available: https://www.nclrights.org/wp-content/uploads/2020/05/Final-SCC-SOGIE-Data-Collection-Practice-Guide-8.8.19.pdf.

Willis, G.B. (2005). *Cognitive Interviewing: A Tool for Improving Questionnaire Design.* Thousand Oaks, CA: Sage.

Wilson, A. (1996). How we find ourselves: Identity development and Two-Spirit people. *Harvard Educational Review*, 66(2), 303-317.

Wilson, B.D.M., Choi, S.K., Harper, G.W., Lightfoot, M., Russell, S., and Meyer, I.H. (2020). *Homelessness Among LGBT Adults in the U.S.* Los Angeles, CA: Williams Institute.

Wilson, B.D.M., Choi, S.K., Herman, J.L., Becker, T., and Conron, K.J. (2017). *Characteristics and Mental Health of Gender Nonconforming Adolescents in California: Findings from the 2015-2016 California Health Interview Survey.* Los Angeles, CA: Williams Institute and UCLA Center for Health Policy Research.

Wilson, B.D.M., Cooper, K. Kastanis, A. and Choi, S.K. (2016). *Surveying LGBTQ Youth in Foster Care: Lessons from Los Angeles.* Available: http://williamsinstitute.law.ucla.edu/wp-content/uploads/TWI_Methods-Report-2016.pdf.

Wilson, B.D.M., Cooper, K., Kastanis, A., and Nezhad, S. (2014). *Sexual and Gender Minority Youth in Foster Care: Assessing Disproportionality and Disparities in Los Angeles.* Los Angeles, CA: Williams Institute. Available: https://escholarship.org/content/qt6mg3n153/qt6mg3n153.pdf.

Wilson, B.D.M., Gordon, A.R., Mallory, C., Choi, S.K., Badgett, M.V.L., and LBQ Women's Report Team. (2021). *Health and Socioeconomic Well-Being of LBQ Women in the U.S.* Los Angeles, CA: Williams Institute.

Wilson, B.D.M., Jordan, S.P., Meyer, I.H., Flores, A.R., Stemple, L., and Herman, J.L. (2017). Disproportionality and disparities among sexual minority youth in custody. *Journal of Youth and Adolescence*, 46, 1547-1561. Available: http://doi.org/10.1007/s10964-017-0632-5.

Wilson, B.D.M., and Kastanis, A.A. (2015). Sexual and gender minority disproportionality and disparities in child welfare: A population-based study. *Children and Youth Services Review*, 58(C), 11-17.

Wilson, B.D.M., and Meyer, I.H. (2021). *Nonbinary LGBTQ Adults in the United States.* Los Angeles, CA: The Williams Institute.

Wilson, B.D.M., O'Neill, K.K., and Vasquez, L.A. (2021). *LGBT renters and eviction risk.* Los Angeles, CA: The Williams Institute.

Wipfler, A.J.N. (2016). Identity crisis: The limitations of expanding government recognition of gender identity and the possibility of genderless identity documents. *Harvard Journal of Law and Gender*, 39, 491-554.

Wolff, M., Wells, B., Ventura-DiPersia, C., Renson, A., and Grov, C. (2017). Measuring Sexual Orientation: A review and critique of U.S. data collection efforts and implications for health policy. *The Journal of Sex Research*, 54(4-5), 507-531. Available: doi: 10.1080/00224499.2016.1255872.

Wylie, S.A., Corliss, H.L., Boulanger, V., Prokop, L.A., and Austin, S.B. (2010). Socially assigned gender nonconformity: A brief measure for use in surveillance and investigation of health disparities. *Sex Roles*, 63(3-4), 264-276.

Yan, T., and Tourangeau, R. (2008). Fast times and easy questions: The effects of age, experience, and question complexity on web survey response times. *Applied Cognitive Psychology*, 22, 51-68.

Zaller, N.D., Neher, T.L., Presley, M., Horton, H., Marshall, S.A., Zielinski, M.J., and Brinkley-Rubinstein, L. (2020). Barriers to linking high-risk jail detainees to HIV pre-exposure prophylaxis. *PLoS ONE*, 15(4), e0231951. Available: https://doi.org/10.1371/journal.pone.0231951.

Zucker, K.J. (2017). Epidemiology of gender dysphoria and transgender identity. *Sexual Health*, 14(5), 404-411. Available. https://doi.org/10.1071/SH17067.

Appendix A

Measures Evaluated
by the Committee

The table in this appendix lists the measures used in federally sponsored surveys and other data collection approaches to measure sexual orientation and gender identity that the committee considered.

TABLE A-1 Sexual Orientation and Gender Identity Measures by Survey

Name of Data Collection Instrument	Sponsor[a]	Measure(s)			Population	Data Type	Mode(s)
		Sexual Orientation	Gender Identity[b]				
			One-Step Approach	Two-Step Approach			
All of Us	NIH	X		X	All ages	Medical	CATI, P&P
American National Election Studies (ANES)	NSF	X		X	Adults (eligible voters)	Survey	Web, CAPI, CASI, CATI, Video
Behavioral Risk Factor Surveillance System (BFRSS)	CDC	X	X[c]		Adults	Survey	CATI
Center for Substance Abuse Treatment—*Government Performance Results and Modernization Act* (CSAT-GPRA)	SAMHSA		X		Youth and Adults	Admin	n/a
Centers for Disease Control and Prevention Recommendations for Health Care Providers (CDC Recs)	CDC	X		X	n/a	Medical	n/a
Gallup	Gallup	X[d]			Adults	Survey	CATI
General Social Survey (GSS)	NSF	X		X	Adults	Survey	CAPI (SAQ)

Study	Sponsor		Population	Type	Mode
Growing Up Today Study (GUTS)	NIH	X	Young Adults (20s)	Survey	P&P Web
Health Center Patient Survey (HCPS)	HRSA ASPE[e]	X	All ages	Admin	CAPI
Health and Retirement Study (HRS)	NIH, SSA, DOL, ASPE, State of Florida	X	Older adults	Survey	CAPI CATI
High School Longitudinal Study of 2009 (HSLS:09)—2016 Collection 3 Years After High School Graduation	NCES	X	Young adults (early 20s)	Survey	Web CAPI CATI
National Adult Tobacco Survey (NATS)	NCHS	X	Adults	Survey	CATI
National Crime Victimization Survey (NCVS)	BJS	X	Ages 16+	Survey	CAPI, CATI
National Epidemiologic Survey of Alcohol and Related Conditions (NESARC)	NIAAA	X	Adults	Survey	CAPI
National Health Interview Survey (NHIS)	CDC	X	Adults	Survey	CAPI CATI

continued

TABLE A-1 Continued

Name of Data Collection Instrument	Sponsor[a]	Sexual Orientation	Gender Identity[b] One-Step Approach	Gender Identity[b] Two-Step Approach	Population	Data Type	Mode(s)
National Health and Nutrition Examination Survey (NHANES)	CDC	X			Adults	Survey	CAPI
National HIV Behavioral Surveillance (NHBS)	CDC	X		X	Adults (high HIV risk)	Survey	CAPI
National Inmate Survey (NIS)	BJS	X	X		Ages 16+[f]	Survey	ACASI
National Intimate Partner and Sexual Violence Survey (NISVS)	CDC, DOD, NIJ	X			Adults	Survey	CATI
National Longitudinal Study of Adolescent and Adult Health, *Wave V* (Add Health)	Multiple[g]	X		X	Adults	Survey	Web, P&P, CAPI, CASI, CATI
National Opinion Research Center (NORC) recommendations for Medicare Current Beneficiary Survey (MCBS)	CMS	X		X	Ages 60+	Survey	n/a
National Outcome Measures, Center for Mental Health Services (NOM)	SAMHSA CMHS	X	X[b]		Adults	Admin	n/a
National Survey of Drug Use and Health (NSDUH)	SAMHSA	X			Adults	Survey	ACASI
National Survey of Family Growth (NSFG)	CDC	X			Ages 15–49	Survey	CAPI, ACASI

National Survey of Older Americans Act Participants (NSOAAP)	AOA	X		Age 60+	Survey Admin	CATI
Population Assessment of Tobacco and Health Study (PATH)	NIDA, NIH, CTP, FDA	X	X	Ages 14+	Survey	ACASI, CAPI
Survey of Today's Adolescent Relationship and Transitions (START)	CDC	X	X	Ages 13–24[i]	Survey	Web, Focus Groups
GenIUSS Report Recommendations	Williams Institute	X	X	Adults	Survey	n/a
Youth Risk Behavior Surveillance System (YRBSS)	CDC	X	X	Grades 9–12	Survey	P&P

NOTES: ACASI, audio computer-assisted self-interview; AOA, Administration on Aging; ASPE, U.S. Department of Health and Human Services Office of the Assistant Secretary of Planning and Evaluation; BJS, Bureau of Justice Statistics; CAPI, computer-assisted personal interview; CASI, computer-assisted self-interview; CATI, computer-assisted telephone interview; CDC, Centers for Disease Control and Prevention; CMHS, Center for Mental Health Services; CMS, Center for Medicare and Medicaid Services; CTP, Center for Tobacco Products; DOD, U.S. Department of Defense; DOL, U.S. Department of Labor; FDA, Food and Drug Administration; HRSA, Health Resources and Services Administration; NCES, National Center for Education Statistics; n/a, not applicable; NCHS, National Center for Health Statistics; NIAAA, National Institute on Alcohol Abuse and Alcoholism; NIDA, National Institute on Drug Abuse; NIH, National Institutes of Health; NIJ, National Institute of Justice; NSF, National Science Foundation; P&P, paper and pencil; SAMHSA, Substance Abuse and Mental Health Services Administration; SAQ, self-administered questionnaire; SSA, Social Security Administration.

[a]Sponsors cited are drawn from websites and publicly available survey documentation.

[b]Single-step gender identity measures use a single question to assess gender identity and transgender experience or identity. Two-step measures use a sequence of two questions that can be compared to identify respondents with transgender experience.

[c]Beginning in 2019, BRFSS added a measure of sex assigned at birth to the approved optional sexual orientation and gender identity module. This module has included a stand-alone measure of transgender status since 2014.

continued

TABLE A-1 Continued

[a] The Gallup measure is a measure of LGBT status that instructs respondents to select all that apply from the following response options: straight or heterosexual; lesbian; gay, bisexual; and transgender.

[c] The U.S. Department of Health and Human Services Office of the Assistant Secretary of Planning and Evaluation (ASPE) provides support for generating public-use data files that can be used for research.

[f] Adults in jails or prisons and juveniles in detention centers.

[g] The National Survey of Adolescent and Young Adults Health (Add Health) is funded by grant P01-HD31921 from the Eunice Kennedy Shriver National Institute of Child Health and Human Development, with cooperative funding from 23 other federal agencies and foundations.

[h] Guidelines recommend asking respondent to report their gender with an open-ended response field. Instructions tell interviewers they may clarify by asking whether the respondent sees themselves as a man or male, woman or female, transgender, or other.

[i] Sexual minority males ages 13–18 years and transgender youth ages 13–24 years when interviewed who were recruited through social media sources.

Appendix B

Agendas for Open Panel Meetings

Panel on Measuring Sex, Gender Identity, and Sexual Orientation
Meeting #1
May 14, 2021

Remote Conference Meeting
Via Zoom

OPEN SESSION

1:00–1:30 pm	Welcome and Introduction to the National Academies *Monica Feit*, Deputy Executive Director, DBASSE
1:30–2:30 pm	Sponsor Interests and Perspectives; Discussion of Statement of Task *Karen Parker*, National Institutes of Health *Irene Avila*, National Institutes of Health
2:30–2:45 pm	*Break*

CLOSED SESSION (COMMITTEE AND STAFF ONLY)

2:45–5:00 pm	Closed to Public
5:00 pm	Adjournment

179

Meeting #2
June 17, 2021

Remote Conference Meeting
Via Zoom

OPEN SESSION

3:00–3:05 pm   **Welcome and Overview of Agenda**
Nancy Bates, Committee Co-Chair
(formerly U.S. Census)
Marshall Chin, Committee Co-Chair
(University of Chicago)

3:05–3:20 pm   **Presentation: Measuring Sex and Gender**
Sari van Anders (Queen's University)

3:20–3:40 pm   **Committee Q&A**
Moderator: *José Bauermeister* (University
of Pennsylvania)

3:40–4:15 pm   **Panel: Use of SGD Measures by Federal Agencies**
Ethan Fechter-Leggett, Research Epidemiologist
(NIOSH [CDC])
Kirk Greenway,
Director (OPHS Division of Program Statistics)
Principal Statistician (Indian Health Service)
Elliot Kennedy, Director, Office of Policy Analysis and
Development (ACL-HHS)
Mahri Monson, Office of General Counsel (EPA)
Jennifer Truman,
Statistician (Bureau of Justice Statistics [DOJ])

4:15–5:00 pm   **Committee Q&A**
Moderator: *Nancy Bates*, Committee Co-Chair

5:00 pm   **Adjournment**

Meeting #3
July 19, 2021

Public Workshop

OPEN SESSION

1:00–1:10 pm   *Welcome and Introductions*
                  Nancy Bates, Co-Chair (formerly U.S. Census Bureau)
                  Marshall Chin, Co-Chair (University of Chicago)

1:10–2:40 pm   *Session 1: Sex and Gender in Populations with*
                  Differences of Sex Development (DSD)
1:10–1:30   *Sex Designation for Individuals with DSD*
                        Courtney Finlayson, Lurie Children's Hospital
                        of Chicago
1:30–1:50   *How Intersex Erasure Sustained the Sex and Gender*
                  Binary: A History
                        Elizabeth Reis, Macaulay Honors College,
                        CUNY
1:50–2:10   *Population Measurement of DSD Populations*
                        Jason Flatt, University of Nevada, Las Vegas
2:10–2:40   *Discussion*
                        Moderator: Katie Dalke

2:40–2:50 pm   *Break*

2:50–4:20 pm   *Session 2: Legal and Administrative Issues*
2:50–3:10   *The Importance of Allowing Non-Binary Legal Sex*
                        Harper Jean Tobin, HJ Tobin Policy Consulting
3:10–3:30   *Medicolegal Issues Related to Legal Sex Designations*
                        Vadim Shteyler, University of California, San
                        Francisco
3:30–3:50   *Statistical Standards for Gender, Sex, and Variations*
                  of Sex Characteristics: New Zealand
                        Jack Byrne, University of Waikato
                        Jaimie Veale, University of Waikato
                        Micah Davison, Statistics New Zealand
3:50–4:20   *Discussion*
                        Moderator: Kellan Baker

4:20–4:30 pm   *Break*

4:30–6:00 pm	Session 3: Sex, Gender Identity, and Sexual Orientation in Health Care
4:30–4:50	*Importance of Collecting Sex, Gender Identity, and Sexual Orientation in Medical Records* Sean Cahill, The Fenway Institute
4:50–5:10	*Sex at Birth and Gender Identity in Transgender Health Care* Juno Obedin-Maliver, Stanford University
5:10–5:30	*Gender, Sex, and Sexual Orientation: A Brief Discussion of Operationalization in Health Care* Clair Kronk, Yale University
5:30–6:00	*Discussion* Moderator: José Bauermeister
6:00 pm	Adjournment

Appendix C

Biographical Sketches of Committee Members and Staff

NANCY BATES (*Co-Chair*) is working as a consultant with Stanford University on a project, supported by the National Institutes of Health, to measure sexual orientation and gender identity. Previously, she served as the senior methodologist for survey research at the U.S. Census Bureau. In that position, she oversaw and contributed to the research that formulated inclusive relationship questions that improved measurement of same sex couples in the 2020 decennial census. She also previously served as co-chair of the research group on sexual orientation and gender identity for the Office of Management and Budget and the Federal Committee on Statistical Methodology. She recently co-edited a *Journal of Official Statistics* special issue on measuring LGBT populations. She is an elected fellow of the American Statistical Association. She has an M.A. in applied sociology from the University of Oklahoma.

MARSHALL CHIN (*Co-Chair*) is the Richard Parrillo Family professor of healthcare ethics in the Department of Medicine at the University of Chicago and a practicing general internist and health services researcher. His work focuses on reducing health disparities through interventions at individual, organizational, community, and policy levels and on elucidating practical approaches to improving care of diverse individual patients and addressing systemic, structural drivers of disparities in the health care system. He and his team created the widely cited *The Roadmap to Reduce Disparities*. He is the principal investigator of the Your Voice! Your Health! Project, funded by the Agency for Healthcare Research and Quality of the U.S. Department of Health and Human Services, that improves shared decision making among clinicians and LGBTQ people of color. He is an elected member of the National Academy of Medicine. He has a bachelor's degree and an M.P.H. from Harvard and an M.D. from the University of California at San Francisco School of Medicine. He completed residency and fellowship training in general internal medicine at Brigham and Women's Hospital.

KELLAN E. BAKER is the Executive Director and Chief Learning Officer at the Whitman-Walker Institute. Previously, he was the centennial scholar and a Robert Wood Johnson health policy research scholar in the Department of Health Policy and Management at the Johns Hopkins Bloomberg School of Public Health. His research focuses on economics, policy, and methodology issues in transgender health. Previously, he was a senior fellow at the Center for American Progress in Washington, D.C., where was a founding steering committee member of Out2Enroll, a nationwide campaign in partnership with the White House and the U.S. Department of Health and Human Services to connect low-income LGBT populations with coverage under the Affordable Care Act. He is the board chair of the Equality Federation and also serves on numerous scientific and community engagement bodies. He has a B.A. with high honors in astrophysics and Russian from Swarthmore College, an M.P.H. from the George Washington University, an M.A. in international development from the Elliott School of International Affairs at the George Washington University, and a Ph.D. in health policy and management with a focus on health services research and health economics from the Johns Hopkins School of Public Health.

JOSÉ A. BAUERMEISTER is the Albert M. Greenfield professor of human relations at the University of Pennsylvania, chair of the Department of Family and Community Health at the Penn School of Nursing, director of the Penn Program on Sexuality, Technology & Action Research, and professor of psychiatry at the Perelman School of Medicine. He chairs the National Institutes of Health (NIH) study section on population and public health approaches to HIV/AIDS and is a standing member of the NIH's Council of Councils' Sexual and Gender Minority Research Working Group. He served as associate editor of the American Psychological Association's inaugural book on human sexuality and of the SAGE Publication *Handbook of LGBT Lives in Context,* and he serves on the editorial board of the *Archives of Sexual Behavior* and the *Annals of LGBTQ Population Health.* He is an Aspen Institute health innovators fellow and a member of the Aspen Global Leadership Network. He has a bachelor's degree in psychology from the University of Puerto Rico and a master's and a doctorate in public health from the University of Michigan.

TARA BECKER (*Study Director*) is a Program Officer for the Committees on National Statistics and Population in the Division of Behavioral and Social Sciences and Education at the National Academy of Sciences. In addition to this study, she serves as the Study Director for a study examining the older workforce and employment at older ages. She has served as a Program Officer for a study examining the well-being of LGBTQI+ individuals and another examining high and rising working age mortality rates in the United States. Before joining the National Academies, she was a Senior Public Administration Analyst and Senior Statistician for the California Health Interview Survey at the Center for Health Policy Research at the University of California, Los Angeles, where she conducted research on disparities in health insurance coverage and access to health care, as well as on survey data quality and methodology. Prior to this, she was a postdoctoral fellow in the Department of Health Policy and Management at the University of California, Los Angeles and a Biostatistician at the University of Wisconsin, Madison Department of Biostatistics and Medical Informatics. She has a B.A. in sociology and mathematics, an M.S. in sociology, an M.S. in statistics, and a Ph.D. in sociology from the University of Wisconsin, Madison.

D'LANE COMPTON is a professor of sociology in the College of Liberal Arts, Education and Human Development at the University of New Orleans. Their two major research interests are social psychology and the demography of sexual orientation, using both perspectives to examine sexual, gender, and family inequalities. Specifically, their research adds to our knowledge about how categorization or labeling processes yield different outcomes in treatment and resources. This work has culminated in a number of peer-reviewed articles, book chapters, education essays, and two co-authored books, *Same-Sex Partners: The Social Demography of Sexual Orientation* with Amanda K. Baumle and Dudley L. Poston and *Legalizing LGBT Families: How the Law Shapes Parenthood* with Amanda K. Baumle. They are interested in research design and methodological issues related to substantive concerns, in particular how methods of measurements can affect inferences about and the study of underrepresented or "hidden" populations. They received a B.S. from Texas A&M, an M.A. from the University of Missouri-St. Louis, and a Ph.D. from Texas A&M, all in sociology.

KATHERINE DALKE has appointments in the Departments of Psychiatry and Behavioral Health and the Department of Humanities at the Penn State College of Medicine. She also serves as the director of the Office for Culturally Responsive Health Care Education, which is responsible for innovating and integrating cultural competency and humility training across the College of Medicine's educational programs. In this role, she focuses on how formal health sciences curricula can promote culturally responsive learning environments and clinical care. Her clinical and scholarly work focuses primarily on the mental health of people who are LGBTQI or who have a difference in sex development (DSD). She currently serves on Sexual and Minority Research Working Group of the National Institutes of Health and the Intersex Working Group for revisions to the standard of care of the World Professional Association for Transgender Health. She has an M.A. in bioethics and an M.D. from the University of Pennsylvania, and she completed psychiatry residency training at the Hospital of the University of Pennsylvania.

ALIYA SAPERSTEIN is the Benjamin Scott Crocker professor in human biology and a professor of sociology at Stanford University. Her research focuses on the conceptualization and measurement of race and ethnicity and sex and gender in surveys and the implications of these methodological decisions for studies of stratification and health disparities. Her co-authored article, "New Categories Are Not Enough: Rethinking the Measurement of Sex and Gender in Social Surveys," and subsequent work on alternative survey measures of sex and gender informed the addition of new self-identification items in the 2018 General Social Survey. She is a recipient of the early achievement award by the Population Association of America. Her research has been supported by the American Sociological Association Fund for the Advancement of the Discipline, the Clayman Institute for Gender Research, and the Russell Sage Foundation. She has a Ph.D. in sociology and demography from the University of California-Berkeley.

KARINA WALTERS is a Katherine Hall Chambers university professor in the School of Social Work, an adjunct professor in the Department of Global Health in the School of Public Health, and the founding director of the Indigenous Wellness Research Institute, all at the University of Washington. She is an enrolled citizen of the Choctaw Nation of Oklahoma. Her work in social epidemiological research focuses on the environmental, historical, social, and cultural determinants of health of American Indian and Alaska Native population and health equity, as well as on Indigenous methodologies and in designing culturally derived chronic disease prevention research. She developed the indigenist stress-coping model that has been cited in over 450 studies. Methodologically, she has expertise in decolonizing methodologies, particularly with respect to developing culturally grounded measures and designing community-based, culturally derived interventions. She is only one of two American Indians (and the only Native woman) ever invited to deliver the director's lecture to the Wednesday Afternoon Lecture Series at the National Institutes of Health and is the first

American Indian inducted as a fellow into the American Academy of Social Welfare and Social Work. She has a B.A. in sociology, an M.S.W., and a Ph.D. in social welfare, all from the University of California, Los Angeles.

BIANCA D. M. WILSON is the Rabbi Zacky senior scholar of public policy at the Williams Institute at the University of California, Los Angeles. Her research focuses primarily on system-involved LGBTQ youth, LGBT poverty, and sexual health among queer women. She has completed studies and reports on the measurement of sexual orientation, gender identity, and gender expression among youth and adults. In addition to multiple peer-reviewed and institution-published reports, she co-edited a special issue of the *Journal of Lesbian Studies* that featured a multidisciplinary collection of work on health and other topics from the perspectives of Black lesbians in the United States, the Caribbean, and South Africa. She has a doctorate in psychology from the Community and Prevention Research Program at the University of Illinois at Chicago, with a minor in statistics, methods, and measurement. She completed postdoctoral training at the Institute for Health Policy Studies and the Lesbian Health and Research Center at the University of California, San Francisco.